Cleveland's Neighborhood Taverns

Cleveland's Neighborhood Taverns

A Pub Crawl Through History

Tom Kaschalk

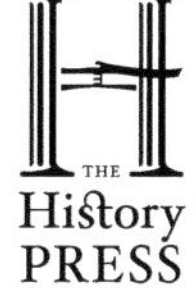

Published by The History Press
An imprint of Arcadia Publishing
Charleston, SC
www.historypress.com

First published 2025

Manufactured in the United States

ISBN 9781467158374

Library of Congress Control Number: 2025933735

Contents

Acknowledgements

My journey through the rich and complex history of Cleveland's taverns and neighborhoods has been guided by a wealth of resources that have shaped my understanding of and deepened my appreciation for the city's past. While much of this book is built on primary sources, interviews and site visits, the foundation of my research was greatly enhanced by numerous newspapers, websites and digital archives.

I owe a debt of gratitude to the *Cleveland Plain Dealer* and the *Call and Post*, whose archives provided invaluable insights into the social and cultural dynamics of Cleveland over the years. The detailed reporting and local perspectives found in these newspapers were instrumental in uncovering the stories that breathe life into the history of Cleveland's taverns.

I also want to acknowledge the *Scoundrel's Field Guide* website, which offered unique perspectives on the city's hidden histories and lesser-known tales that might otherwise have been overlooked. The wealth of information available on ClevelandHistorical.org was equally crucial, providing context and depth to the narrative with its rich collection of stories and historical records. I would especially like to thank Brian Meggitt and Mark Tidrick from the Cleveland Public Library, Photo Collection Department. Your tireless efforts to dig deep into the photo collections and provide invaluable images have greatly enriched this book. Your dedication to preserving Cleveland's visual history has made a significant impact on this project, and I am truly grateful for your help.

Elizabeth Piwkowski at Cleveland State University and the Cleveland Memory Project (http://clevelandmemory.org) has been an indispensable resource throughout this journey. The extensive digital archives of the Cleveland Memory Project allowed me to access historical photographs, documents and publications that were essential in painting a vivid picture of Cleveland's past. I am deeply grateful to the dedicated individuals who maintain and contribute to these digital archives, ensuring that Cleveland's history is preserved and accessible to all.

I would also like to extend my heartfelt thanks to Chuck Mocsiran, chief archivist for the City of Cleveland, and Dr. Judith Cetina, Cuyahoga County archivist, whose guidance and mentorship have significantly expanded my understanding of Cleveland's history and its rich historical documents. Judy's invaluable expertise and dedication to preserving the county's legacy have been a constant source of inspiration throughout this project.

Together, these sources have not only informed the factual content of this book but also enriched my understanding of the broader historical and cultural landscape in which Cleveland's taverns have existed. While this book focuses on the stories and spaces that have defined Cleveland's drinking culture, it is also a tribute to the many researchers, archivists and writers who have documented this city's vibrant history.

On a personal note, I would like to express my deepest appreciation to those who have been my pillars of support throughout this project. To my wife, Natalie Kaschalk: your unwavering encouragement and thoughtful critique have been the backbone of this work. Your belief in this project kept me going, even when the path seemed long and uncertain.

To my good friend and lifelong Clevelander Tony Brancatelli: your service and deep connection to this city and its history provided invaluable perspectives that greatly contributed to the authenticity of this narrative. Your stories, knowledge and love for Cleveland have left an indelible mark on this work.

I am also profoundly grateful to Brian Passell, whose friendship and inspiration have been constants in my life. Your encouragement and insights have not only shaped this book but also enriched my journey as a writer.

Cheers!

Introduction

This is a story of gathering places known by many names: taverns, bars, pubs, nightclubs, lounges, cafés, saloons and beer joints. Cleveland has always been a city of neighborhoods, each with its own unique character and history, woven together by the shared experiences of its people. In these neighborhoods, taverns have stood as cornerstones, serving as gathering spots where generations have come together to share a pint, a story and a sense of community.

For me, this history is deeply personal. Some of my earliest memories are of visiting neighborhood bars with my father. When I was growing up, in Cleveland, no matter where you lived, there was always a tavern on the corner. As a young boy, stepping into those bars was thrilling. To my innocent eyes, the money left on the bar looked like it was there just for me—for pop, chips and endless games of pinball or bowling.

As I grew older, these corner bars became even more familiar. By my teens, my friends and I knew which places would serve us a bottle of beer—and if you bought two, you'd often get a third on the house. These bars weren't just hangouts; they were also part of my education. I sharpened my math skills on video poker and football betting slips and played on tavern-sponsored softball teams, always rallying back to the bar for a drink—win or lose.

Over time, I learned life lessons that extended far beyond the games. You could sit next to an old-timer at the bar and hear stories of life in the neighborhood, working at the GM or Ford plants or spending decades in the steel mills. If you got laid off, the tavern became a refuge of opportunity: just leave your car keys on the bar, and like magic, your car—and its payments—would disappear. These taverns weren't just spots to celebrate or commiserate; they were the heart of our community. On hot summer nights, their air-conditioning offered cool relief, and no matter how badly the Cleveland Indians played, there was always a reason to stay for one more round.

This book charts a course through Cleveland's history, as seen through the lens of its beloved watering holes. We begin with the pioneering days of Lorenzo Carter and trace the waves of immigration that brought new communities—and new taverns—into the city's fabric.

We'll explore the rise of industrial Cleveland and the thriving saloons that catered to steelworkers, iron laborers and dockhands. We'll confront the dark days of Prohibition, when speakeasies and bootleggers kept the city's thirst alive, and then move through the Great Depression and subsequent economic upheavals that tested the endurance of these cherished establishments.

As we journey through the decades, we'll explore the postwar boom and the rise of downtown nightlife, when neon signs lit up the streets and bars became gathering places for both white- and blue-collar workers celebrating their hard-earned wages. We'll dive into the vibrant African American taverns that became cultural and musical landmarks on Cleveland's East Side, hosting legendary live performances and defining the city's nightlife.

We'll witness the tumultuous shifts of the 1960s and '70s, when Cleveland's economy faltered, inner-city neighborhoods deteriorated and suburban flight drained the population—yet tavern culture persevered. Finally, we'll examine the impact of modern urban renewal: long-standing neighborhood bars now struggle to maintain their identity in the face of gentrification and the rise of corporate-owned chains.

Throughout this journey, we'll celebrate not just the taverns that withstood the test of time but also those that, while no longer standing, remain immortal in the collective memory of the communities they once served. These establishments have witnessed the full spectrum of human experience, from exuberant celebrations at the end of World War II to solemn gatherings in the wake of both local and national tragedies.

Through these stories, we'll meet the bartenders, regulars and owners who infused life into these spaces. We'll journey across Cleveland's diverse neighborhoods on a pub crawl that takes us from the East Side to the West Side, visiting the corner bars, jazz clubs and legendary dives that have anchored communities for generations. From the legendary Flat Iron Café to the iconic Harbor Inn, from Collinwood to the cozy corner bars of Tremont: these are the places where Cleveland's history has been written, one drink at a time.

I embark on this journey with both a caveat and an apology: Cleveland's rich tavern history is vast, with countless stories spanning generations. If your favorite spot does not find its mention in these pages, please know it's not for lack of significance or affection. Rather, it reflects the deep, often untapped well of tales that Cleveland's drinking establishments offer—far too plentiful for one volume to fully encompass.

With this book, I invite you to join me in a heartfelt toast—not just to the bars, taverns and gathering places that have shaped our personal journeys but also to the vibrant spirit of Cleveland itself. Let's raise a glass to the narratives that bind us, to the rich history that defines our identity and to the memorable spaces where we've come together.

To conclude, I turn to the insightful words of James Wallen, published over a century ago in *Cleveland's Golden Story*: "The city's hostelries, mellow in memories, deserve a book of 'Friendly American Taverns.'" Time has marched on since Wallen's observation, but its relevance endures. This book answers his call, diving deep into Cleveland's taverns, which embody not just the spirit but also the soul of the city. Let this work stand as a tribute to Wallen's vision, exploring the storied establishments that have anchored Cleveland's community through the ages.

Chapter 1

Pioneers, Pints and New Arrivals

Cleveland's Tavern Culture from Settlement to the Civil War

In 1796, General Moses Cleaveland, working for the Connecticut Land Company, led a survey team into the undeveloped territories of the Western Reserve. Their objective was clear: to map the land and initiate its sale, which would soon attract settlers from New England. These early settlers, driven by the promise of new opportunities, also brought with them deeply rooted traditions from their colonial past. Among these was the establishment of taverns, which quickly became central gathering spots in the emerging community, essential for both social life and local commerce.

These establishments served a far greater purpose than simply quenching thirst. As Edward Field highlights in his book *The Colonial Tavern*, taverns in New England shared a close relationship with meetinghouses. Taverns were usually located in proximity to churches. Unlike the unheated meetinghouses, taverns offered a warm refuge and relaxation after long Sunday services. This practical function made taverns essential community hubs for social interaction and lively discussions.

Founding Father: Major Lorenzo Carter and the Birth of Cleveland's Tavern Tradition

Lorenzo Carter, originally from Rutland, Vermont, is celebrated as Cleveland's first permanent settler. He arrived on the banks of the Cuyahoga River in 1797, when the area was home to only seven other inhabitants.

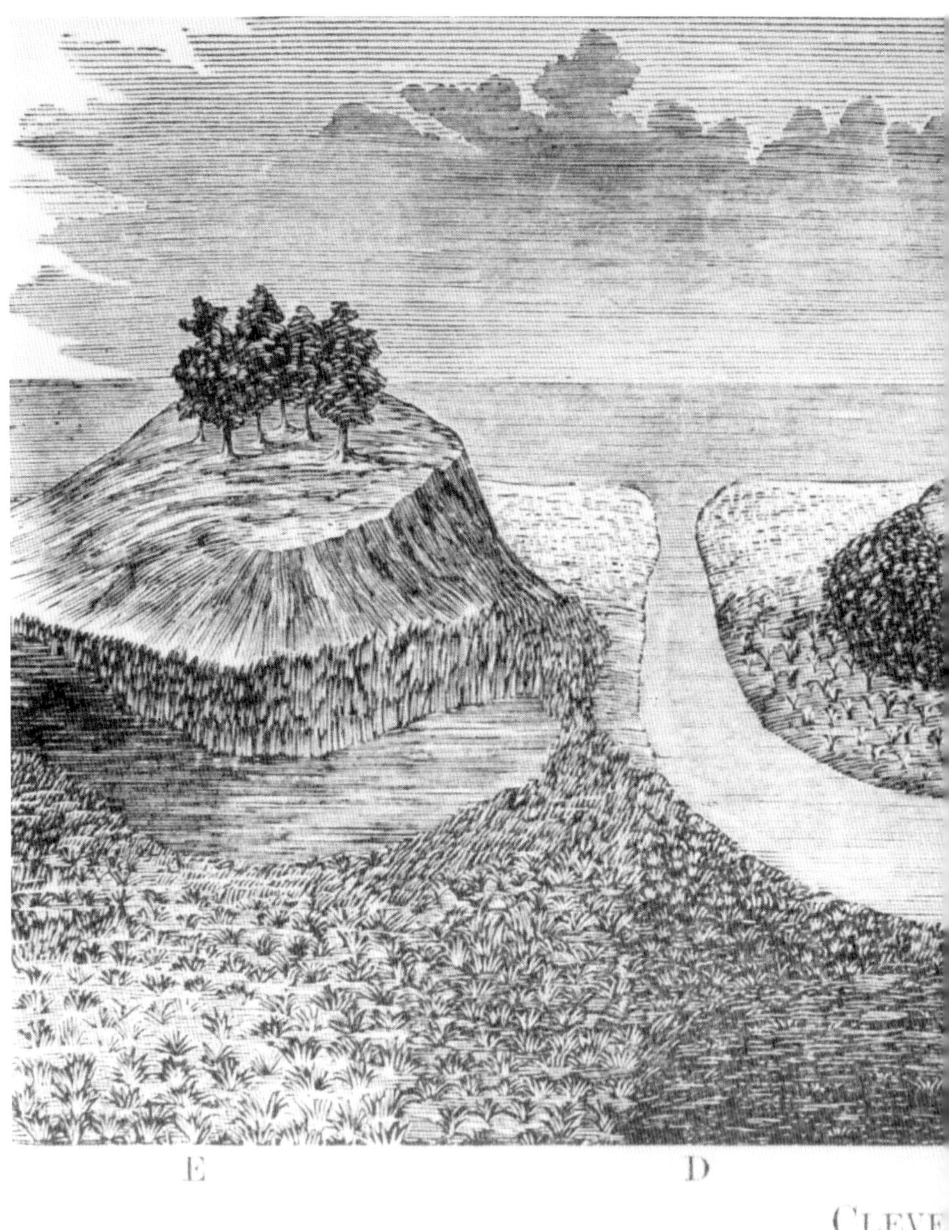

Early Cleveland settlement on the banks of the Cuyahoga River, featuring Lorenzo Carter's homestead and tavern. *Cleveland Public Library/Photograph Collection.*

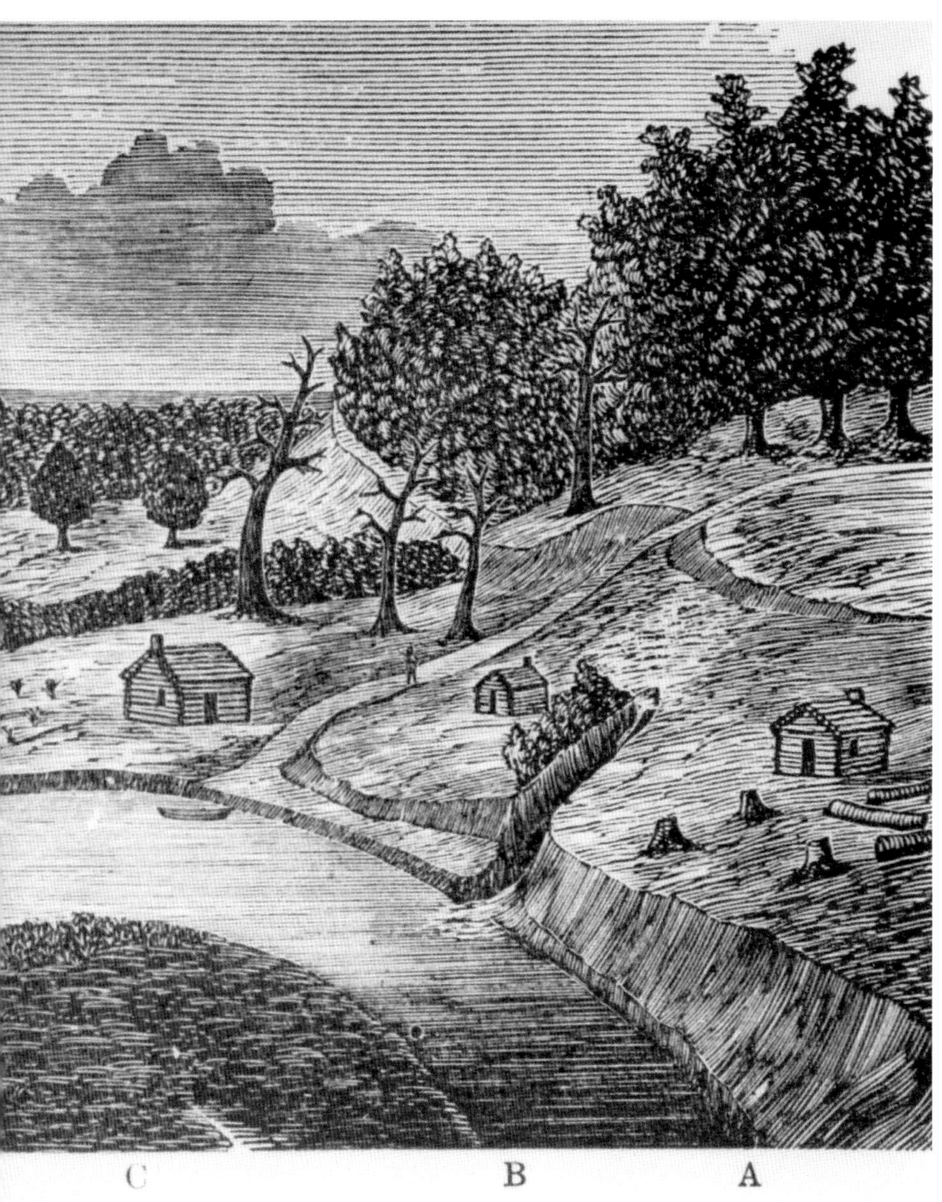
C
B
A
1800

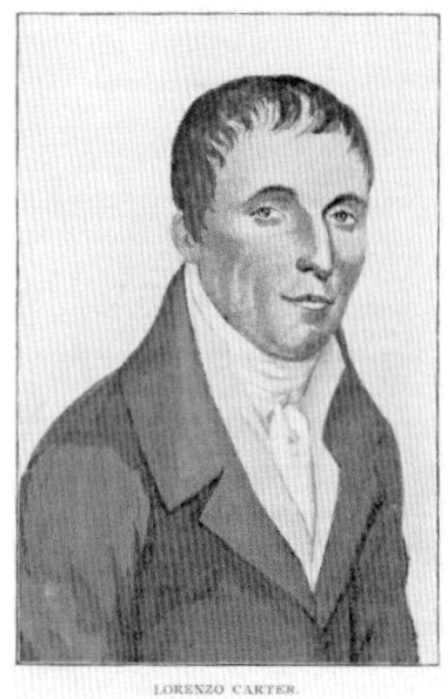

Lorenzo Carter, first settler and tavern owner, sparked the city's rich tavern culture from its very founding. *Cleveland Public Library/ Photograph Collection.*

Despite numerous hardships, including harsh conditions from January 1799 to April 1800 that drove away all other settlers, Carter and his wife, Rebecca, steadfastly remained on the swampy banks of the Cuyahoga. Carter was a fur trader and farmer before he established the first inn and tavern in Cleveland.

Carter's tavern was the site of several notable milestones in Cleveland's history, hosting the city's first wedding, dance and church service. These events underscore its central role in the early social and cultural life of the city. In his book *Cleveland's Golden Story*, James Wallen includes a narrative from Gilman Bryant, an early settler. Bryant recounts his eagerness to visit the tavern with Miss Nancy Doan, offering a personal glimpse into the significance of the establishment.

> *It was a long four-mile ride through the woods to the Carter tavern, but the thought of Major Jones fiddling "Hie Betty Martin" and the "Sailor's Hornpipe" kept us in good spirits.*

Carter's influence in the area grew significantly as he amassed several dozen acres of land on both the east and west sides of the Cuyahoga River. He played a pivotal role in the city's development by constructing the first log warehouse in 1810 and launching the *Zephyr*, the region's first trading ship on Lake Erie, in 1808. Like many future tavern owners, he was actively involved in public service, serving as a constable and a major in the Ohio Militia. Carter died of cancer at the age of forty-seven in 1814 and is buried with Rebecca at Erie Street cemetery in downtown Cleveland.

Lorenzo Carter's impact on the small community and his leadership paved the way to more formal governance in Cleveland. In 1802, the city established its first governing board; its primary focus was on generating community revenue, notably through issuing tavern licenses. The first of these four-dollar licenses, likely governed by New England's principle of maintaining "good rule and order," were awarded to Carter and fellow pioneer Amos Spafford by town clerk Nathanial Doan, who later became a tavern owner himself. This early licensing of taverns—notably at a time when regulation was already being established so early in the township's

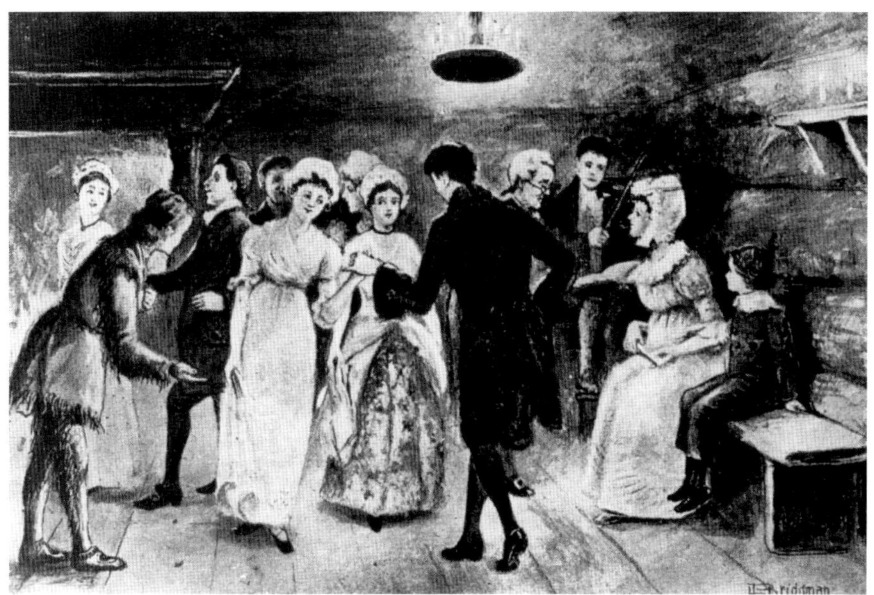

Early settlers gather in the Carter tavern, dancing, enjoying music and fostering a sense of community. *Cleveland Public Library/Photograph Collection.*

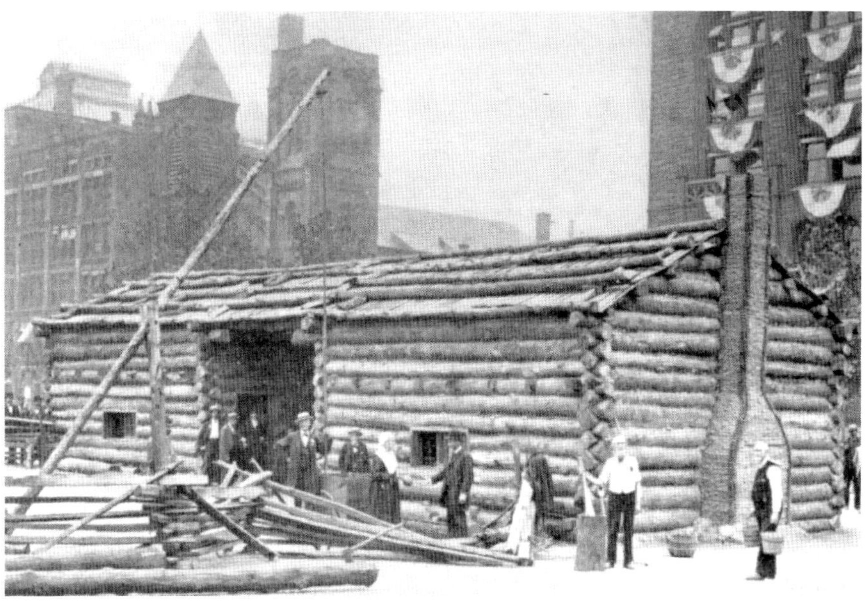

An 1896 re-creation of Lorenzo Carter's original log cabin for Cleveland's centennial celebration. *Cleveland Public Library/Photograph Collection.*

history—highlights not only the importance of taverns in social life but also underscores Carter's foundational role in shaping Cleveland's community and governance.

As the settlement expanded, Cuyahoga County was established, and by 1810, it had assumed responsibility for licensing from the City of Cleveland. Cleveland's population grew slowly during the early 1800s: only fifty-seven residents were recorded in 1810, and this number had risen modestly to just over six hundred by 1820. Despite these slow beginnings, the tavern industry flourished, growing from five establishments in 1814 to ten in 1823.

Spafford's Tavern was positioned along the Cuyahoga River on Merwin Street, which is now part of an area currently managed by Cleveland Metroparks. Merwin's Wharf, a popular restaurant offering boat slips on the river, blends the historical footprint of the area with modern recreational facilities. Spafford ultimately continued westward and was an early pioneer in Perrysburg, Ohio. He transferred ownership of his tavern to George Wallace, who subsequently renamed it the Wallace House.

As Cleveland grew, the higher ground east of the Cuyahoga River became a sought-after area for new inns and taverns. Among them was Doan's Tavern, situated on Euclid Road and East 107th Street, which served the expanding

At a meeting of the Commissioners of Cuyahoga County, June 6, 1810

Ordered by the Board that the County pay on Dollar for each Wolf Scalp for the year in sueing

Ordered by the Board that the State price for Ferriage crost Cuyahoga for the year ensuing be as follows:

Footman Six Cents

Man and Horse Ten Cents

Loaded Waggon and Team Fifty Cents

For each empty Wagon and Team Twenty five Cents

Loaded cart and team Thirty two cents

For each horse, mule or ass, or head of meat cattle Six Cents

For each hog or sheep Two cents.

Ordered by the Board that the price of Taverns License for the year ensuing be four Dollars.

Ferry Lisence for do be one Dollar

Excerpt from the inaugural 1810 Cuyahoga County commissioners meeting, transcribed by the Works Progress Administration (WPA) from the original commissioners' journals. *Courtesy of the Cuyahoga County Archives.*

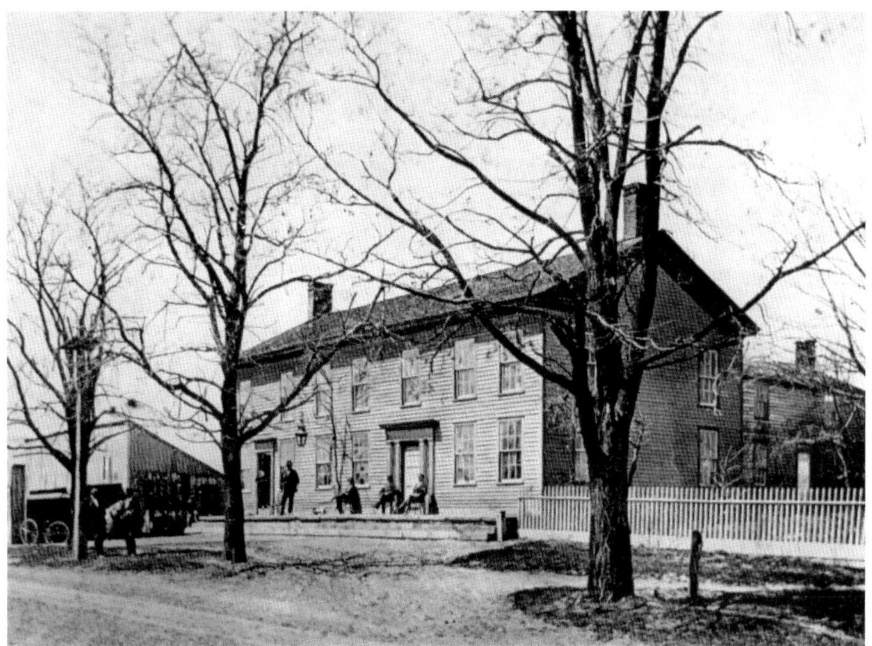

McIlrath Tavern at Superior and Euclid in 1860. *The Cleveland Press Collections, courtesy of the Michael Schwartz Library Special Collections, Cleveland State University.*

community beyond the initial riverfront settlements. The tavern was a popular stop for settlers heading to Newburgh along the stagecoach route. According to William Ganson Rose in his seminal work *Cleveland: Making of a City*, Doan's Tavern hosted the inaugural service of the Plan of Union Church. During this event, Reverend William Wick denounced dancing as an "unscriptural, vain and vicious practice." Despite his call for repentance, Sarah McIlrath Shaw, a charter member of the church, openly refused to condemn her participation in a dance held at Doan's Tavern, leading to her ostracism from the congregation. Local lore holds that Nathaniel Doan met his untimely end within the walls of his own tavern in 1815. To this day, the area is affectionately referred to as Doan's Corner, preserving his legacy.

If Sarah McIlrath Shaw found herself unwelcome at Doan's Tavern, she might have sought the hospitality of her family's own establishment, the McIlrath Tavern, located at the intersection of Superior and Euclid. This tavern was a favored gathering place, renowned for its lively foxhunts and social gatherings. It was so integral to local culture that early Clevelanders vividly remembered the bear that was kept chained to a tree outside. The tavern remained a popular spot until it was demolished in 1890.

As travelers continued along Euclid Avenue from McIlrath Tavern, they would soon come across Dunham Tavern, another significant historical landmark just a few miles down the road.

The Dunham Tavern: A Living Legacy Since 1824

The Dunham Tavern, Cleveland's oldest structure still standing on its original site, was established in 1824 by Rufus Dunham and his wife, Jane Pratt Dunham, on land acquired from the Connecticut Land Company. In 1833, Cuyahoga County granted Rufus a tavern license for five dollars, marking the beginning of his tavern's role as a stop to refresh travelers navigating the route between Buffalo and Detroit. Initially a simple log cabin, the structure was expanded to include a taproom and a larger main house, becoming a popular social hub and meeting place for members of the local Whig Party. The tavern was sold in the 1850s and converted into a private residence. In 1932, a renowned architect undertook an extensive restoration, and by 1941, it had been transformed into a museum. The Dunham Tavern is now not only a beloved historic site but also listed on the National Register of Historic Places.

Throughout the early 1830s, Cleveland was in a state of dynamic transition, evolving from a quaint village into a flourishing town. This decade witnessed unprecedented growth: the city's population expanded from slightly over one thousand to more than six thousand by decade's end. The city's demographics shifted, from a community of predominantly native-born eastern pioneers to a diverse melting pot: immigrants constituted nearly 25 percent of the population by 1840. Irish and German immigrants, who formed a significant part of this influx, brought with them distinct skills that contributed to the local economy. The Germans, often skilled workers, enhanced local craftsmanship and industry, while the Irish, primarily laborers, were instrumental in the physical building of the city.

A pivotal event during this period was the construction of the Ohio and Erie Canal. The canal, 308 miles from Cleveland to the Ohio River, was completed by 1832 and was largely excavated by hand by Irish and German immigrants. This monumental engineering feat not only played a crucial role in establishing Cleveland as a key transportation hub but also significantly boosted the city's economic growth. The canal facilitated the efficient movement of goods and people, enhancing Cleveland's strategic importance and transforming its port into an epicenter of trade.

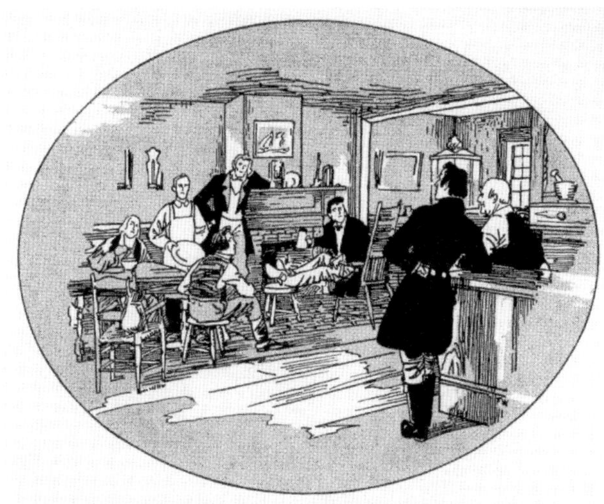

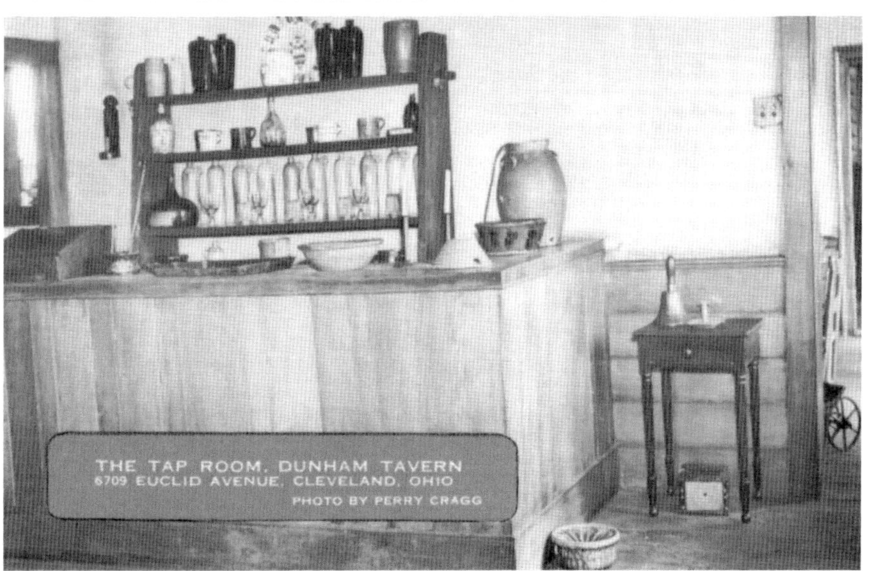

Top: Postcard depicting the Dunham Tavern's taproom. *Michael Schwartz Library Special Collections, Cleveland State University and courtesy of Dunham Tavern Museum & Gardens.*

Bottom: A re-creation of the Dunham Tavern taproom. *Cleveland State University, Michael Schwartz Library Special Collections and Dunham Tavern Museum & Gardens, photo by Perry Cragg.*

Amid this swift growth, the inaugural edition of the Cleveland City Directory in 1837 stood out as a significant indicator of the city's coming of age. The directory offered a comprehensive overview of the urban landscape, including businesses, services and residents, effectively

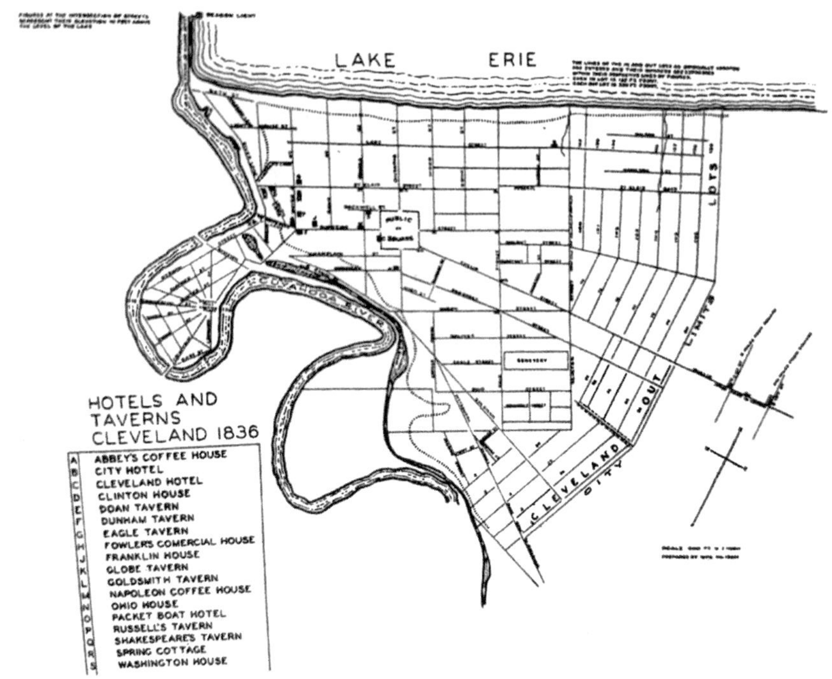

An 1836 map from *Historic Sites of Cleveland: Hotels and Taverns. Ohio Historical Records Survey Project.*

cataloging the life of Cleveland. At this time, the town supported eighteen taverns and inns, highlighting the demand for social spaces within the rapidly growing community.

The Shakespeare Tavern, located at the intersection of Superior Avenue and Water Street (now West Ninth), traces its origins to 1823, when it was first operated by Joel Hood. By 1836, the tavern's character had begun to change, and the Shakespeare developed a reputation as a rougher saloon, frequented by a clientele considered less respectable than those of more refined establishments of the time. As the author of the Ohio Historical Records Survey Project's *Historic Sites of Cleveland: Hotels and Taverns* put it, "The romance was gone." The Shakespeare continued to evolve and was a frequent advertiser in the daily and weekly editions of the *Cleveland Advertiser*. Together with its neighboring hotel, the Shakespeare attracted visitors from across the Western Reserve and became a favored dance venue. Joel Hood, like many tavern keepers of his time, was politically active within the Whig Party; in 1840, he pursued a role in local politics, running for the office of city constable.

As the Panic of 1837 ushered in an era of economic uncertainty, the Shakespeare Tavern inevitably began to feel the impact, reflecting the broader challenges faced by the city of Cleveland. Like much of the nation, Cleveland was profoundly affected by the economic turmoil following the panic and the depression that dominated the 1840s. The city's previously thriving economy took a sharp downturn. Despite these challenges, Cleveland's strategic importance as a key transportation and trade hub uniquely positioned it for a robust recovery as the economic climate began to improve toward the decade's end. This resilience underscored the city's adaptability and its critical role in the regional economy, setting the stage for renewed growth and development in the subsequent years. By the end of the decade, the waterfront was beginning to take its current form, marked notably by the construction of Stockly's Pier in 1849. This development was just part of a broader expansion and continuous enhancement of the lakefront area.

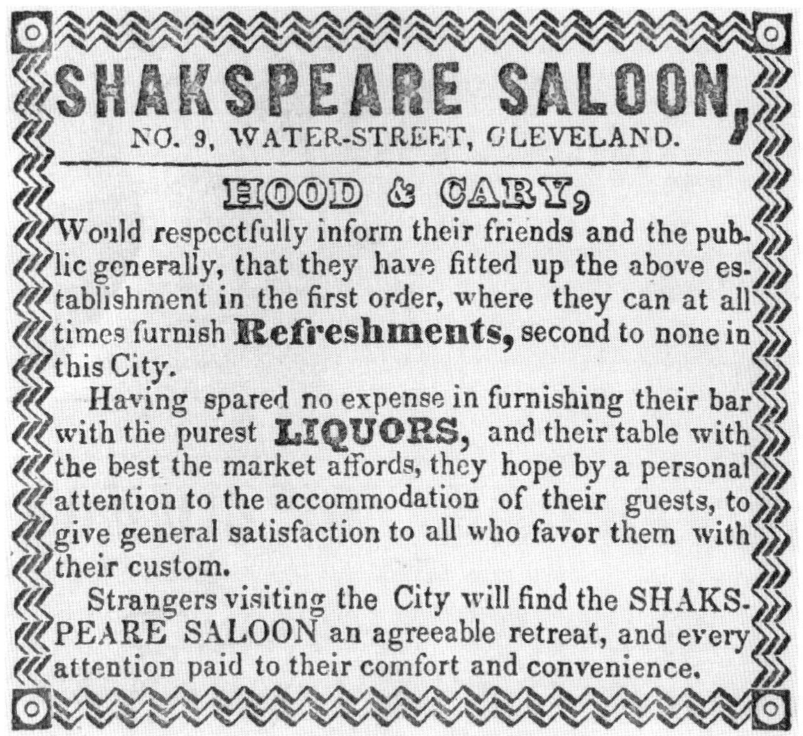

SHAKSPEARE SALOON,
NO. 9, WATER-STREET, CLEVELAND.

HOOD & CARY,

Would respectfully inform their friends and the public generally, that they have fitted up the above establishment in the first order, where they can at all times furnish **Refreshments**, second to none in this City.

Having spared no expense in furnishing their bar with the purest **LIQUORS**, and their table with the best the market affords, they hope by a personal attention to the accommodation of their guests, to give general satisfaction to all who favor them with their custom.

Strangers visiting the City will find the SHAKSPEARE SALOON an agreeable retreat, and every attention paid to their comfort and convenience.

Advertisement in the first Cleveland City Directory in 1837 (the tavern's name was misspelled "Shakspeare"). *Courtesy of the Cuyahoga County Archives City Directory Collection.*

First Waves and Wartime: Early German and Irish Arrivals to Civil War–Era Cleveland (1850s–1860s)

The 1850s marked a period of explosive growth in Cleveland. The success stories of early German and Irish settlers quickly spread back to their homelands, igniting a new wave of immigrants eager to capitalize on the city's economic potential. Cleveland's population swelled to seventeen thousand, and in 1853, the city directory listed fifty-seven taverns. These establishments were primarily concentrated around the Cuyahoga River, with the busiest hubs located on Superior and Pittsburgh Avenues near what is now Broadway. The east bank of the Cuyahoga alone boasted nine bars, offering plenty of options for the city's growing population.

The Foundations of German Tavern Culture in Cleveland

During this decade, German taverns became pivotal social hubs, laying the foundation for a thriving culture of beer gardens and breweries that flourished until the eve of Prohibition. Entrepreneurs like Paul Schmidt, who opened an old-world wine shop on Michigan Street in the 1850s, contributed to this growing landscape. His shop was part of a dense cluster of German taverns around Public Square. These venues, as depicted in a November 1950 series by Theodore Andrica in the *Cleveland Press* titled "Friendship Glowed in Old German Cafes," were more than just drinking spots—they provided German immigrants with a sense of belonging and solidarity in their new homeland. A notable feature was the affordable fifteen-cent lunch, which included a stein of beer, soup, a potato, a cut of meat and an optional cup of whisky for five cents more. For the adventurous, Wright's Tavern, located where the Jack Casino now stands, even offered a free bear meat lunch.

According to Andrica, influential tavern keepers such as William Richter, a pioneer in serving lager beer on tap, played pivotal roles in shaping the city in the 1850s. Once Clevelanders discovered lager beer, Richter's tavern became one of the most popular gathering places in the city. Articles from the *Cleveland Press* vividly illustrate how the "stammtisch," or regulars' table, became a cornerstone of these German taverns, nurturing a sense of community and a shared identity among the city's German immigrants. One beloved establishment, Haltnorth's beer garden, founded by German immigrant Frederick Haltnorth, established itself as a cultural epicenter in Cleveland. Situated at the intersection of Woodland and Wilson Avenues,

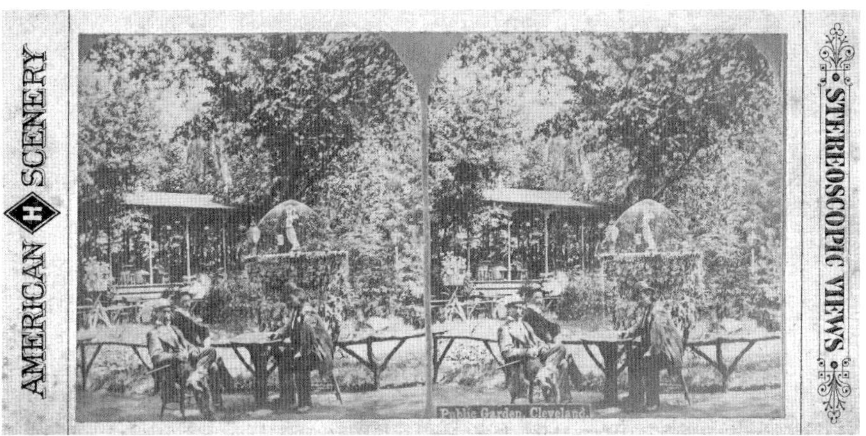

Stereograph image of Haltnorth's Beer Garden at Woodland and Wilson (East Fifty-Fifth Street), today the site of Haltnorth Court. *Cleveland Public Library/Photograph Collection.*

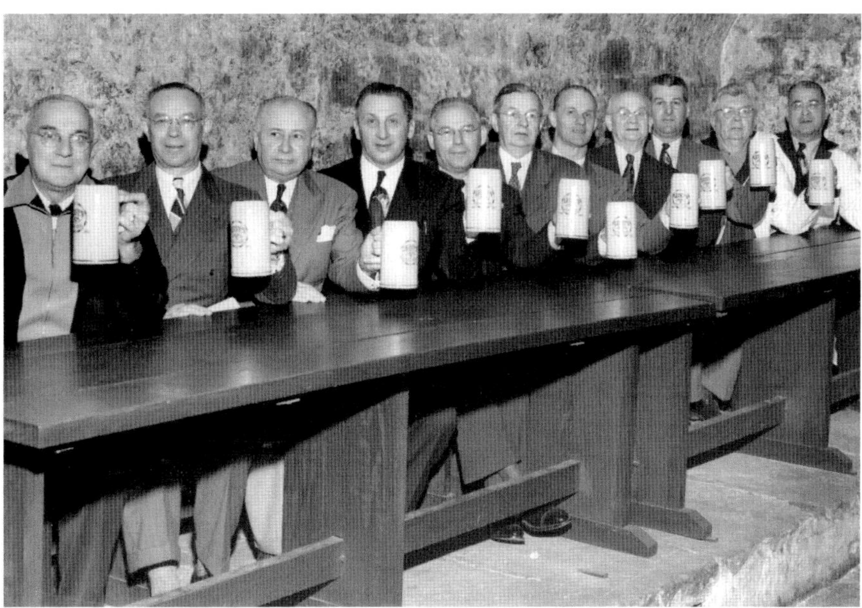

Leisy Brewery old-timers hoist a toast in a rathskeller, a classic underground beer hall, circa 1952. *Left to right*: Harry Weiser, George Schleicher, George S. Diehm, Otto Kalsen, William M. Linsenmann, David B. Tarr, Ray W. Ruch, Louis Naegle, Leo Staskopf, Carl Bohn and Peter Lauerhahs. *Cleveland Press Collection, photographer Lou Moore, Cleveland State University, Michael Schwartz Library Special Collections.*

this beer garden emerged as a vibrant gathering place for community organizations to host special meetings and celebrations. German singing societies and other musical groups frequently graced its grounds with performances well into the early 1900s.

As Cleveland's German tavern culture thrived in the 1850s, so too did its brewing industry, laying the groundwork for the city's distinguished role as a major brewing hub. With the completion of the railroads, exports of Cleveland's lager beer began, expanding its reach and reputation. German brewing traditions continued to influence the industry for decades, and the cultural impact of these breweries remains a part of Cleveland's heritage. The early Germans began brewing shortly after their arrival. Brewing was initially simple, with small-scale breweries and beer production closely tied to saloons and taverns. The introduction of the first ice cellar establishments marked a significant advancement in brewing, allowing for larger production volumes. The first notable brewery, which ultimately became known as the Cleveland Brewing Company, was opened in 1852 by Schmidt and Hoffman on Ansel Road. Soon after, names like the Stumpf Brothers, Gund, Leisy, Schlather and Carl Ernest Gehring emerged as prominent German brewers. For further reading on this topic, the bibliography includes several books that discuss the rich history of Cleveland's brewing industry in detail.

Hope and Hardship: Irish Saloons in Mid-Nineteenth-Century Cleveland

The devastating Great Famine in Ireland (1845–52) triggered a substantial wave of Irish immigration to Cleveland throughout the 1850s. Two years after the famine, Cleveland's Irish population exceeded one thousand—and it was growing by the day. These early settlers, attracted by the city's booming economy and growing status as a transportation hub, primarily made their homes on Whiskey Island, a marshy, mosquito-infested land situated along the banks of the Cuyahoga River. This small tract of land housed thirteen saloons by the century's end. According to William Hickey in *Irish Americans and Their Communities of Cleveland*, "The nineteenth-century Irish loved their saloons. They would sit in them many an evening and, spurred on by 'the creature,' dream their dreams and scheme their schemes."

As the Irish population expanded, their settlements stretched up the east and west banks of the Cuyahoga River's mouth, into areas known as the Angle and Irishtown Bend, eventually spilling over into Ohio City. This area

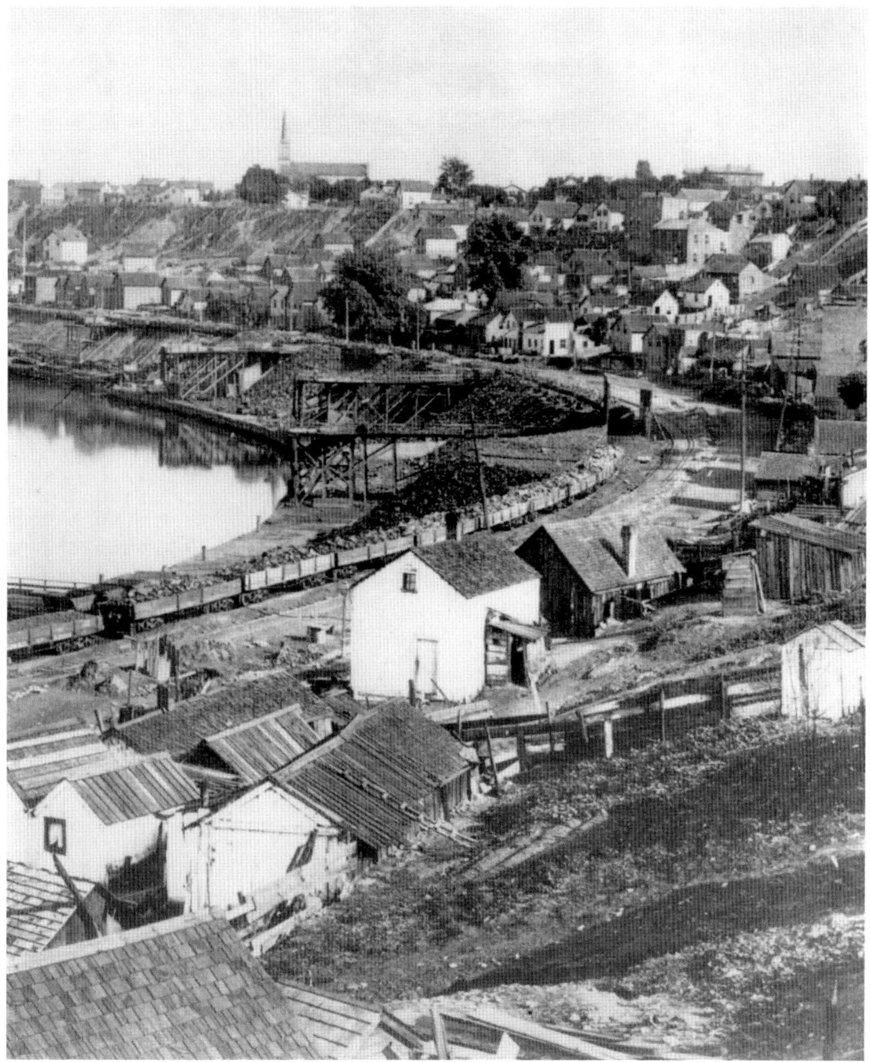

Cleveland Flats Irish settlement, Irish Bend, circa 1885. *Cleveland Public Library/Photograph Collection.*

evolved into a bustling, rough-and-tumble immigrant neighborhood with twenty-four saloons in its heyday. Unlike their predecessors, who might have worked on canal construction, these new immigrants found employment on the railroads, as dock laborers and in iron ore production at the early rolling mills. The work was exhausting and dangerous, making the saloons crucial retreats where they could unwind after long hours at work.

As saloons multiplied throughout the city, local newspapers, including the *Cleveland Leader*, began reporting on the issues arising from their proliferation. On October 11, 1858, the *Cleveland Newspaper Digest* reported, "There are scattered throughout our city an alarmingly large number of drinking and gambling saloons, where young men make another step towards disgrace each time they enter the doors." Despite the grim portrayals in the press, the taverns of the Angle and Whiskey Island remained the heart of Cleveland's Irish community. They were gathering places where the Irish shared their hopes and sorrows—sanctuaries that kept alive the memories of their homeland.

The unity between the German and Irish communities in Cleveland during the Franco-Prussian War celebrations, as reported by the *Cleveland Leader* on September 5, 1870, exemplifies a remarkable instance of cross-cultural solidarity. This collaboration underscores how these distinct immigrant groups could come together to celebrate shared victories despite their different backgrounds. The *Leader* noted, "The wine and beer saloons were crowded, and nearly every man had the Prussian colors flying on his coat lapel. One would naturally think these jubilant people were all Germans, but they were no such thing. We could distinguish the rich Irish brogue high above the sweet German accent."

This blending of German and Irish celebrations can be seen as a symbol of unity among immigrant communities who, despite originating from different European backgrounds, came together in a shared environment when facing common challenges or, in this case, celebrating shared sympathies toward European political shifts.

PINTS AND PATRIOTISM: CLEVELAND TAVERNS DURING THE CIVIL WAR

As the 1860s began to unfold, Cleveland stood on the brink of profound transformation. The decade was a period of rapid growth: the population exploded from forty-three thousand to ninety-two thousand by 1870. The city's boundaries expanded substantially as it annexed neighboring communities, including Ohio City and Brooklyn Village. German and Irish immigration continued, while Eastern European immigration began to take shape, driven by economic opportunities in industrialization and manufacturing. Saloons also boomed; the 1863 city directory contained more than three dedicated pages of listings and almost two hundred saloons.

During this period of expansion and economic growth, the Civil War exerted a profound influence on the nation, and Cleveland felt its impact deeply. The war affected every aspect of city life, turning taverns into essential gathering spots where citizens and soldiers could exchange news, debate the issues of the day and find comfort during uncertain times. As young men enlisted and departed for the battlefields, those remaining sought the camaraderie and support found in these local establishments.

Cleveland made significant contributions to the Union cause during the Civil War. The city provided thousands of troops to the Union army and millions of dollars in supplies, equipment, food and support to the soldiers. Camp Cleveland, which opened in 1862, in what is now northeast Tremont, was one of several Civil War camps that operated in the Cleveland area during the Civil War period. It was the only camp to remain in operation throughout the conflict. The camp included barracks, hospitals and administrative buildings to support the soldiers stationed there. As the Civil War reached its conclusion in 1865, Camp Cleveland transitioned from a training ground to a demobilization center. Over ten thousand soldiers were mustered out from service, receiving their final wages and reentering civilian life. With their earnings, many sought the welcoming atmosphere of taverns, a place to celebrate their return and ease back into the rhythms of home.

The Civil War contributed to the saloons' reputation for rowdiness. Taverns like August Fay's on Ontario Street became notorious hubs for soldiers either on leave or awaiting mustering from Camp Cleveland. In

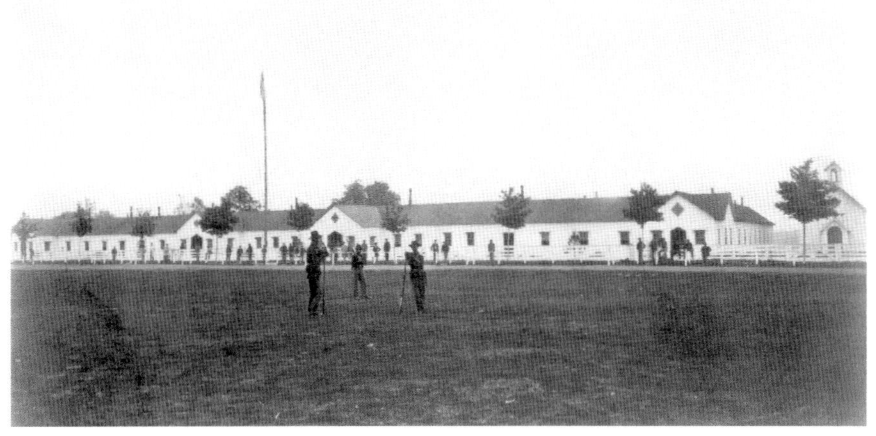

Civil War Camp Cleveland, 1865. Today the location is in Tremont, at the towpath entrance. *Cleveland Public Library/Photograph Collection.*

April 1864, one of these gatherings turned tragic at Fay's Tavern, due to the volatile mix of alcohol, high emotions and the rough company often found in such establishments, where gambling, fighting and prostitution were common.

John Fay, the brother of August Fay, and a soldier himself, became embroiled in a deadly altercation while defending August from an irate patron. The dispute had begun when the patron, swindled by a prostitute operating within the saloon, turned his anger on August. In the heated exchange, John was fatally stabbed.

This incident led to a highly publicized trial, chronicled in the *Cleveland Leader*. It was not John's first brush with death. Ironically, he had been shot two years earlier by another drunken soldier but had survived. John Fay's ultimate sacrifice is commemorated on the Roll of Honor at the downtown Soldiers and Sailors Monument.

Due to the problem of rowdy inebriated soldiers, laws were passed to prohibit soldiers from drinking at the local taverns. However, a letter to the editor of the *Cleveland Leader* dated June 12, 1865, revealed that the City of Cleveland failed to enforce this directive. "Proprietors of saloons not only allow soldiers to buy drinks, but give them liquor and then swindle them out of their earnings."

While many establishments during the Civil War era were known for their rowdiness, not all shared this notorious reputation. The tradition of integrating taverns with hotels persisted, giving rise to several more refined venues that catered to a distinguished clientele. The renowned Weddell House, situated on Superior and Bank Street, was a grand, five-story hotel and tavern that opened in the mid-1840s. The hotel's tavern served as a meeting place for locals and distinguished travelers to partake in political discussions.

On the eve of the Civil War, on February 12, 1861, the *Cleveland Plain Dealer* reported that Lincoln was going to visit the Weddell House the following week and hold a reception for the public. Lincoln was known to sip champagne slowly, ensuring that he remained composed and congenial rather than becoming a "stick in the mud." Shortly after the Confederate surrender in 1865, General George Armstrong Custer visited the hotel and tavern during a journey to meet General Philip Sheridan. Despite Custer's youthful indiscretions with alcohol, which once led a judge to harshly forbid him from seeing his daughter, he had sworn off liquor entirely by this point in his life.

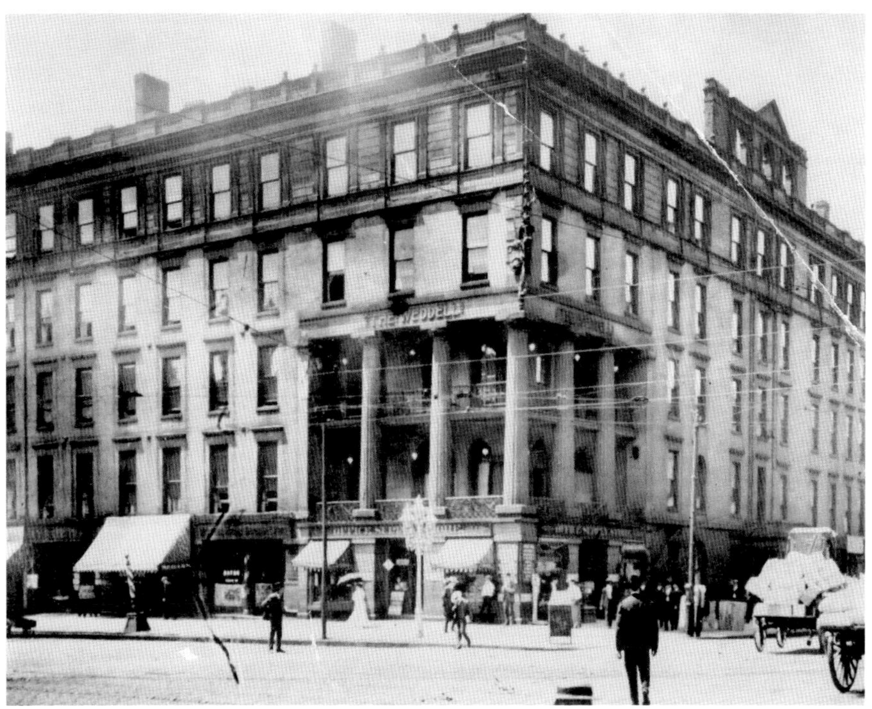

Weddell House, opened in 1847 at Superior and West Sixth Street, circa 1900. Visitors to the tavern include Abraham Lincoln and General George Custer. *Cleveland Public Library/ Photograph Collection.*

As the Civil War drew to a close and the nation began to heal and rebuild, the United States opened its arms to a new wave of change. The postwar era was not only a time of reconstruction but also marked the beginning of significant demographic shifts. Substantial Eastern European immigration began, as thousands crossed the Atlantic in search of the freedoms and opportunities that the rejuvenated Union promised. This period of transformation laid the groundwork for the rich multicultural tapestry that would come to define the American experience.

Chapter 2

Forging a New Era

Immigration and Industrialization

The 1870s marked the beginning of an era of unprecedented growth for Cleveland, setting the stage for an impressive expansion that continued well into the early twentieth century. By 1900, the city's population had surged from 92,000 in 1870 to over 381,000, more than quadrupling with the influx of immigrants from central, eastern and southern Europe. By 1890, three-quarters of the city's population was foreign-born or born of foreign parents. As 1920 approached, this growth trend persisted, and Cleveland's population reached nearly 800,000, making it the seventh most populous city in the United States. These new residents brought with them their unique ethnic identities and traditions, significantly enriching the city's cultural fabric. This dramatic population growth was driven by continued immigration and the city's industrial strength, which attracted a diverse workforce seeking opportunities and stability.

As the nineteenth century ended, Cleveland not only experienced a surge in population but also underwent significant physical expansion. The city extended its boundaries by annexing neighboring Newburgh and Brooklyn Village, along with several smaller surrounding villages. This expansion prompted the establishment of new industrial and residential areas, which was essential for supporting the growing workforce. These developments were crucial for bolstering Cleveland's industrial base, supplying the necessary infrastructure to foster the city's growth as a hub of manufacturing and commerce.

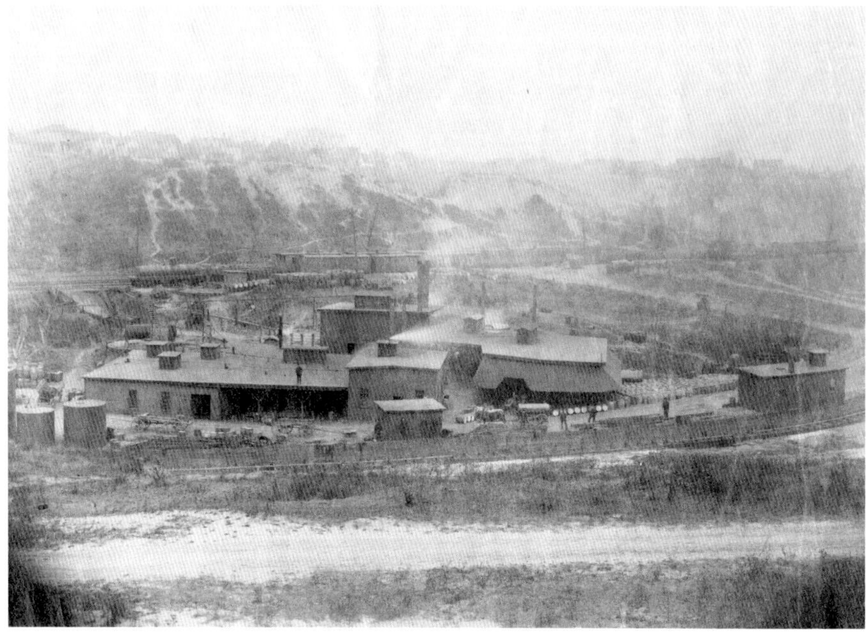

Standard Oil plant on Wiley Avenue, circa 1870–80. *Cleveland Public Library/Photograph Collection.*

This era of expansion was characterized by not just a dramatic increase in population but also a significant economic transformation that continued into the new century. The influx of new residents coincided with the rise of influential companies. Beyond traditional employment opportunities on the docks and railroads, major firms such as Cleveland Rolling Mills, Standard Oil, Sherwin-Williams, Otis Elevator and Warner and Swasey emerged, offering substantial economic opportunities to the new immigrants. Furthermore, the early twentieth century saw the rise of the automobile industry in Cleveland, with companies like White Motors and Winton Motor Carriage leading the way in motor vehicle production. General Electric also expanded its operations during this time, contributing to a boom in electrical manufacturing and innovation. These companies became household names and were instrumental in shaping both the local and national economy, turning Cleveland into a major hub of industry and innovation.

Immigrants typically selected their neighborhood based on its closeness to their workplace and the existing communities of their ethnic peers. After long, exhausting days of manual labor at the mills or factories, they could be surrounded by others who shared their culture, language and religious practices. The neighborhood tavern provided essential comfort and support, creating a sense of home and community in the new country. Living among their ethnic peers helped preserve their traditions and provided a familiar environment where they could relax and recharge. The immigrants could not only unwind but also speak their native languages, share news from their homelands and discuss life and the challenges in the United States.

Each neighborhood's story is a testament to the resilience and contributions of its residents. They built churches, established schools and opened businesses that catered to their specific cultural needs, all while contributing to the broader economy of Cleveland. The city is still defined by these diverse neighborhoods, each evolving in its own way, shaped by the unique characteristics and makeup of its residents.

The Early Ethnic Neighborhoods

While most immigrants were confined to particular areas of the city, the Haymarket District was home to forty different nationalities. This area was originally Cleveland's first marketplace, where farmers would congregate to sell their produce. Starting in 1870, Italians arrived, moving in among eastern Europeans, Syrians and other ethnic groups. Jews of all eastern European origins organized their first congregation right at Central Market. The Haymarket District was situated where the Gateway Complex stands today, just above the flats.

It would be an understatement to say this was a colorful area. These newly arrived immigrants worked down the hill in the flats, in very harsh working conditions, in the most dangerous jobs. As the housing stock continued to deteriorate, many families lived in poverty, and the area became the first slum in the city. Rampant crime and gang activity, led by the notorious gangster Blinky Morgan, persisted in the area. Alfred Henry Lewis, a former city prosecutor turned prominent writer, captured the struggles of working-class neighborhoods like the Haymarket District in his book *Field Notes of a Reformer*. Much of this firsthand account was later published in a series of articles in the *Cleveland Plain Dealer*, in 1920. The neighborhood was so rough that police patrolled in threes and used wheelbarrows to transport drunks to jail. Lewis remarked that every other house was either a saloon or bawdy house. While some of Lewis's accounts may blend fact with fiction, they nonetheless offer a vivid and largely accurate portrayal of the area. Some of the most popular saloons were Sailor Boy's, Big Mike's Place and Gypsy George's, a Western bar and dance hall. Gypsy George's had seven

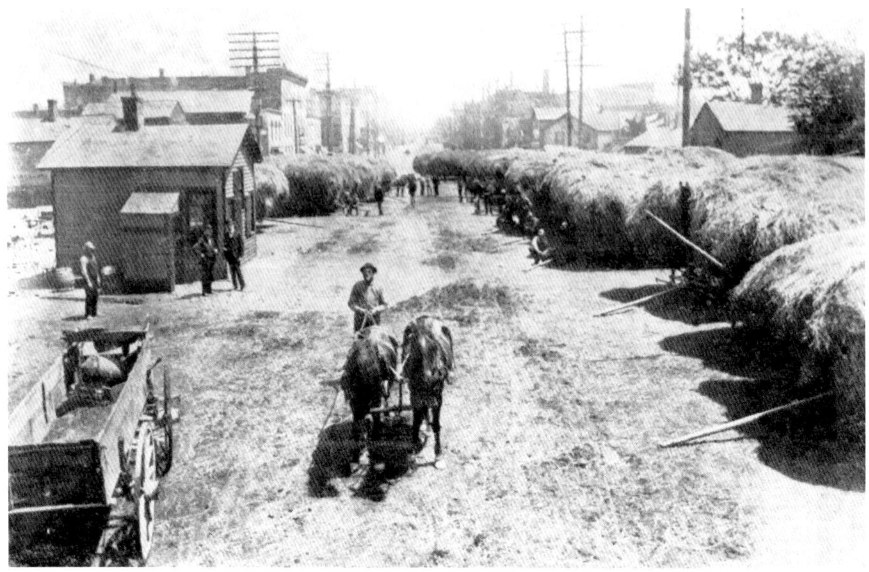

Haymarket District, circa 1890. *Cleveland Public Library/Photograph Collection.*

entrances, including two underground passages. Overall, the Haymarket area was home to thirty saloons on Commercial Street. Ultimately, the construction of the Central Viaduct and, later, the Terminal Tower led to the area's demise.

While the Haymarket District was a melting pot housing over forty nationalities, many other immigrant communities formed more insular, concentrated ethnic enclaves throughout the city. The Irish were already established on Whiskey Island and in the Angle, and the Germans had settled on the near East and the West Side. The last twenty-five years of the nineteenth century saw Czechs and Poles clustering in neighborhoods south of Broadway, such as Praha and Warczawa. Italians formed concentrated communities in Big Italy off Woodland Avenue and Little Italy along Mayfield Road. The area now known as Tremont was home to Carpathian-Rusyn, Greek, Polish, Slovak and Syrian populations. Hungarians settled along Buckeye Road, while Croatians, Serbs and Slovenians claimed sections of Saint Clair Avenue as well as Collinwood. Jewish immigrants established communities on Woodland and Kinsman Road. These groups formed their own places of worship and social institutions, which were vital for maintaining their culture, language and traditions.

Throughout the immigrant neighborhoods, there was no shortage of saloons. By 1885, there were 1,418 saloons serving a total population of

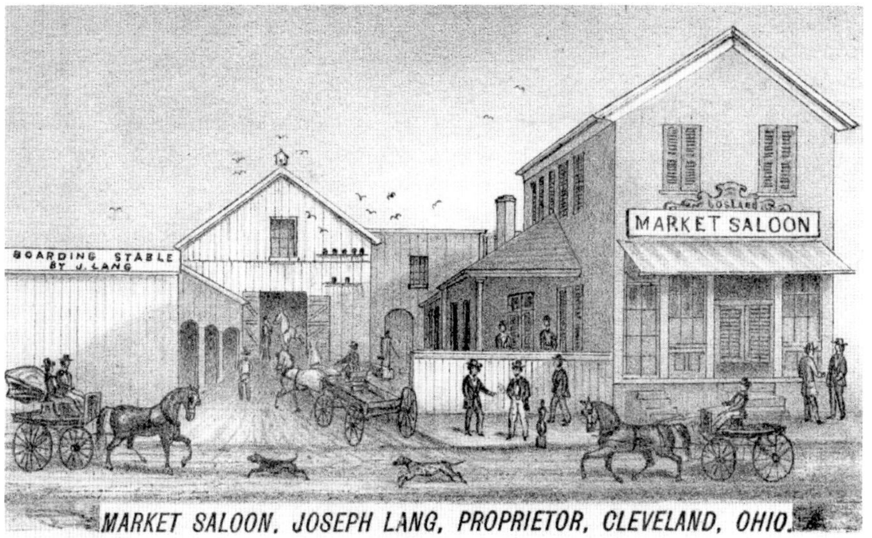

Market Saloon on 86 Lorain Street, Ohio City, 1874. Proprietor Joseph Lang was arrested for violating the election liquor law in 1877. *Cleveland Public Library/Photograph Collection.*

about 200,000 city residents. These tavern keepers were often colorful and notable figures within their communities. Around the turn of the century, Karl Roskoph, the son of Moses Roskoph (a member of the second Jewish family to settle in Cleveland, in the 1830s) opened his own tavern at Perry Street (East Twenty-Second) and Woodland. Both Moses and Karl had several encounters with the law, including an arrest for intent to kill during a confrontation on Perry Street.

Just a few miles south of Roskophs' Tavern, the Scczerbacki Tavern stood at 3565 East Eightieth, near Broadway and Aetna. It was strategically positioned to cater to the needs of the early eastern European immigrants returning home from the mills. Serving those residing closer to the heart of Warczawa, John Grucza's tavern could be found at the corner of East Fifty-Seventh and Orey Streets. While this establishment changed hands over the years, it remained a welcoming local tavern and was known as the Polish Roman Catholic Union throughout the 1970s.

A few miles to the north and east, most Hungarian immigrants settled in the Buckeye Road neighborhood. The city's Hungarian immigrant population boomed from 9,558 to 43,134 by 1920. Hungarians constituted 8 percent of the city's foreign-born population in 1900 and 18 percent in 1920. In contrast to members of other immigrant groups, many Hungarians initially planned to return to Hungary after accumulating enough savings to

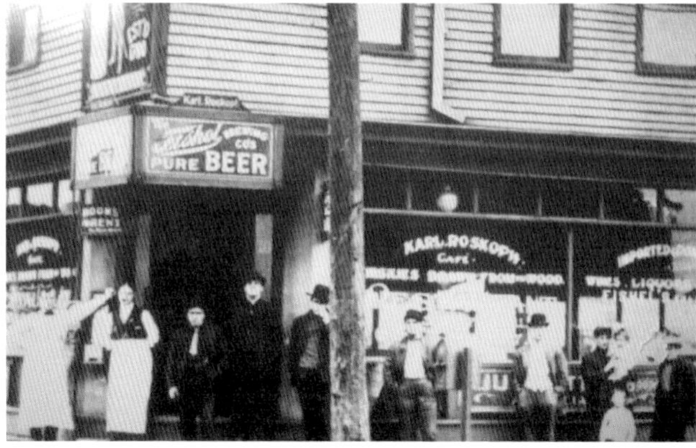

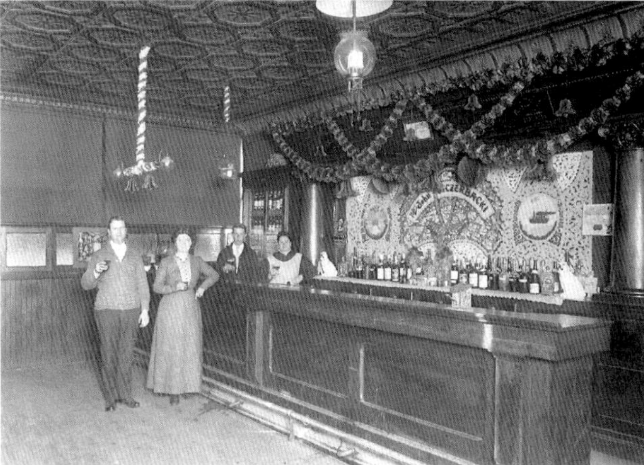

Top: Early patrons in front of Karl Roskoph's tavern at Perry (East Twenty-Second) and Woodland, date unknown. *Courtesy of Slavic Village Historical Society.*

Bottom: Scczerbacki Tavern, circa early 1900s. Take note of the battleship *Maine* picture and the canary cage. In an era when lighting relied on natural gas fixtures, the presence of a deceased canary served as an indicator of gas being turned on without a flame. *Courtesy of Slavic Village Historical Society.*

purchase land. However, due to continued immigration and the impact of World War I, many ultimately chose to stay in the United States. From 1925 to 1960, the Hungarian-supported establishments in the Buckeye-Woodland area, including twenty-five taverns, remained relatively unchanged. A well-documented early Hungarian tavern was Takacs Saloon, which was located at 172 South Woodland Avenue in Cleveland.

The massive influx of European immigrants to Cleveland slowed dramatically with the onset of World War I, even as the city's industrial base continued to expand to support the war effort. The new labor force was drawn largely from the American South, part of the Great Migration that reshaped the demographic landscape of northern cities. By 1920, the African American population in Cleveland had surged, from 8,500 in 1910 to over 34,000; many newcomers settled predominantly in the Central Avenue area.

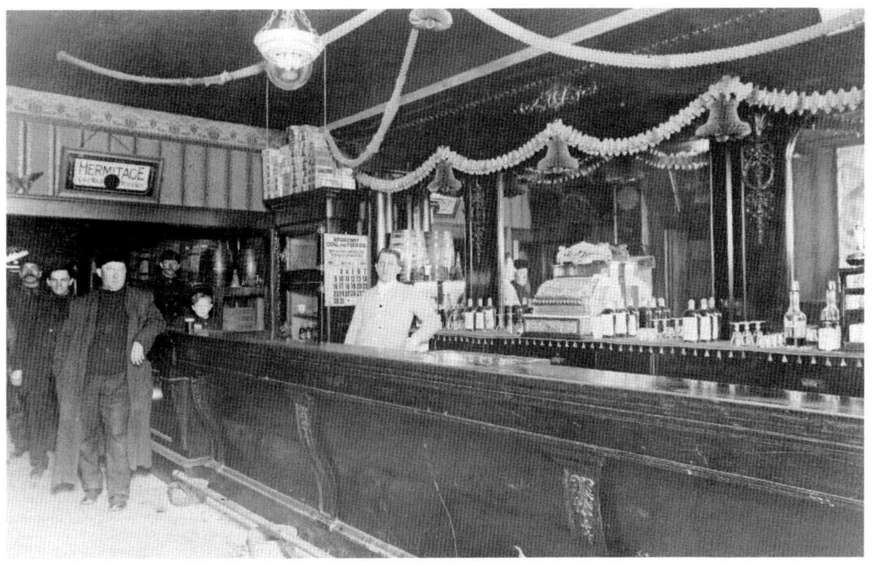

The Grucza Tavern at 3906 East Fifty-Seventh Street in Warczawa. The calendar is dated January 1911. *Cleveland State University, Michael Schwartz Library Special Collections.*

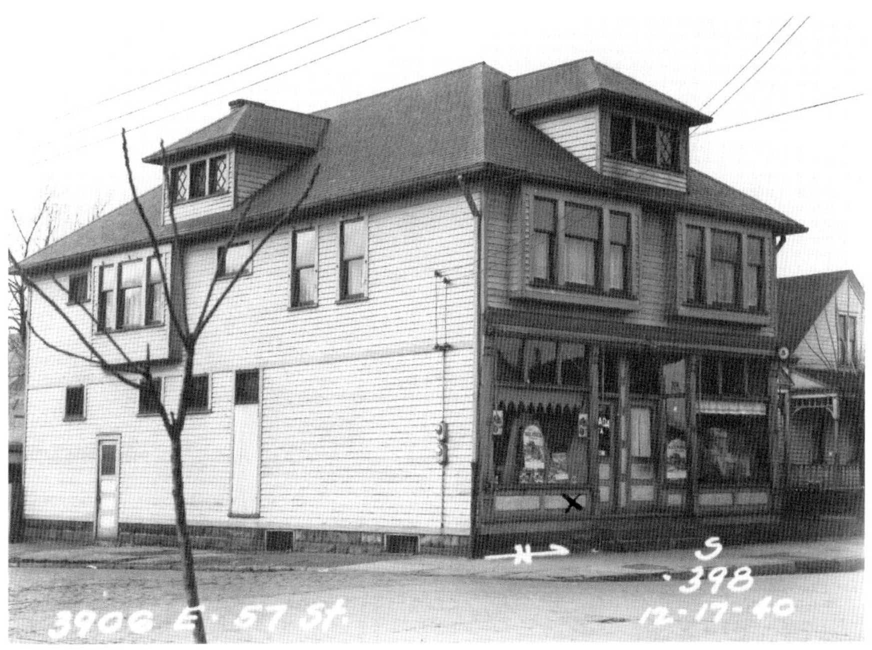

The Grucza Tavern, which became the Polish Roman Catholic Union (PRCU) bar, a popular neighborhood spot in Slavic Village through the 1970s. *Cleveland Public Library/ Photograph Collection.*

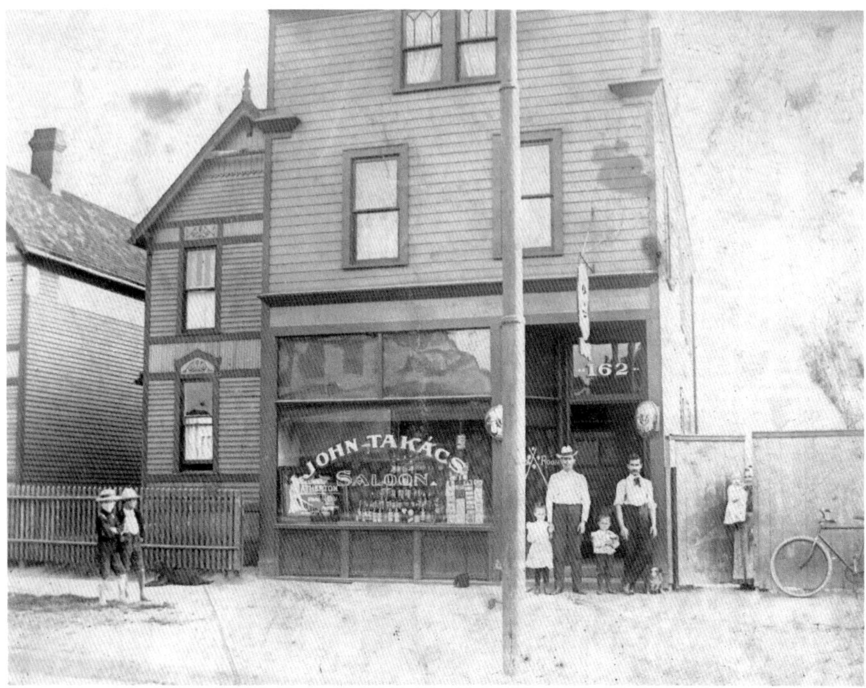

Elizabeth Takacs (holding the hand of an unknown male), Louis Takacs, John Takacs and Barbara Takacs. The other individuals are unknown. *Photo by Andras Zambroszky date unknown, Cleveland State University, Michael Schwartz Library Special Collections.*

By the turn of the twentieth century, Cleveland was home to over two thousand taverns and twenty-six breweries, a proliferation that significantly exacerbated the societal challenges linked to alcohol abuse. While the temperance movement had long been advocating for stricter laws and regulations, it was now gaining considerable momentum and political support. As the twentieth century unfolded, this movement was poised to intensify, garnering widespread backing and resulting in the implementation of more stringent laws and regulations. The shift toward prohibition was not solely a reaction to alcohol-related issues but also reflected broader societal desires for reform across the United States to eliminate the purchase and consumption of alcohol.

Chapter 3

Dry Laws and Wet Counters

The Battle over Booze in Cleveland

The growing influence of the temperance movement led to the formation of the Cuyahoga County Temperance Society, followed by the Cleveland City Temperance Society in 1836. These early organizations preached total abstinence and squarely blamed poverty and immorality on alcohol consumption. The 1837 Cleveland City Directory revealed that the Cleveland City Temperance Society boasted an impressive 260 members, apparently one of the largest associations in the city at that time. Its sizable membership demonstrated the early prevalence of and dedication to the temperance cause in Cleveland.

Since many tavern owners were also public officials, the city was slow to enact any laws controlling the consumption or production of spirits. While legislative efforts to control liquor licenses were proposed, they remained stalled in debate with little action. Finally, a compromise was reached, and on May 6, 1840, an ordinance was passed to regulate taverns and to prohibit the sale of spirits or other intoxicating liquors in quantities less than one quart. This was an attempt to limit immediate consumption and reduce disorderly conduct. However, the law was rarely enforced, and in 1850, a group of prominent women formed the Cleveland Ladies Temperance Union, which grew to over 1,400 members by 1853. At the same time, Catholic temperance groups formed, joining other temperance societies advocating political involvement, both locally and nationally, to exert pressure to enact more substantive regulations. In 1852–53, the temperance organizations recruited a third-party gubernatorial candidate

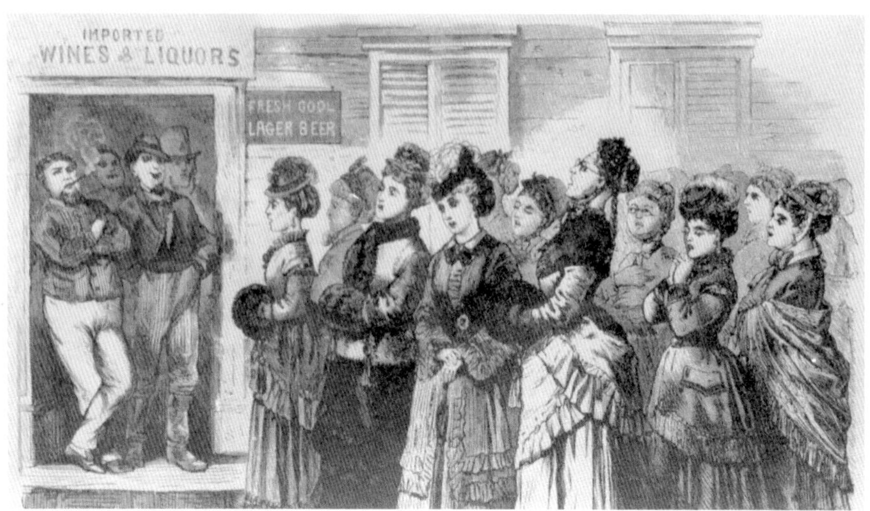

Women in Logan, Ohio, singing hymns in front of a saloon during the temperance movement. *The Cleveland Press Collections, courtesy of the Michael Schwartz Library Special Collections, Cleveland State University.*

who endorsed total prohibition of alcohol manufacturing and sales. The Prohibition Party remains in existence and is the oldest third party in the United States. The party has put forth a presidential nominee in every election since 1872.

As the Civil War ended, the temperance movement gained momentum with the Women's Crusade, a series of widespread protests across the state. During these protests, which became known as the Ohio Whiskey War, women entered saloons aiming to shame those who sold and consumed alcohol. These protests not only disrupted the daily business of taverns but also spotlighted the growing societal push against alcohol. Cleveland's temperance forces joined this escalating campaign of raids and demonstrations against the city's saloons and breweries.

In 1893, a new organization, the National Anti-Saloon League, was formed in Oberlin, Ohio, as a political pressure group. It was backed by evangelical Protestants, and its paid staff employed tactics such as sending mass mailings to lists of registered voters with the goal of eliminating saloons. In Cleveland, the branch shared a headquarters with the local Woman's Christian Temperance Union as both groups worked together toward their common prohibitionist goals.

The temperance movement had a significant impact on laws in Cleveland during the last quarter of the nineteenth century. The Civil War–era laws

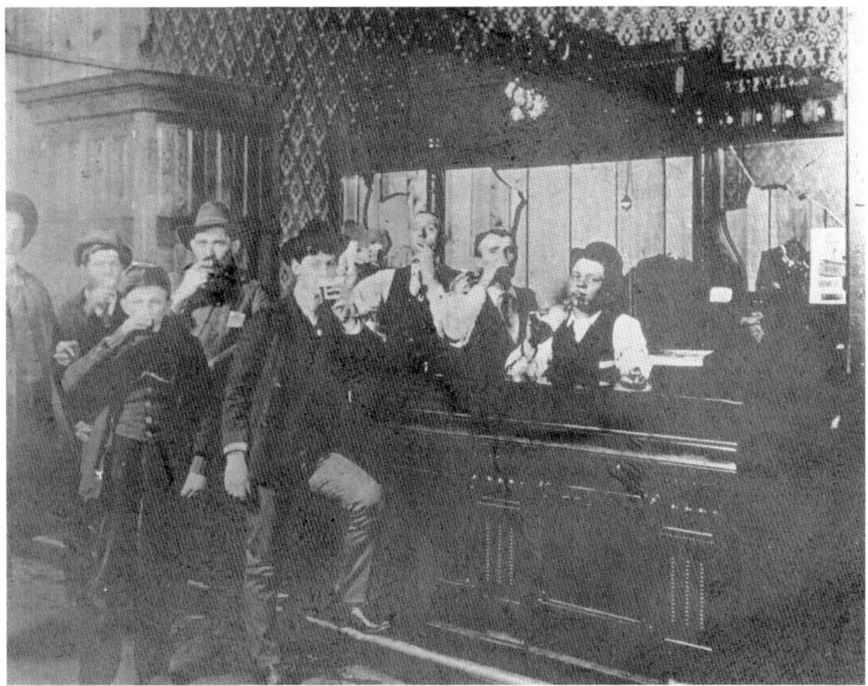

Men and teenagers drinking at a bar, circa 1890. *Courtesy of the Western Reserve Historical Society.*

prohibiting soldiers from drinking in taverns and restricting alcohol sales on Sundays proved to be ineffective and were ultimately repealed. This led to more innovative attempts to limit alcohol consumption and sales. For instance, a city ordinance dating to at least 1875 allowed family members to file formal objections prohibiting the sale or gifting of liquor to specific relatives. However, this measure had limited effectiveness, as notices had to be properly distributed to all establishments that sold and served beer and spirits.

The longest-standing regulation was the prohibition of the sale of alcohol on the Sabbath. On September 10, 1900, the *Cleveland Leader* reported on an unsuccessful operation by the Cleveland police, who attempted to infiltrate local taverns on a Sunday. The tavern owners were tipped off by paid lookouts to refuse entry to anyone unknown to them. This limited the sting to the arrests of only eighteen bartenders and saloonkeepers along what was known as Saloon Row on Superior. Despite ongoing police efforts, many tavern keepers continued to disregard the Sunday closing laws. Their sentiments were captured in a quote from a tavern keeper in the *Plain Dealer*

Name. William Watkins
Residence No 608 Central Ave, Rear.

Notice is hereby given to all Liquor Dealers and all owners or lessors of premises where Intoxicating Liquors are sold in the City of Cleveland not to sell or give intoxicating liquors to William Watkins who resides at rear of #608 Central Ave., after ten days from date of filing this notice.

Dated Cleveland Oct 5th, 1896. Signed. Mrs. Julia Watkins
Filed Oct 8, 1896.

City of Cleveland notice prohibiting the sale of intoxicating liquors to William Watkins, October 5th 1896. *Courtesy of the City of Cleveland Archives.*

on April 26, 1909: "It is inhuman on a day so warm as this to allow the good people of Cleveland to go thirsty."

The turn of the century brought more challenges to the saloonkeepers as the temperance movement continued to gather support and political clout. In 1904, Ohio passed the Brannock Law, which represented a major setback for the state's liquor interests. The Brannock Law allowed districts to vote on going "dry," which would result in taverns losing their liquor licenses and being forced out of business. The *Cleveland Plain Dealer* reported on the voting results on Friday, August 12, 1904, revealing that sixty tavern licenses were revoked across the city. But it was a minor victory for the temperance movement, as the "wets" emerged convincingly victorious across most districts. This trend continued later that summer in Newburgh, where the wets prevailed across all four wards.

Anti-Saloon League advocates continued to garner political support, leading to increasingly restrictive legislation against saloonkeepers. The Dean Law, enacted in 1909, imposed harsh penalties on tavern owners who failed to comply with regulations concerning moral conduct. One tavern keeper gave a tongue-in-cheek response to the new law in an interview with the *Plain Dealer*: "Obey the Dean Law? Of course, whoever heard of a saloonkeeper selling to a minor or an intoxicated person or harboring an immoral woman?" This sarcastic remark was reflective of the attitudes of tavern keepers across the city.

The Anti-Saloon League and the Ohio Liquor Association engaged in a fierce battle over a proposed amendment to the Ohio Revised Code that would limit the number of taverns across the state to one for every five hundred residents. The Anti-Saloon League emerged victorious, as the amendment passed and became effective in 1913. This resulted in the closure of eight hundred taverns in Cuyahoga County.

The selection criteria for closures were based on four categories: taverns deemed undesirable due to crime, disorderly conduct or poor sanitary conditions; those owned by unnaturalized citizens; those owned by breweries; and transient establishments, which lacked a permanent owner. The surviving saloonkeepers supported the amendment, as it could limit competition and potentially improve their reputation. The following year, Cleveland was able to add nearly fifty saloons due to the city's estimated population growth. This set the stage for the final battle: Prohibition.

When Cleveland Went Dry: The Prohibition Battleground

The nearly century-long effort of the temperance crusaders achieved its ultimate goal with the ratification of the Eighteenth Amendment to the U.S. Constitution in 1919, instituting the era of nationwide Prohibition as the law of the land. This national ban on the manufacture, sale and transportation of alcohol, intended to curb the perceived moral decay associated with drinking, resulted in a plethora of unintended consequences. The impact of Prohibition rippled across Cleveland, giving rise to bootlegging, speakeasies and a surge in organized crime. While organized crime existed prior to Prohibition, the dynamics of supply and demand necessitated further structure and organization among crime families. In *The Rise and Fall of the Cleveland Mafia: Corn Sugar and Blood*, author Rick Porrello, who is not only an expert on the history of organized crime in Cleveland but also the grandson of a leading crime family, discusses the three stages of Prohibition: initially, the consumption of alcohol already in stock; subsequently, the manufacture of homemade booze; and finally, rumrunning or importing.

The underground alcohol trade that emerged from these stages fueled the rise of a vast illicit supply chain, encompassing production, distribution and smuggling. As the city's Italian immigrants migrated from the Woodland area to the Little Italy neighborhood, this area became the epicenter of bootlegging activity.

As Prohibition's unintended consequences unfolded, the strict enforcement of the law stirred deep resentment among immigrant communities, who felt targeted and marginalized from mainstream society. On April 17, 1919, a *Cleveland Plain Dealer* article titled "85,000 Saloons—For Rent" poignantly questioned the future of traditional community gathering spots. The article highlighted the integral role these establishments played in the lives of poorer residents: "The poorer people have their christenings, their weddings, their dances. Unless they are connected with the church, they regard the saloon as the social clearinghouse of the neighborhood." This sentiment underscored how deeply Prohibition reshaped everyday social interactions and community bonds.

It was apparent from the start that the local police were not enthusiastic about supporting the new law. On November 9, 1920, the *Cleveland Plain Dealer* reported that Police Chief Smith, under the mayor's direction, had declared an intensified crackdown on vice, gambling and illicit liquor. The police force doubled its vice squad to fifty officers to crack down on Volstead Act violations. The city also enacted new measures, including stricter licensing for all establishments that sold any type of drink, since soda fountains were operating as speakeasies. The city also increased fines, setting the penalty for first offenses at $1,000 and establishing a mandatory sixty-day jail sentence for second offenses. While Cleveland police struggled to secure convictions compared to federal authorities, Prohibition agents at one point boasted that they recorded 1,600 convictions since the onset of Prohibition.

On January 6, 1932, the *Cleveland Plain Dealer* reported on the typical federal raid: Agents gained the doorman's trust and found patrons enjoying illegal beer, liquor, gin and wine. The proprietors operating the speakeasy were promptly arrested, and the agents dismantled and hauled away every fixture and bottle from the club. One such raid targeted the Tom Thumb Club, which was raided four times before the establishment was finally shut down.

Despite the official closure of taverns, the 1924 Cleveland City Directory, surprisingly, listed 496 saloons across the city. Eventually, the directory eliminated the saloon category altogether and directed readers to the soft drinks section, where forty-two retailers were listed. Faced with a stark choice, Cleveland's taverns had to either shut down, transform into soda shops or restaurants or defy the law by operating as speakeasies. For many tavern owners, running an illicit speakeasy became the only viable way to remain in business.

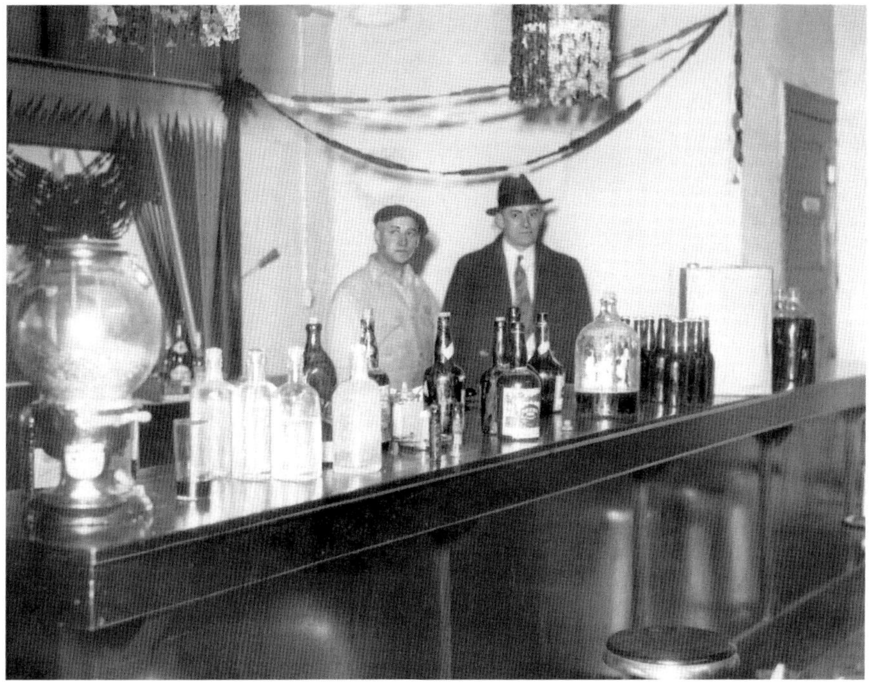

Raid at Tom Thumb Club, East Thirteenth and Central Avenue, 1932. *Cleveland State University, Michael Schwartz Library Special Collections.*

The term *speakeasy* is believed to have originated from the practice of advising patrons to "speak easy," or maintain a low profile, to avoid attracting the attention of law enforcement. These underground drinking establishments had nondescript exteriors and often disguised themselves as other businesses, granting access only through rear alleys or side doors using passwords. Inside, speakeasies were dimly lit, with heavy curtains blocking the view from the outside. Despite the constant threat of police raids, speakeasies were widespread and immensely popular, serving as a symbol of public resistance against Prohibition laws. The speakeasies served Clevelanders from all walks of life, from the working class to local and visiting celebrities.

On July 19, 1927, the *Plain Dealer* reported the arrest of Billy Fergus, a well-known boxing promoter, for running a large-scale "saloon" at 1270 West Fifty-Eighth Street. Authorities uncovered over two hundred cases of beer stashed inside Fergus's establishment, which agents dubbed the "biggest beer oasis on the west side." The word on the street was that bartenders claimed "everybody was fixed except the Feds, and they were

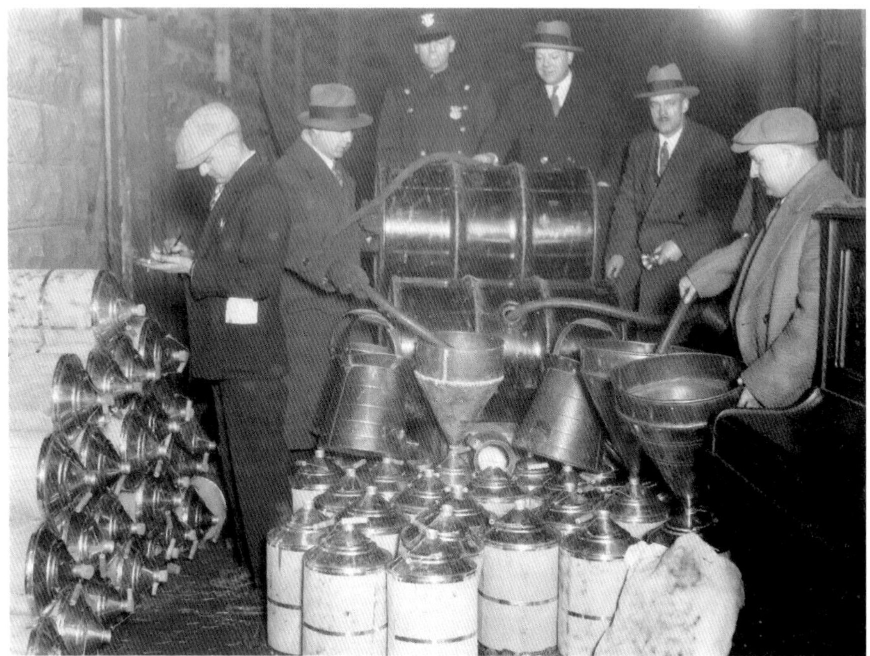

Local and federal law enforcement surrounding evidence found in a Prohibition raid, April 6, 1927. *Cleveland Press Collection, Cleveland State University, Michael Schwartz Library Special Collections.*

scared to come near." Like most speakeasies, the illegal saloon featured a secret entrance leading to a dark and dusty area where the beer was stored. This wasn't the first raid on the Fergus family: Billy's brother Eddie had previously been caught operating his own underground tavern on Fulton Road and Bridge Avenue.

Despite occasional "wins" for Prohibition agents, these minor victories barely made a dent in the rampant Prohibition violations that were sweeping across Cleveland and the nation. Local and federal law enforcement agencies found themselves outnumbered and outmaneuvered by the surge of new speakeasies and the public's contempt for liquor laws. As the Eighteenth Amendment neared repeal, political organizations began to surface, aiming to abolish Prohibition and return to the temperance movement. Among these groups, the Crusaders took a more moderate approach to temperance, advocating for the regulation of alcohol rather than its complete elimination. They envisioned a society where alcohol remained legal but was accompanied by comprehensive education about its dangers. They believed this approach would be more effective and help stem the rise in organized crime. To support their cause, the Crusaders sponsored a study that was featured in a *Plain Dealer* article on June 26, 1932, titled "Map of City Shows Speakeasies Exceed Old Saloons By Far." The article highlighted the extent to which speakeasies had proliferated throughout the city, surpassing the number of taverns that existed prior to Prohibition. The map, created by Irving Starworth for the Crusaders, pinpointed the locations of 2,545 speakeasies in Cleveland that were in operation in 1931. The data suggested a dramatic increase in the availability of alcohol, with one speakeasy for every 358 residents compared to one saloon for every 670 residents in the pre-Prohibition era. During the year of the study, Cleveland police recorded 3,551 liquor law violations.

The anti-Prohibition movement garnered support from the Federation of Women's Clubs of Greater Cleveland, which had previously been an advocate for the Eighteenth Amendment. Mrs. Amasa Stone Mather, the Ohio chairwoman of the Women's National League for Prohibition Reform, concurred with the Crusaders' assessment that speakeasies significantly outnumbered taverns and that young men and women were drinking more

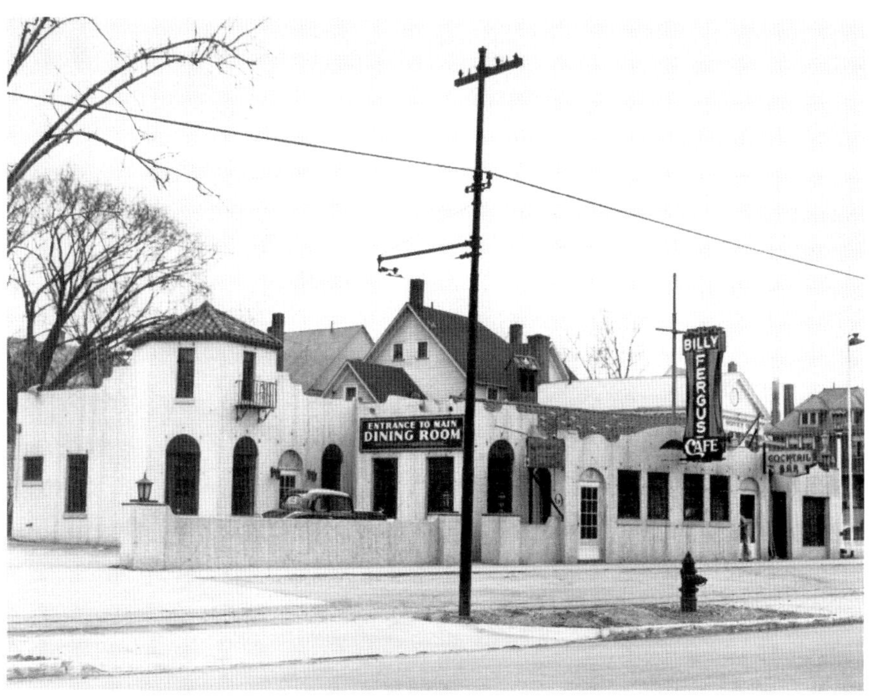

Café and Cocktail Lounge, run by Billy Fergus, fight promoter, in 1927. *Cleveland Press Collection, Cleveland State University, Michael Schwartz Library Special Collections.*

now than before Prohibition. There was a prevailing belief that people frequented saloons for social purposes, while many visited speakeasies with the sole intention of getting drunk.

Widespread public disillusionment, coupled with the unstoppable proliferation of illegal speakeasies, culminated in immense local and national pressure for repeal. On December 5, 1933, this growing momentum resulted with the ratification of the Twenty-First Amendment, which officially ended the country's experiment with banning alcohol. This was a sobering acknowledgment that legislating morality through blanket prohibition was impractical and doomed to fail; the demand for alcohol was deeply woven into the national fabric.

The Battle Continues: Crime, Corruption and Tavern Survival in Post-Prohibition Cleveland

During Prohibition and throughout the 1930s, Cleveland was a city of stark contrasts. With a booming population of over 900,000, it had become the sixth-largest city in the nation. Meanwhile, Cuyahoga County's total population surpassed 1.2 million, making Cleveland the center of the third-largest metropolitan area in the United States. The 1920s saw the construction of the iconic Terminal Tower, a towering symbol of the city's ambition, alongside the elegant public library and the Federal Reserve Bank of Cleveland, which boasted one of the world's largest vaults. The newly established Terminal complex not only served as a vital nexus for national rail travel but also provided local commuters with access to the new rapid transit line. The 1930s brought further landmarks to the city: Severance Hall was completed, and the Cleveland Stadium opened on the lakefront.

Taverns in Cleveland quickly began to reopen their doors, reclaiming their place as essential social hubs in the community. The Cleveland City Directory resumed publishing locations where patrons could grab a drink, listing 947 "retail beer" dealers in 1936. By the end of the decade, this number had grown to slightly over 1,500. At the same time, technological advancements were transforming home life for working-class Clevelanders post-Prohibition. Although early versions of refrigeration existed in the 1800s, used by wealthier households, it wasn't until the late 1920s and 1930s, with the invention of freon, that refrigerators became commonplace in American homes. This new convenience allowed people to purchase and store beer for home consumption, making a small dent in the tavern business.

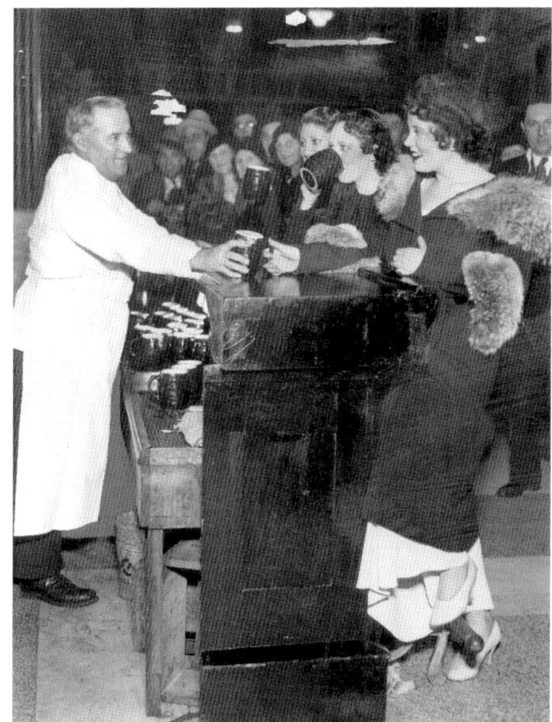

Left: Bartender Tommy Allen serves free beer at the Loew's State Theatre, March 21, 1933, the day before President Roosevelt signed the repeal of Prohibition. *Cleveland Press Collection, Cleveland State University, Michael Schwartz Library Special Collections.*

Below: Otto Moser at his bar at the end of Prohibition. *Cleveland Press Collection, Cleveland State University, Michael Schwartz Library Special Collections.*

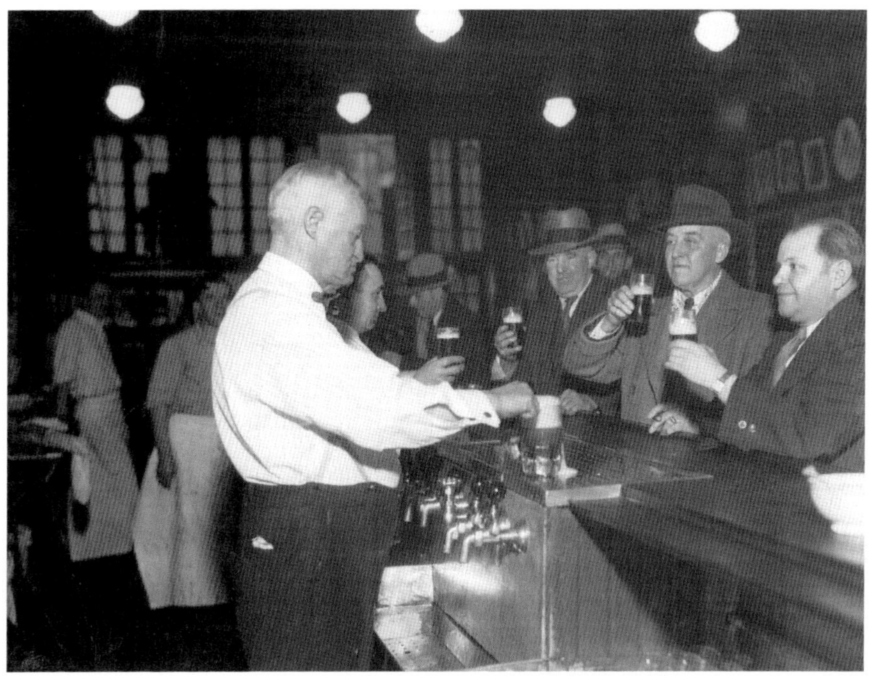

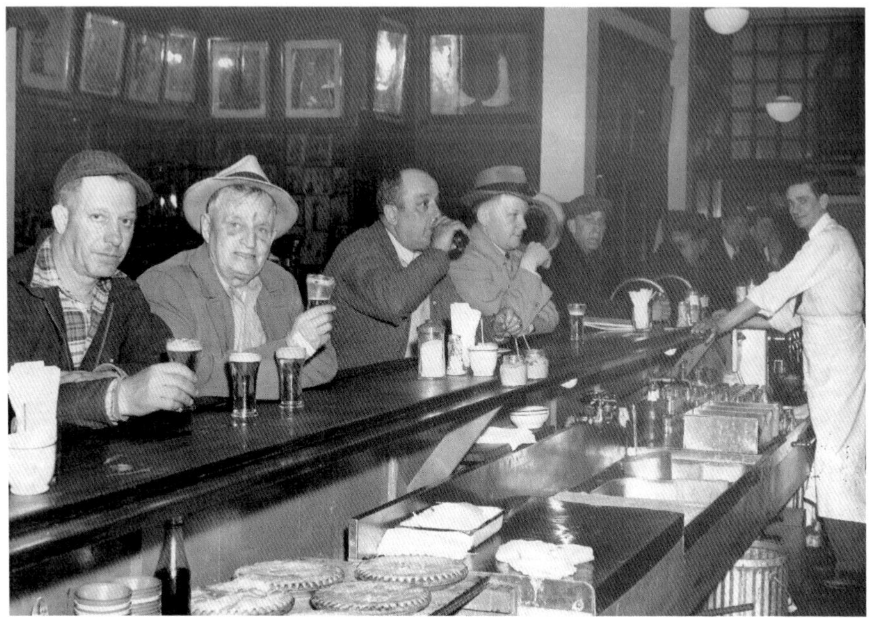

Otto Moser's bar, 1949. *Cleveland Public Library/Photograph Collection.*

However, the impact was limited, as the social and cultural elements of the neighborhood tavern could not be replaced at home.

Taverns remained vibrant centers of community life, offering a sense of camaraderie and connection that home refrigeration simply couldn't replicate. This spirit of community and revival was exemplified on March 23, 1933, just one day after President Roosevelt signed landmark legislation allowing the manufacture and sale of low-alcohol beer and wine. That day, the famed Otto Moser's bar at 2044 East Fourth Street in downtown Cleveland prepared to reclaim its status as a preeminent watering hole. The *Plain Dealer* reported that during the thirteen years of the "noble experiment," Moser had been forced to convert his ornate mahogany bar into a lunch counter to stay in business. But with the constitutionally mandated drought finally over, Moser eagerly looked forward to reopening as a proper saloon. "The last thirteen years have been pretty sour," the sixty-eight-year-old proprietor lamented. "Everyone hates their neighbor."

In its late-nineteenth-century heyday, Otto Moser's captured the lively atmosphere of the bustling theater district. Actors, musicians and entertainers frequented the bar three deep, knocking back ten-cent beers and twenty-cent imported pilsners. Photographs of celebrities adorned the walls of the

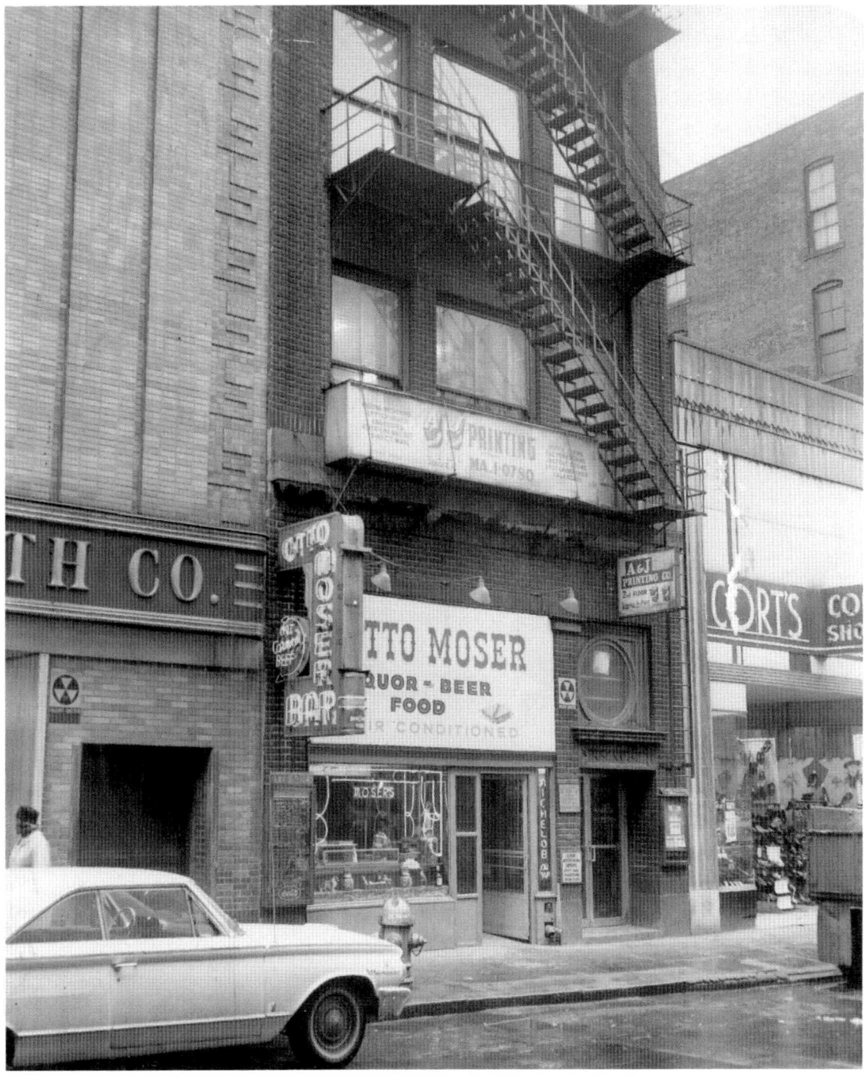

Otto Moser Restaurant and Bar, 2044 East Fourth Street, 1960. *Cleveland Public Library/ Photograph Collection.*

bar throughout its extensive history. Prohibition's enforced closure of this civic anchor represented the death of an era. But with the repeal of the Eighteenth Amendment, Moser and his patrons looked to the future with renewed optimism. As the Encyclopedia of Cleveland History recounts, the famed bar would go on to enjoy another eighty-five years as a celebrated city institution before its closure in 2018.

THE GREAT DEPRESSION

While Cleveland experienced remarkable growth and development in the early twentieth century, the late 1920s and 1930s marked a period of profound hardship for its residents as the Great Depression cast a long, dark shadow over the city. The brutal economic downturn took hold swiftly after the infamous stock market crash on Black Tuesday, October 29, 1929. Within a year, over one hundred thousand Clevelanders found themselves jobless as factories and businesses shuttered.

The Depression plunged countless families into poverty and financial ruin. If you didn't lose your job, you might be forced to accept a pay cut of 50 percent to keep it. Workers in the steel and auto manufacturing industries were also faced with labor unrest and strikes as the unions continued to demand better working conditions. The daily struggle to put food on the table and make ends meet became an all-consuming battle for survival. Long bread lines formed, and Cleveland's ethnic neighborhoods were particularly hard hit, as the immigrant working class disproportionately lost their livelihoods in mills, plants and workshops.

The years of deprivation also prompted a fundamental redefinition of the federal government's role and obligations to its most vulnerable citizens. The desperation witnessed in cities like Cleveland laid the groundwork for the expansive social safety net programs and labor protections that would emerge from the New Deal in the coming decades. This period of collective hardship, perseverance and resilience marked a turning point—a catalyst for significant economic reforms that permanently reshaped the nation's socioeconomic landscape. For Clevelanders who endured this bleak era's breadlines, shantytowns and ever-present hunger, the Depression years left indelible physical and psychological scars that were passed on to the next generation.

While Prohibition was officially over, the challenges surrounding alcohol regulation were far from resolved. Organized crime and the underground liquor trade adapted to the new legal landscape, providing fertile ground for ongoing clandestine activities. This period highlighted the complexities of transitioning from an era of outright bans to regulated freedom as law enforcement grappled with the remnants of Prohibition's illicit networks. Stringent liquor laws and high taxes continued to fuel bootlegging operations, with federal taxes alone giving bootleg liquor a more than $1.00 per quart advantage. Judge Ackerman of the Cleveland Municipal Court stated on January 15, 1936, that "the bootleg situation was as bad if not worse than

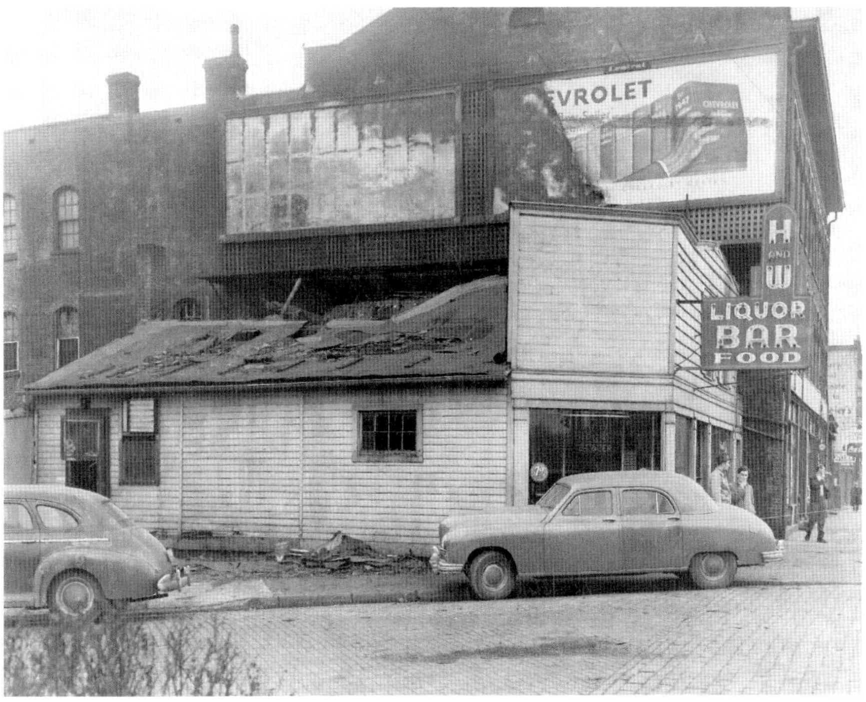

H&W Bar, a Depression-era tavern, and crumbling neighborhood infrastructure. *Cleveland Press Collection, Cleveland State University, Michael Schwartz Library Special Collections.*

during the dry regime," estimating that there were five thousand bootleg joints in Cleveland, with illicit liquor being sold to beer joint operators for $1.75 a gallon.

Eliot Ness: Crusader Against Corruption in Cleveland

After gaining national notoriety for corruption and organized crime related to bootlegging during Prohibition, Cleveland took a bold step in 1935 by appointing thirty-three-year-old Eliot Ness as its safety director. After his famous days fighting Al Capone in Chicago, Ness was assigned to the Cincinnati enforcement division of the Treasury Department's Alcohol Tax Unit. The following year took him to the Cleveland regional office to lead thirty agents in enforcing the new laws surrounding production and distribution of alcohol. As head of the Alcohol Tax Unit, Ness had gained a reputation for closing down illegal stills at a rate of one per day.

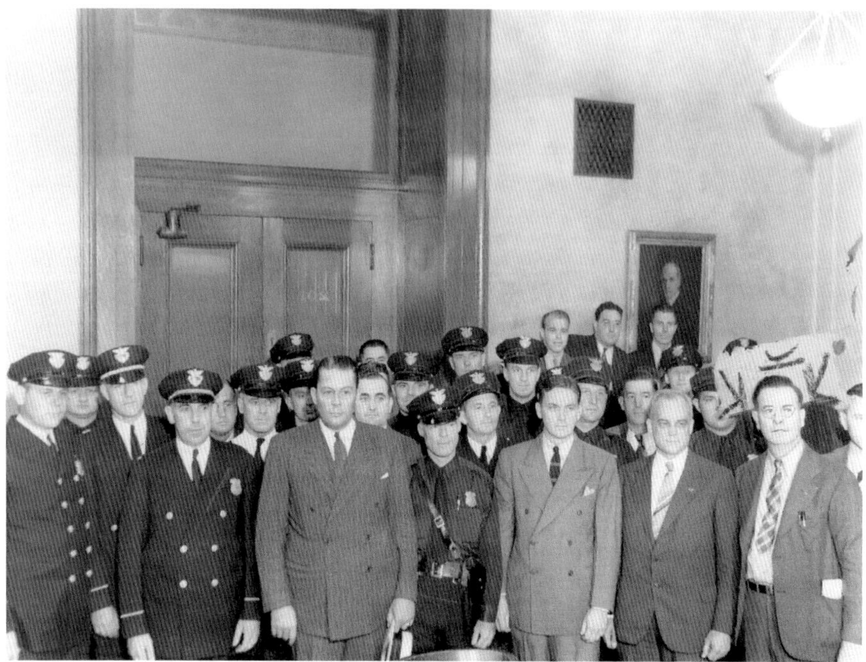

Eliot Ness (*front row, third from right*) on July 15, 1939, with Cleveland policemen receiving bronze medals from the annual revolver tournament. *Cleveland Public Library/Photograph Collection.*

In his new role as safety director, Ness vowed to investigate and root out corruption within the police force. He implemented stricter licensing requirements and inspections, ensuring that only legitimate establishments were allowed to serve alcohol. Ness's efforts paid off: Cleveland experienced a significant drop in crime rates during his first eighteen months in office. In addition to sending several high-profile mobsters to prison, he also eradicated corruption within the police department. On October 6, 1936, the *Plain Dealer* reported that Ness submitted a report to the Cuyahoga County grand jury implicating twenty officers, including Captain Harwood, in protecting bootleggers during Prohibition. Casper Korce, a saloonkeeper and bootlegger, testified that Captain Harwood was paid bribes of twenty to twenty-five dollars during meetings at East 152nd and Saint Clair Avenue. These meetings, which took place regularly, were part of a broader system of corruption in which Harwood and other officers shook down saloon owners and bootleggers in exchange for protection from law enforcement crackdowns. Korce also delivered ten free cases of beer to the Harwood residence. Harwood was convicted on six counts of soliciting and accepting bribes for providing police protection to bootleggers and was subsequently sentenced to serve time in the Ohio Penitentiary.

Thanks to Eliot Ness's efforts to clean up corruption and restore order, Cleveland began to look toward a brighter future. His relentless pursuit of justice brought significant changes within the police force and instilled a renewed sense of integrity and trust in law enforcement. Ness went on to run unsuccessfully for mayor of Cleveland and move to Cloudersport, Pennsylvania, where he died of a heart attack in 1957.

Chapter 4

On the Cusp of Change

Cleveland Taverns from War to Postwar Prosperity

In the early 1940s, Cleveland was once again in a state of transition, grappling with the enduring effects of the Great Depression and the looming impact of World War II. During this pivotal period, the city experienced a significant demographic shift: its population declined to 878,336, a 2.5 percent decrease from 1930. This marked the first time in its history that Cleveland saw a reduction in its population. According to the census, 20 percent of the population was foreign-born White and 10 percent was Black. In contrast, Cuyahoga County experienced a modest growth of 1.3 percent, reaching a population of 1,247,000. This demographic change signaled the beginning of a substantial migration, as first-generation Clevelanders began moving to the new suburbs.

While the suburbs grew, the inner-city steel and manufacturing industries experienced a significant rebound and began to play a vital role in supporting the European war effort. Cleveland's mills and factories were now operating at full capacity to produce aircraft, tanks and other military equipment. The typical worker put in twelve-hour days in the hot, loud and dangerous mills. Their labor involved operating blazing furnaces and meticulously shaping red-hot steel. By 1944, the average Cleveland manufacturing worker was earning $66.25 per week, compared to the national average of $46.68. Skilled workers were earning $1.15 to $1.35 per hour; common laborers were paid $.70 to $.90 per hour. High wages and overtime pay allowed many Clevelanders to save for their eventual move to the suburbs.

After enduring these grueling shifts, workers were eager to climb the hill from the mills and visit their neighborhood tavern. These local establishments provided a much-needed respite, serving as places for workers to unwind, share stories and enjoy the camaraderie of fellow laborers. The taverns were convenient locations for workers to cash their checks, quench their thirst and perhaps try their luck at slot machines, often leaving a significant portion of their earnings with the tavern owner. On July 22, 1942, the *Plain Dealer* reported that some saloons would cash up to $28,000 each payday, making the saloon owners targets for robbers. However, tavern owners and patrons did not take lightly to being victims. According to one account, at the Croatian Tavern at 3244 Saint Clair, two hundred bar patrons fought off two masked gunmen, attacking them with beer bottles and chairs and thwarting the attempted robbery.

At the top of Dille Hill and Broadway stood the Open-Hearth Tavern and the Hilltop Tavern, two establishments that drew a steady crowd of mill workers. In January 1957, one laborer fresh off a shift at Republic Steel calmly sipped a drink at the Open Hearth while confessing to robbing two other bars on Broadway earlier that night. Detectives arrived and escorted the nonchalant criminal to jail.

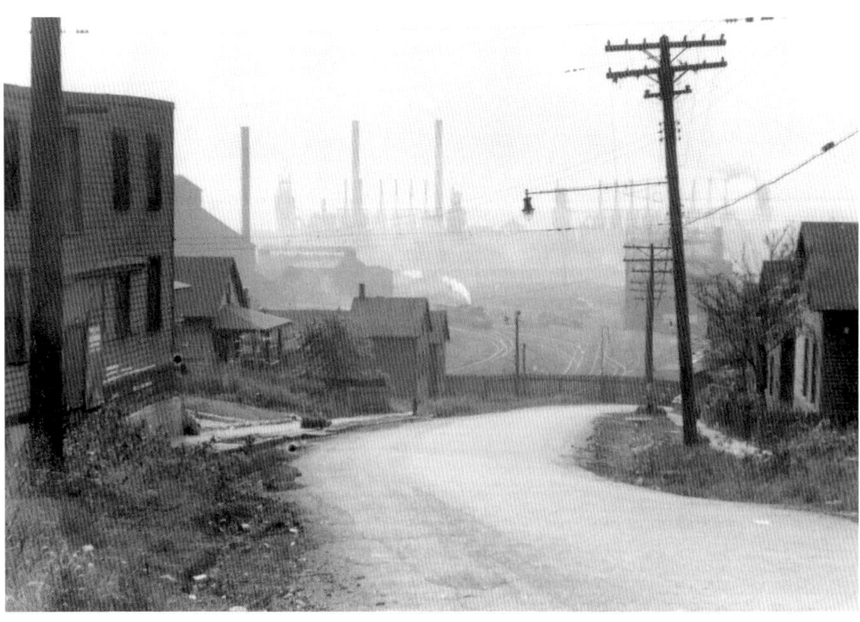

Steelworkers would climb Dille Hill at Broadway Avenue and East Forty-First Street, often stopping at one of the many taverns on Broadway. *Cleveland Public Library/Photograph Collection.*

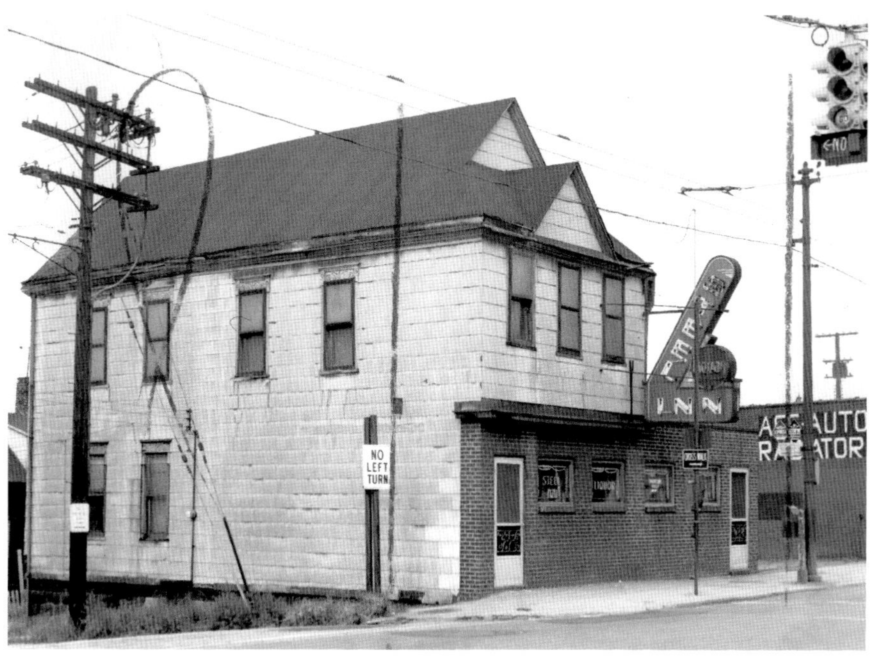

Steel Inn, a neighborhood tavern catering to mill workers, 1940. *Cleveland Press Collection, Cleveland State University, Michael Schwartz Library Special Collections.*

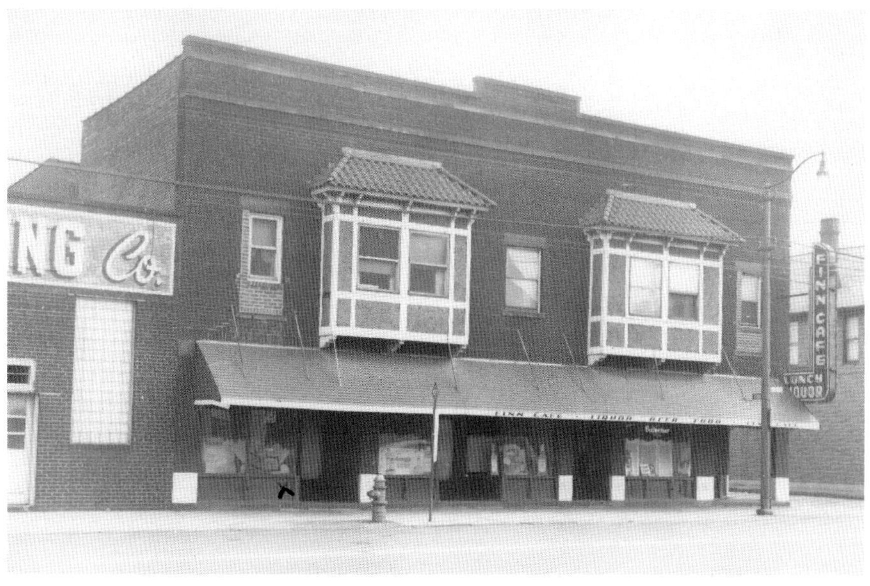

The Finn Café on Broadway served mill workers for decades. *Cleveland Public Library/ Photograph Collection.*

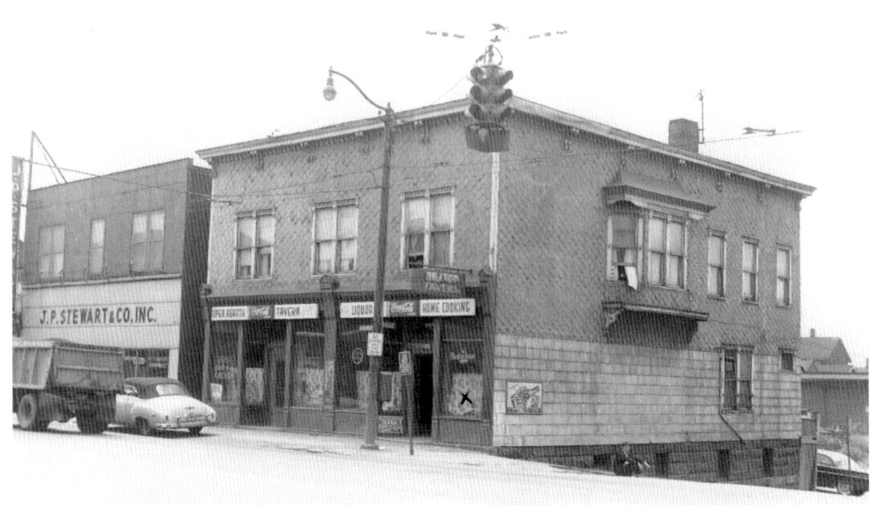

Looking southwest on Dille Avenue with a view of the Open-Hearth Tavern and the Hilltop Tavern, 1956. *Cleveland Public Library/Photograph Collection.*

The Open Hearth and the Hilltop were just the start. Within a five-minute walk along Broadway, thirsty patrons had their pick of watering holes like the Track Inn, the Blue-Sky Café, Chief's Café, the New Broadway Café, the Tower Grill and the popular Finn Café. The Finn was an iconic tavern on Broadway and a great supporter of local sandlot and softball teams. Its first published box scores date to 1939, when the café fielded a team in the Aetna League. The Finn Café maintained a powerhouse softball team up through the 1980s, cementing its place in Cleveland's amateur sporting culture. After being closed for some time, the beloved tavern was refurbished and reopened as the Sunny Spot @ Finn Café in October 2022, ushering in a new era while paying homage to its history.

The Cleveland Arsenal: Fueling the War Effort on the Home Front

The entry of the United States into World War II ushered in a period of profound transformation, one that would reshape the city's industrial landscape and social fabric for years to come. The hardworking men who once filled the taverns along Broadway would soon trade in their mill coveralls for military uniforms, a change that would alter their lives forever.

In Cleveland, the impetus of war production led to a substantial increase in employment, which rose 34 percent from 1940 to 1944. This growth was primarily in the manufacturing sector, where employment rose from 191,000 to 340,000 during this time frame. Cleveland offered ample job opportunities for draft-exempt individuals. The Cleveland Electric Illuminating Company (CEI) created the tagline "the best location in the nation" as part of a public relations campaign to promote Cleveland. This slogan aimed to highlight Cleveland's strategic advantages, including its strong manufacturing base, proximity to major markets and location within a day's drive of over 50 percent of both the U.S. and Canadian populations.

It was widely believed that every airplane and automobile made in the United States contained parts or accessories manufactured in Cleveland. Several major companies played pivotal roles in Cleveland's wartime economy. The Thompson Aircraft plant in Euclid expanded in 1941 and became the city's largest employer, with a workforce of twenty-one thousand. The White Motor Company also contributed by manufacturing military vehicles, and the I-X Center, originally built in 1942 as the Cleveland Bomber Plant and later known as the Cleveland Tank Plant, played a significant part in Cleveland's wartime production. The facility, owned by the War Department during World War II, was operated by General Motors as the Fisher Body Aircraft Plant No. 2, producing the B-29 bomber. The plant was located just outside the city in Brook Park and played a crucial role in supporting the war effort and shaping Cleveland's massive wartime output.

Cleveland's local taverns found themselves playing a unique and crucial role in supporting the war effort on the home front. Many transformed into hubs for advertising and promoting the purchase of war bonds, and owners and patrons alike rallied behind the patriotic cause. As more women entered the workforce to aid in wartime production, it became increasingly common to see them bellying up to the bar alongside men in these neighborhood watering holes.

Bob Williams was a columnist for the *Cleveland Call and Post*, a predominantly African American newspaper. His column, Bobbing Along with Bob Williams featured an editorial on December 30, 1944, in which he observed:

> *Café and night spots, whether we like to admit these things or not, have played an important role in the alleged building up and maintaining civilian morale, since not withstanding whatever general fault or criticism we may level against them, at some time or another we have found therein most of the high and low of virtually every grade of society.*

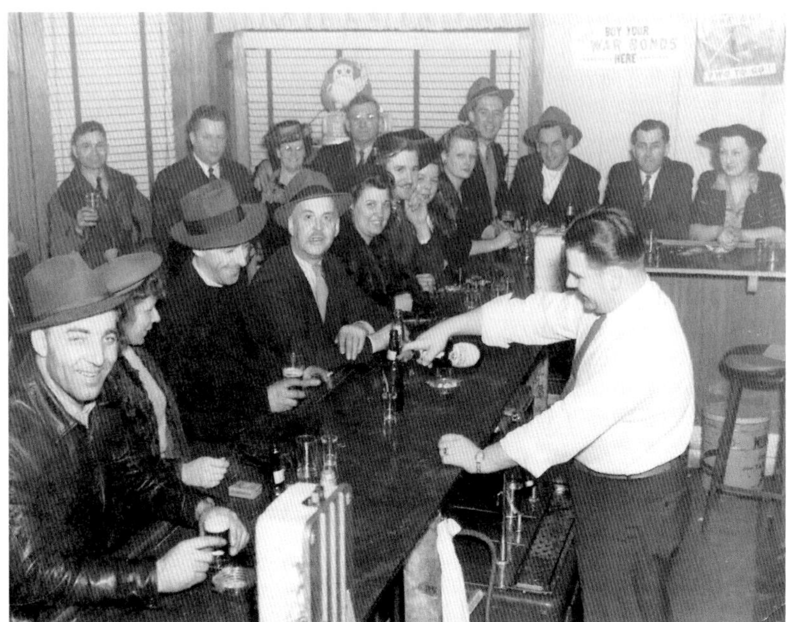

Crowded wartime bar scene in Old Brooklyn. *Frank Libal Collection, courtesy of the Old Brooklyn Historical Society.*

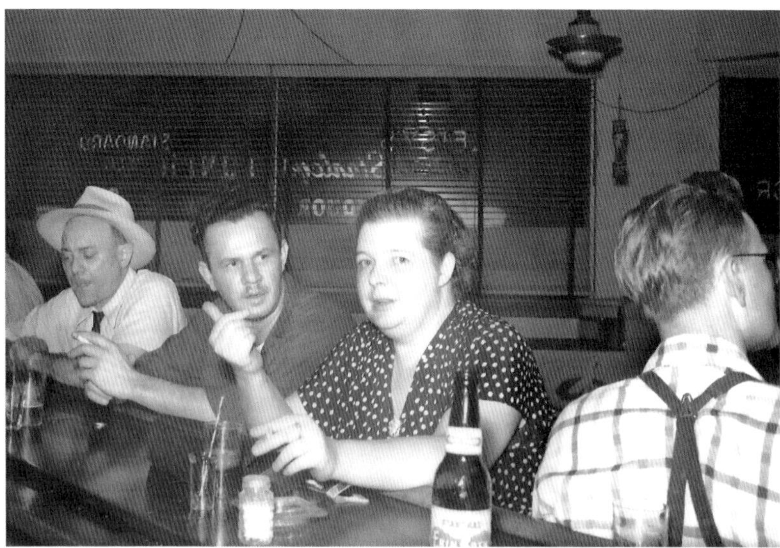

Wartime bar scene in an Old Brooklyn neighborhood tavern: "shots and beer," and don't forget to sprinkle the salt in the beer. *Frank Libal Collection, Courtesy of the Old Brooklyn Historical Society.*

These establishments further demonstrated their commitment to the war effort by strictly adhering to the wartime curfew law, which mandated that they close promptly at midnight. The *Plain Dealer* reported that tavern owners willingly complied with this measure aimed at conserving resources and maintaining order during a time of national crisis. Furthermore, when victory arrived in Europe on May 8, 1945, and, three months later, in Japan, Mayor Thomas Burke ordered all bars closed to honor the momentous occasion.

As the war ended and the nation transitioned into a period of postwar prosperity, Cleveland underwent significant changes that would redefine its identity. The influx of returning veterans and the economic boom brought about new opportunities and challenges. The manufacturing sector continued to thrive over the next decade, fueling the city's economy and job market. The population swelled, resulting in the rapid expansion of suburbs and further transforming the close-knit inner-city ethnic neighborhoods.

Raising a Glass to Prosperity: The Downtown Taverns of Postwar Cleveland

In 1950, Cleveland reached its peak population—914,808 residents—making it the seventh largest city in the nation. This marked a 4.2 percent increase since the 1940 census, reflecting the city's robust postwar growth. The number of watering holes remained on par with the prior decade; the Cleveland City Directory listed 1,460 "beer parlors" in 1955. The demographic makeup of the population was also changing: Cleveland's foreign-born population declined to 15 percent, while the Black population rose significantly, from 10 percent a decade earlier to 16 percent in the new decade. This growth was fueled by a wave of migration from the South, particularly Appalachia. Many Appalachian families, facing economic hardship and limited opportunities in their rural communities and coal mining towns, sought a better life in Cleveland's booming manufacturing industry. Steel mills, auto plants and other factories offered steady jobs and the chance for upward mobility.

Meanwhile, Cuyahoga County witnessed even more explosive growth, reaching a population of 1,389,532, with 34 percent of the county's residents now living outside the city limits. This suburban migration was heavily influenced by returning veterans who benefited from the GI Bill and FHA loans, which made homeownership more accessible than ever before. These veterans sought new beginnings and found opportunities in the expanding suburban areas, where developers were rapidly constructing tracts of homes to meet the demand. These new neighborhoods featured single-family homes, green spaces and community amenities that appealed to young families. This shift not only transformed the physical landscape of Cuyahoga County but also reshaped the social and economic dynamics of the region.

The rise of the automobile industry and the development of extensive road infrastructure further accelerated suburban migration. As car ownership became more common, residents could easily commute to work in the city. Even before the interstate highways were constructed, improved road networks connected the inner city with outlying areas, accelerating the outward migration.

One of the most striking examples of Cleveland's suburban migration was the explosive population growth experienced by the city of Parma. In 1950, Parma had a modest population of just twenty-eight thousand. However, by 1955, that number had skyrocketed, more than doubling to an estimated sixty-five thousand as families flocked to the burgeoning suburb. This trend showed no signs of slowing: Parma's population surpassed eighty-two thousand by the end of the decade. Former Clevelanders maintained their affinity for the neighborhood tavern. In 1951, Parma boasted twenty-five taverns, one-third of them concentrated along State Road alone. As migration continued, the demand for local watering holes grew, and by 1960, the number of taverns had swelled to thirty-eight, with a staggering fifteen establishments lining the Pearl Road corridor.

While suburbs like Parma experienced a tavern boom to accommodate the influx of former city residents, downtown Cleveland remained a hub for neighborhood bars and taverns. Despite the exodus to the suburbs, the city center retained its status as the region's premier economic, retail and entertainment district, drawing commuters from across Cleveland and the surrounding counties. The steady stream of office workers, shoppers and night owls kept downtown's tavern culture thriving, ensuring the heart of the city remained lively. Whether workers were grabbing a quick drink after work, meeting friends for a nightcap or settling in for an evening of entertainment, the downtown taverns buzzed with activity through the decade.

The Heart of Downtown Nightlife: Short Vincent

Despite spanning a mere 485 feet between East Sixth and East Ninth Streets in downtown, Vincent Avenue, nicknamed Short Vincent, attained legendary status as the epicenter of Cleveland entertainment for over three decades, starting in the 1930s. The diminutive street's illustrious history and notorious reputation were so captivating that author Alan F. Dutka dedicated an entire book, *Cleveland's Short Vincent: The Theatrical Grill and Its Notorious Neighbors*, chronicling the exploits and happenings along this short but lively corridor during its heyday.

Short Vincent became a central gathering spot for newspaper reporters, politicians, visiting athletes and local celebrities. It was especially popular with the New York Yankees, who treated the street as their home base whenever they were in town playing the Indians. On any given night, tourists and locals alike could rub elbows with sports stars, gangsters and famous entertainers while enjoying the concentration of bars, restaurants, music clubs and racy burlesque shows that lined the street. According to Dutka, in 1944, there were as many as fifteen distinct drinking establishments operating on Short Vincent, all packed with locals and visitors alike.

One of the most iconic establishments on Short Vincent was Mickey's Theatrical Grill, which opened its doors in 1937. It took its name from Mickey Miller, brother-in-law of the principal owner, Morris "Mushy" Wexler. Wexler himself was a character straight out of Cleveland's underworld. His involvement in illicit gambling operations frequently landed him in legal trouble; he was once subpoenaed to testify before the 1951 Kefauver Committee during its investigation into organized crime. Despite these brushes with the law, Wexler maintained ownership of the Theatrical Grill until his death in 1979.

From its inception in 1937, the Theatrical Grill quickly gained renown not just as an entertainment venue hosting top musical acts like Judy Garland and Dean Martin but also as a hotbed of gambling and mob activities. Although notorious Cleveland mobster Alex "Shondor" Birns was legally barred from holding a liquor license due to a prior felony conviction, he was still a part owner of the establishment.

During the 1950s, the Theatrical Grill underwent several expansions, including the addition of a distinctive curved bar with a raised stage inside for performers. Private rooms like the Burgundy Room and the Penthouse were created to host meetings and private parties. In 1960, a fire in the

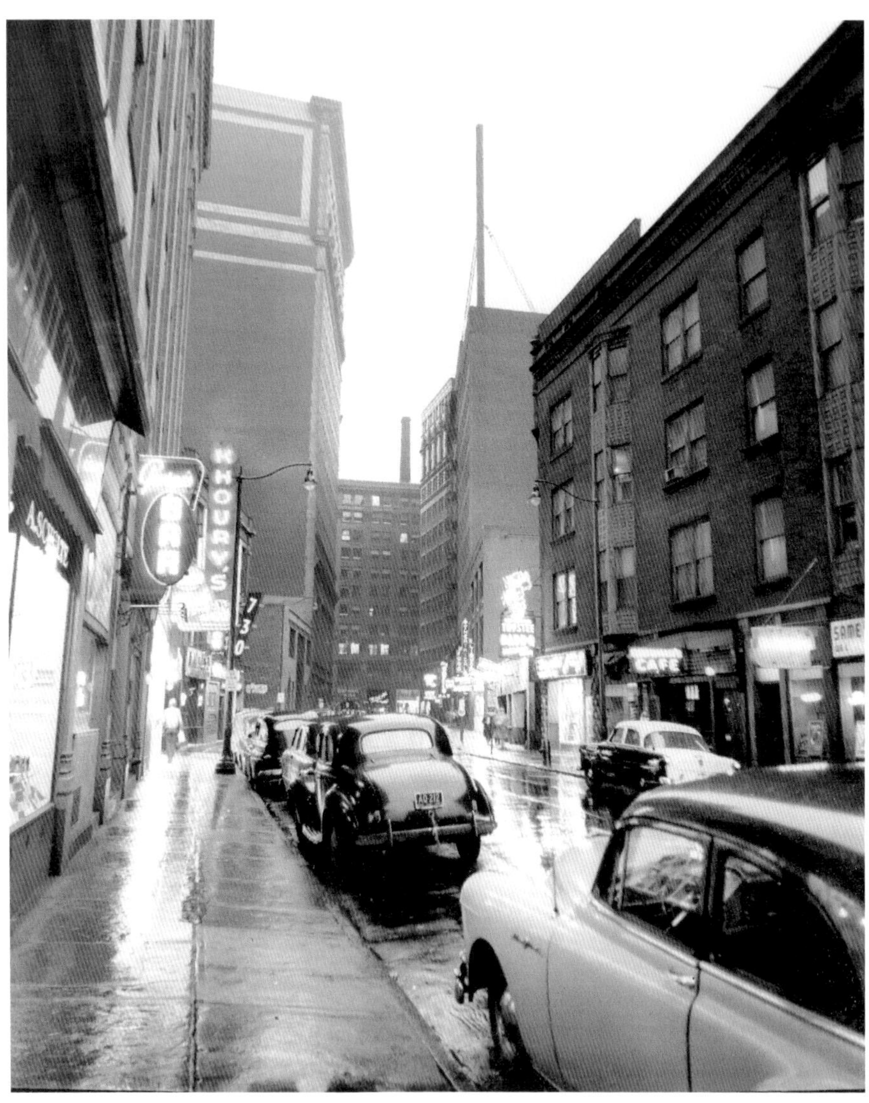

basement destroyed the bar and restaurant; however, Wexler immediately rebuilt and reopened the following year.

The venue continued attracting a steady stream of celebrities throughout the early 1960s; newspaper clippings mention high-profile guests including Art Modell, George Steinbrenner, Frank Sinatra and boxer Joe Louis. Over the next decade, Short Vincent and the Theatrical lost their appeal and experienced a continual decline. The street faced increasing pressure

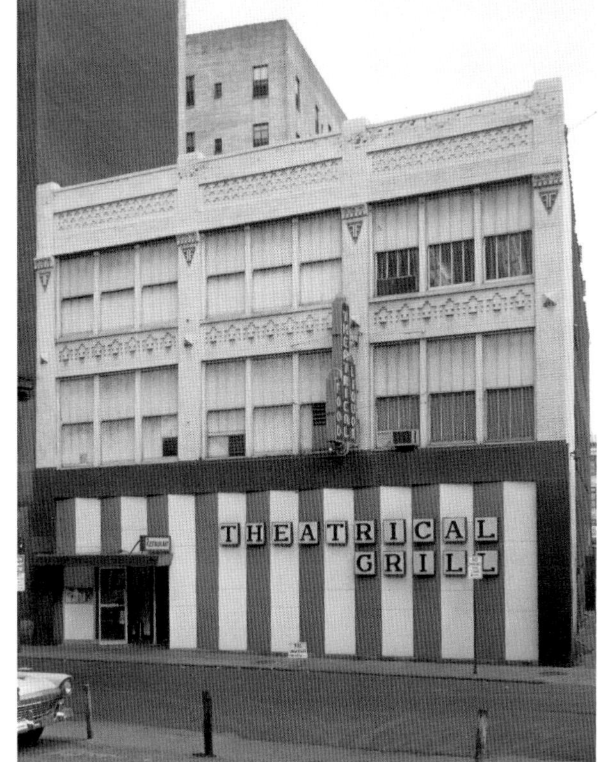

Opposite: Vincent Avenue, view toward East Sixth Street, 1953. *Cleveland Press Collection, Cleveland State University, Michael Schwartz Library Special Collections.*

Right: Theatrical Grill after being rebuilt in 1961. *Cleveland Public Library/Photograph Collection.*

Below: A typical night at the Theatrical in the 1960s. *Cleveland Public Library/Photograph Collection.*

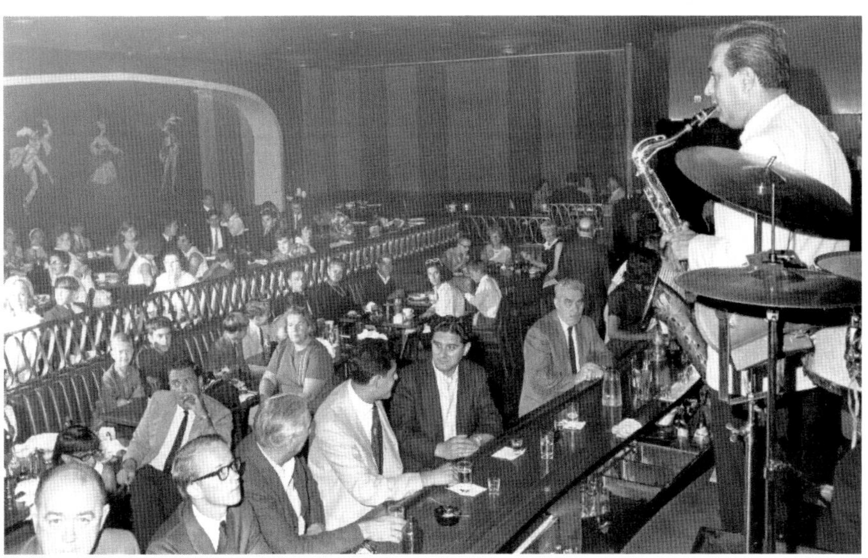

from urban redevelopment plans and a trend toward sanitizing downtown entertainment. By the early 1960s, much of the north side of Short Vincent had been razed to make way for new office buildings, and by 1978, its entire south side had been demolished for the National City Bank Center. The Theatrical, the last business standing, had transitioned to a strip club by the time it closed in 1999.

While the Theatrical Grill attracted celebrities, many other establishments along Short Vincent during the 1950s and '60s cultivated a very different, more disreputable reputation. Venues like Mickey's, the 730 Lounge Bar and Frolics Café, all just a few doors apart, were continually on the radar of law enforcement and the Ohio Liquor Control Commission. This dichotomy was highlighted in the November 1963 *Plain Dealer* article "Night Life Report," which contrasted the Theatrical Grill's approach to nightlife with other clubs that prioritized adult entertainment. Owner Mushy Wexler summed up the venue's philosophy: "Food first, entertainment second, and no girls."

What set places like Mickey's, the 730 and Frolics apart was their reliance on aggressive "B-girls," or "bar girls," to lure in male patrons. These employees engaged men in flirtatious conversation with the objective of encouraging excessive drinking, as they earned a commission based on the number of overpriced cocktails they could convince customers to purchase. A shot of scotch was one dollar, a bottle of champagne twenty-five dollars. This unchecked exploitation, combined with widespread rumors of prostitution, gambling and illegal liquor sales, made these bars frequent targets of liquor control stings and police raids.

Mickey Miller was not only a co-owner of the Theatrical, but he also had a stake in Mickey's Lounge Bar, located just a few doors down at 732 Short Vincent. His partner in this venture was a known bookie, Fuzzy Lakis. Over its eighteen-year run, Mickey's was repeatedly cited and temporarily shut down for a variety of violations, including prostitution, unsanitary conditions and liquor violations. The police would padlock the doors whenever a violation was discovered, but the Liquor Control Board would routinely lift the suspension, allowing the bar to continue operations. On July 8, 1962, the *Plain Dealer* reported that vice cops would take turns monitoring the bar from 8:30 p.m. until closing every night, vigilantly looking out for any violations. However, in February 1965, Fuzzy Lakis finally surrendered his liquor license, leading to the permanent closure of Mickey's Lounge Bar.

In 1947, the Pony Lounge was rebranded as the 730 Lounge. Leonard Cohen managed the lounge, while notorious gangster Angelo Lonardo

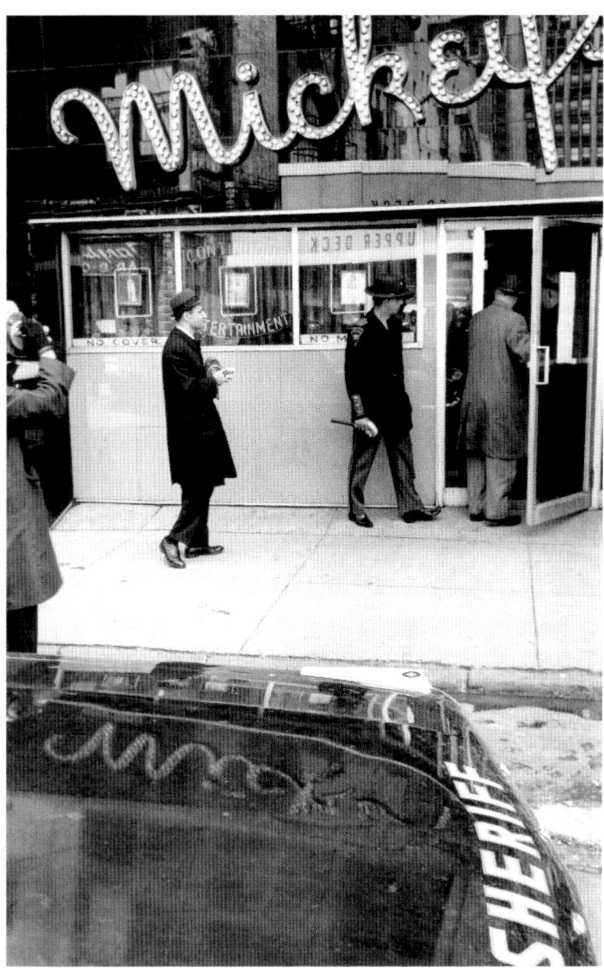

Sheriff and officials entering Mickey's Bar to close it down due to liquor violations, 1961. *Cleveland Press Collection, Cleveland State University, Michael Schwartz Library Special Collections.*

oversaw restaurant operations. Throughout its history, the establishment frequently violated liquor laws. In 1964, Judge Harry Jaffe deemed the club a "common nuisance" and ordered it to be padlocked for a year. Cohen refuted these charges, accusing the authorities of harassment.

In a March 1, 1967 *Plain Dealer* article, Cohen defended the bar's reputation, sarcastically referring to Short Vincent as "Saint Vincent," a jab at the idea that the area was ever considered innocent. Tensions between Cohen and the authorities continued for years. In 1974, Cleveland Municipal Judge Salvatore Calandra, acting in response to the ongoing issues with the city, ordered the bar's eviction.

Just a few doors down from the 730 stood another notorious bar: Frolics Cafe at 814 Vincent Avenue. This establishment also had ties to the city's underworld figures, with ownership links to mobsters Charles Polizzi, in the 1950s, and, later, Angelo Lonardo. Frolics embraced its seedy reputation, with the bartender Gino brazenly advertising "no beer, here we got only whiskey and women." Frolics repeatedly clashed with the Ohio Liquor Control Commission over allegations of harboring prostitution and permitting aggressive B-girl sales tactics. In September 1964, after having its liquor license revoked, Frolics asked the licensing authorities to hold it in "safe keeping" while it contested the closure. However, the commission permanently revoked the club's license, citing rampant illegal activities—including a March incident that year in which a dispute originating inside the bar led to the beating death of a man around the corner on East Ninth Street.

The next notable tenant of the building moved in in 1973, when Larry Flynt opened the Hustler Club on the site. Flynt pledged to the *Plain Dealer* that he intended to run "a more reputable joint," including by prohibiting unescorted women during the evening. The Hustler Club was short-lived, and the location is now part of the PNC Bank complex.

Today, only parking garages and the back façades of several office buildings remain along the 485-foot stretch that was once Cleveland's infamous Short Vincent. The racy burlesque theaters, mob-owned gambling dens and dives where hustlers and high rollers once mingled have all been razed, erased from the downtown landscape by the forces of urban renewal and shifting cultural tides.

East Ninth Street: The Windy Walk from the Lake to Erie Street Cemetery

Let's start back in 1938 when East Ninth Street was anchored at both ends by bars. At the northeast end, near the lake, stood the Deutsche Küche, or German Kitchen, famous for its Italian spaghetti and Mexican chili. At the other end, near the Erie Street Cemetery, was Hank's Café. This one-mile street of surprises hosted a variety of establishments that catered to visitors' eclectic tastes. The route was lined with bars, a tearoom that advertised "readings," the infamous Roxy Theater and Jean's Funny House. The bustling corridor drew people from all walks of life.

The bars on East Ninth faced the same issues—and drew a similar clientele—as those on Short Vincent. One of the most renowned tavern owners of the time was Norman Khoury, famously known as the Nightclub

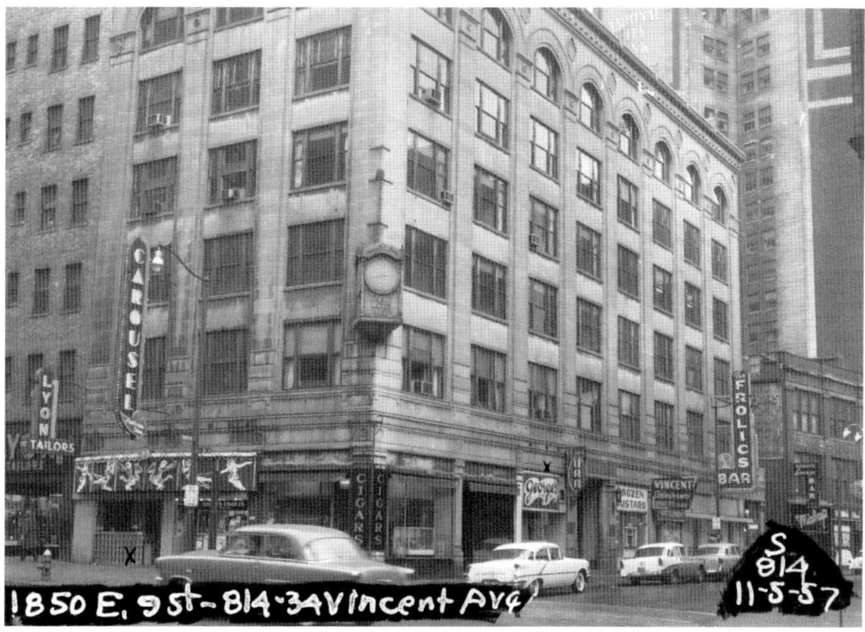

The corner of East Ninth and Vincent Avenue. Norman Khoury owned both Club Carousel and George's Bar. *Cleveland Public Library/Photograph Collection.*

King of Cleveland. Khoury began his nightclub business in 1935 and owned over twenty taverns across Cleveland, Solon and Akron during his thirty-year career. His influence extended beyond the Cleveland area when he purchased Club Savoy in Las Vegas in 1949. However, it wasn't long before an associate of the mobster Bugsy Siegel encouraged Khoury to sell 50 percent of his stake in the club. Ultimately, the club became a target of the Las Vegas tax commission, which suspended Khoury's license, leading to its closure in 1953.

Khoury's legal issues were not limited to Las Vegas. On July 9, 1955, the *Plain Dealer* reported that Khoury had a five-page history of liquor violations. Khoury, who was also a significant real estate owner in downtown Cleveland, continued to battle the liquor commission and tax agents throughout the 1950s and into the mid-1960s. Over the years, the *Plain Dealer* covered his legal disputes extensively, once reporting, "Khoury, King of Clubs, Abdicates." Toward the end of his life, Khoury expressed bitterness, stating, "They treat me like they treat a man who gets a life sentence for speeding." He died at the age of sixty-two and is buried in Studio City in Los Angeles.

From the 1940s to the 1960s, numerous bars along East Ninth Street opened and closed. Some closed due to revoked liquor licenses, while others fell victim to urban renewal as new buildings began to rise along the street. One notable example is Champion Café, located at 1374 East Ninth near Saint Clair Avenue. Known as a hot spot, it became infamous during a liquor board hearing on June 8, 1949. Patrolman Raymond Wahl testified that he had arrested more than a dozen drunks at the bar, and the owner was charged with selling liquor to intoxicated persons and permitting solicitation of prostitution. By 1955, the location had been converted to Kay's Book Shop.

In April 1946, the popular Roxy Musical Bar opened at Chester and East Ninth, drawing large crowds of downtown shoppers with its marathon music shows. It's important to note that this establishment should not be confused with Cleveland's legendary burlesque house the Roxy Theatre, located at 1882 East Ninth. To eliminate confusion, the Roxy Musical Bar was renamed Gould's Musical Bar; after several years, it reverted to its original name. However, the Roxy Musical Bar's history was marked by a series of violations including failure to serve hot food on the premises as required by its license, diluting liquor and soliciting drinks. Notably, the Roxy Musical Bar was also called into municipal court in January 1947 for refusing to serve people due to their skin color or race. These incidents marred the establishment's reputation, and in March 1965, the liquor board charged the Roxy with twenty-two violations and denied its license renewal, bringing an end to its nineteen-year run.

At East Ninth and Euclid, the crossroads of downtown, stood the Cadillac Lounge, a pioneering establishment that provided a relatively tolerant social space for Cleveland's gay community. Restaurateur Gloria Lenihan opened the Cadillac, housed within the Schofield Building, in 1946. The upscale lounge served straight clients during the day and transformed into a safe space for gay men at night. The opulent interior featured eight tropical murals, sixteen strategically placed mirrors, red velvet booths and blond wood paneling. Lenihan enforced strict rules, including a dress code requiring men to wear a jacket and tie. Her "twelve-inch rule" mandated that men maintain at least twelve inches' distance from each other. In 1951, the bar faced legal trouble when undercover agents purchased liquor there on New Year's Eve just after closing time. The lounge claimed confusion over whether to follow standard closing hours or extend them for New Year's Eve, as the holiday fell on a Sunday night. Ultimately, the charges were dropped. Throughout its twenty-seven-year run, the bar attracted popular visiting piano, organ and saxophone musicians.

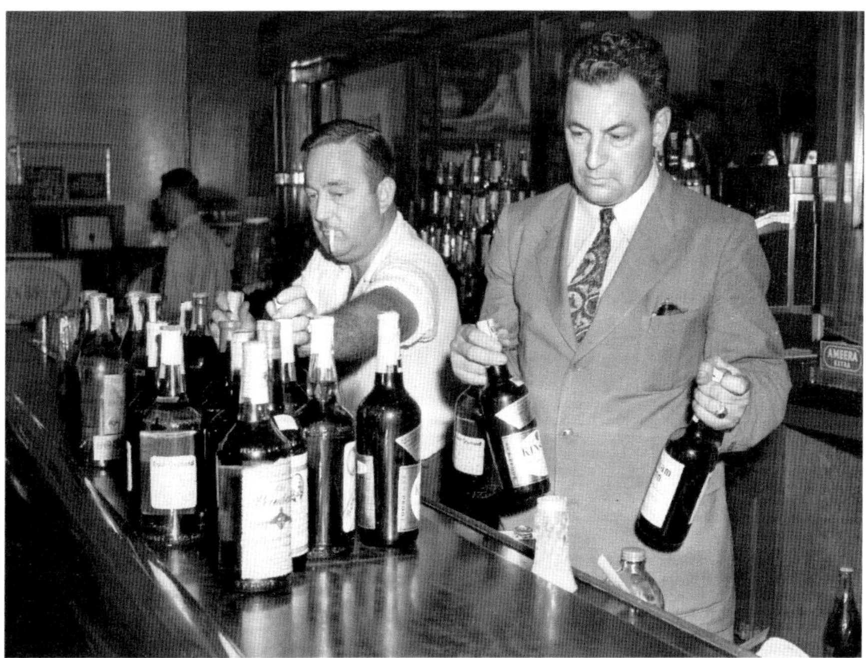

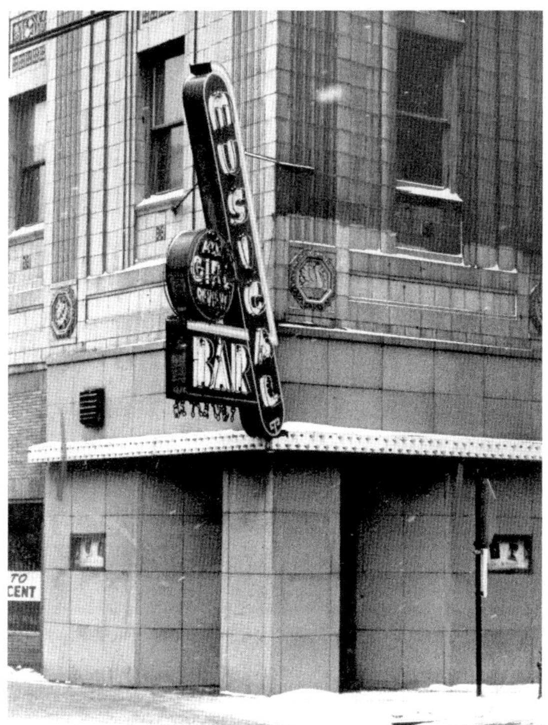

Above: State liquor agents close down Champion Café, June 30, 1949. *Cleveland Press Collection, Cleveland State University, Michael Schwartz Library Special Collections.*

Left: Roxy Musical Bar, 1857 East Ninth Street, 1965. *Tony Tomsic, creator, Cleveland Press Collection, Cleveland State University, Michael Schwartz Library Special Collections.*

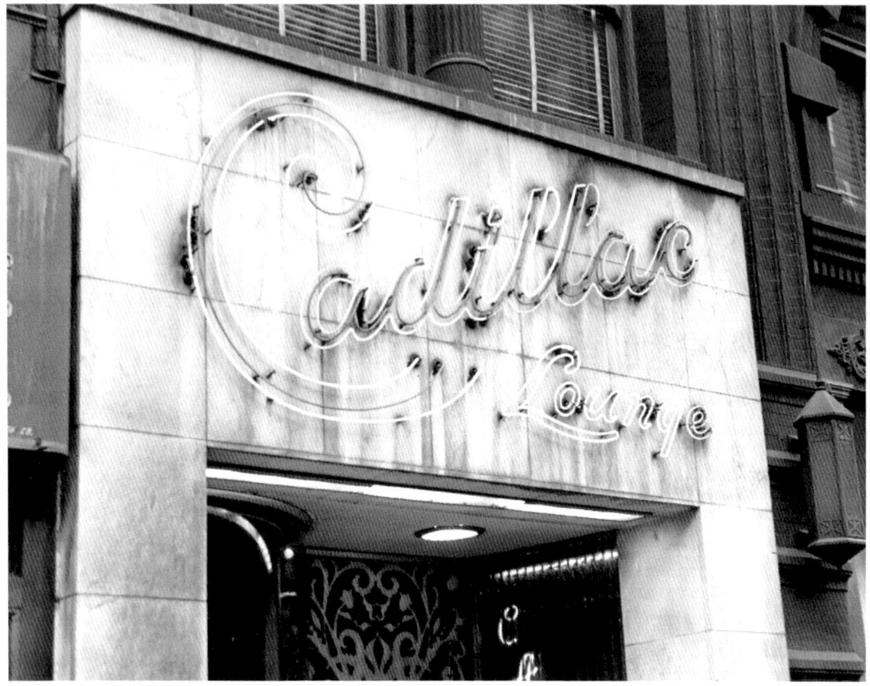

The Cadillac Lounge, 2016 East Ninth Street, 1949. *Cleveland Press Collection, Cleveland State University, Michael Schwartz Library Special Collections.*

In 1970, Lenihan sought to relocate the Cadillac Lounge to Prospect Avenue but encountered resistance, forcing its closure that year. Many patrons followed Lenihan to the Pickwick Bar on Clifton near Lakewood, which became another prominent gay bar until its closing in 1987. On the Cadillac's closure, an auction was held to sell off its property, including the sixty-foot mahogany bar and piano. The eight tropical murals that once adorned the Cadillac's interior now reside at the Western Reserve Historical Society, preserved as relics of this pioneering establishment.

If you didn't happen to be dressed properly or inadvertently violated one of Gloria's rules at the Cadillac, you could simply stroll a stone's throw away and stop at Little Ted's Restaurant and Bar at Superior and East Third Street. The bar in the basement of this establishment catered to the gay community and, notably, lacked the dress code or distance restrictions enforced at the Cadillac Lounge. Little Ted's was named after its five-foot, five-inch owner Ted Miclau, who acquired the nickname during his time operating restaurants in Chicago. Ted's journey took him from fleeing unfriendly mob activity in Chicago to returning to Romania, his homeland,

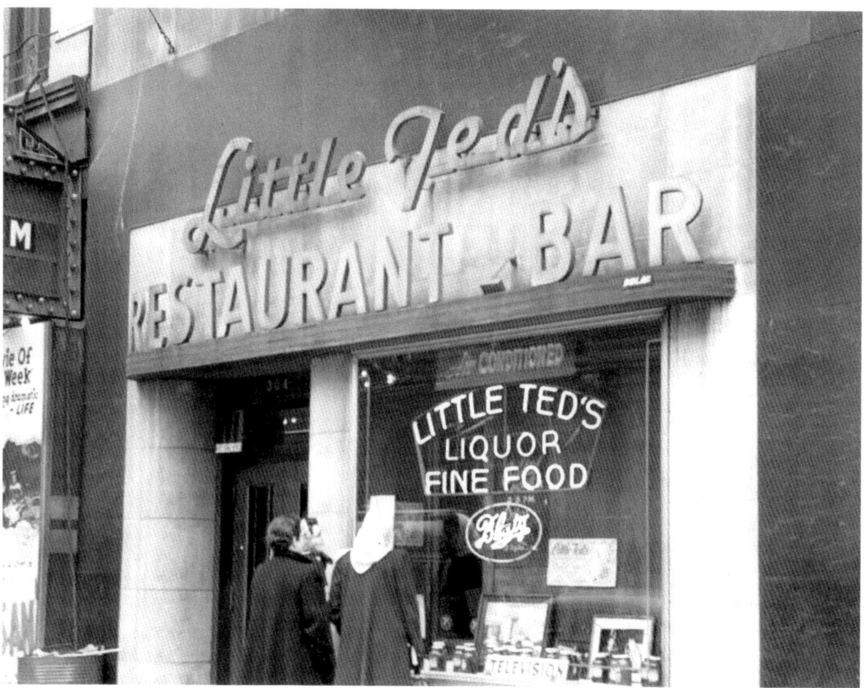

Little Ted's, Superior and East Third Street, May 1949. *Cleveland Press Collection, Cleveland State University, Michael Schwartz Library Special Collections.*

before ultimately settling in Cleveland in 1943. In 1947, he opened a second establishment called Ted's Loop Café on Prospect Avenue.

Over the years, Ted proved himself to be a formidable restaurateur, establishing the successful Black Angus Steakhouse and several other venues, including a hotel on Pearl Road. Ted's venues were prime locations for prominent events, while the basement bar offered popular piano entertainment. Ted's basement bar remained open until 1955, when he decided to focus on his more profitable establishments. Ted eventually retired in 1967 and sold all his business interests. Over the years, Ted and his wife, Cornelia, helped over three hundred Romanian families immigrate to Cleveland. His legacy lived on as he enjoyed a long life, passing away at the age of eighty-eight in 1991.

Downtown was a vibrant hub for nightlife through the 1960s. These establishments were more than just places to enjoy a drink; they were integral parts of the downtown landscape. While this chapter highlights some of the notable bars in the East Ninth and Short Vincent districts, it merely scratches the surface of the rich tapestry that was downtown's bar scene. On that mile-long stretch of East Ninth Street alone, there were additional popular spots not mentioned, such as Fleet's Inn, DeParee's, Young's and the Brass Rail. Each venue had its own loyal patrons and contributed to the lively downtown atmosphere. One block over on East Sixth Street, Moriarty's Irish Pub was a downtown staple that remained open for nearly one hundred years before closing its doors in 2020. It was a well-known hangout spot for celebrities, politicians, judges and lawyers to unwind after long days or grab a midday drink and talk shop.

Chapter 5

A Parallel Scene

The Rise of African American Taverns in Segregated Cleveland

The 1950s in Cleveland remained entrenched in racial segregation and discrimination toward the city's Black population. The Great Migration brought an influx of African Americans from the South seeking economic opportunities. The city's Black population grew dramatically, from 85,000 in 1940 to 147,847 in 1950 and over 250,000 by 1960. Nearly 98 percent of Black residents lived on the East Side of the Cuyahoga River. By the early 1960s, African Americans were over 30 percent of the city's population.

As Cleveland's population expanded, housing issues such as overcrowding, deteriorating conditions, and the subdivision of single family homes into multiple apartments, all previously seen earlier in Cedar-Central, began affecting the Hough neighborhood located north of Euclid between East Fifty-Fifth Street and East 105th Street. Other areas of significant growth included Glenville, Mount Pleasant and the old Miles Heights area. Much of the housing stock in these neighborhoods was over fifty years old and in poor condition, further strained by density and lack of upkeep.

In 1933, the Cedar Tavern, located at 6608 Cedar Avenue, became the first bar to secure a liquor license following the Prohibition era. The establishment was owned by Jack Kowit, a Hungarian immigrant. Initially, it served as a neighborhood bar for the working class, welcoming patrons of all races. Kowit's decision to employ Black bartenders and host events such as birthday parties and weddings for the Black community quickly established the bar as a popular venue.

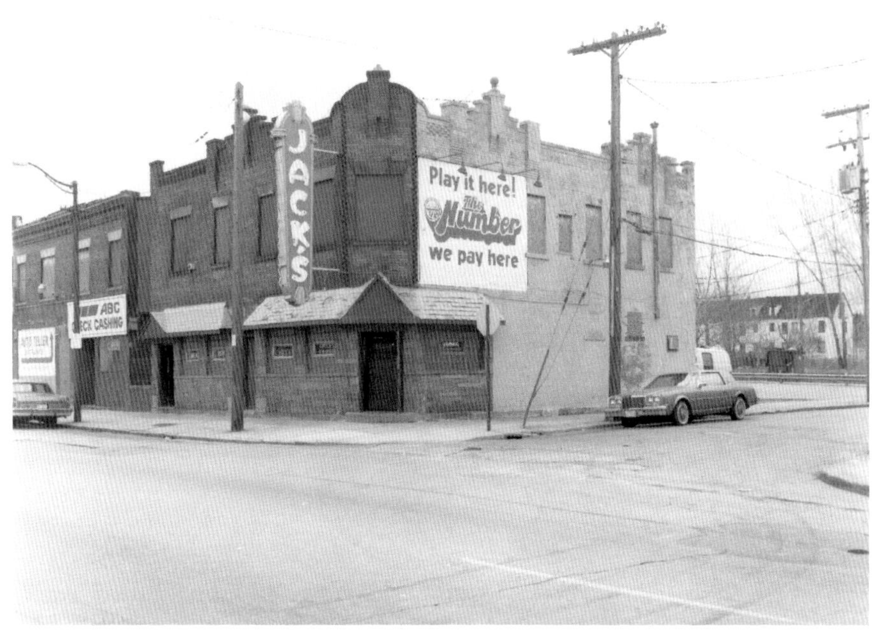

Jack's Musical Bar, 6608 Cedar Avenue, 1992. *Cleveland Public Library/Photograph Collection.*

Jack's son, Ed, joined the business, and over time, the tavern evolved. In 1936, the Kowits hired Fred Reed, a renowned pianist from Chicago, which significantly boosted the bar's popularity. The tavern further expanded its musical offerings by featuring local and traveling jazz bands. To distinguish itself from other taverns with *Cedar* in their names, it rebranded as Jack's Musical Bar in 1950.

However, the tavern wasn't immune to the criminal activities of the time. It fell victim to the infamous "white handkerchief" bandit, who, despite police surveillance in the Cedar-Central area, managed to rob the Cedar Tavern of $1,329 on July 28, 1941—the largest loot from over fifty robberies committed by the bandit. Like other bars in the neighborhood, Jack's was a target for robbers due to its practice of cashing patrons' payroll checks. Ed fought back, injuring a robber on Christmas Eve 1952 and fatally shooting another in October 1963. Eventually, Ed diversified into the check cashing business, opening several outlets on the East Side. Despite the city and the neighborhood's changes, the bar remained operational until the early 2000s.

In February 1934, the *Call and Post* reported that the first Black-owned establishment to sell beer and liquor by the glass in the city was Eugene Brown's Lunch Room, located at 4604 Central Avenue. Brown advertised a daily cocktail hour at 4:00 p.m., offering dinners priced between twenty-five and fifty cents. In addition to the affordable meals, he provided top-notch musical entertainment. Unfortunately, liquor licenses were not routinely approved for Black applicants. In the 1940s, the State of Ohio Liquor License Application required applicants to list their race on the form. State Representative Chester Gillespie protested this and urged all applicants to refuse to comply, but discrimination in granting licenses persisted. Lawyer Gillespie persisted; known as Mr. Civil Rights, he fought to establish the antidiscrimination clause in Ohio's liquor laws.

During the 1940s and '50s, Cleveland's Woodland-Cedar-Central area transformed into a vibrant hub of live music. On May 9, 1953, the *Call and Post* opined that there was no need to travel to Broadway when one could simply stroll over to Woodland Avenue to enjoy some of the finest music this side of the equator.

One of the premier music venues in the area was the Chatterbox Musical Bar at 5121 Woodland Avenue. The bar was the brainchild of John "Chin"

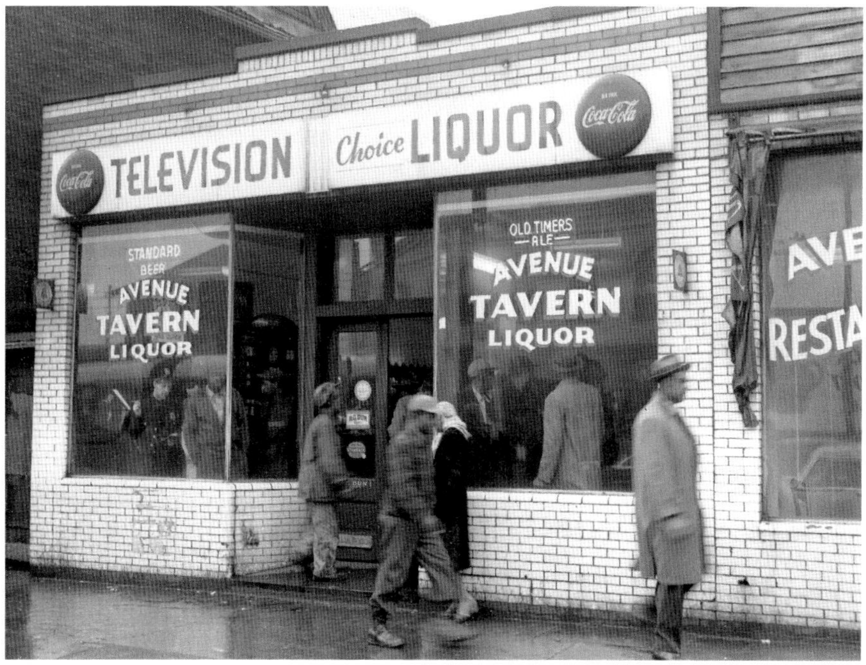

One of many bars on Woodland: the Avenue Tavern, at 3021 Woodland, in 1953. Note the policeman talking with customers. The bartender shot an eighteen-year-old Black customer in 1938. *Cleveland Press Collection, Cleveland State University, Michael Schwartz Library Special Collections.*

Ballard, who was committed to providing an elevated experience for his patrons. To enhance the allure of the tavern, Ballard enlisted the help of designers to optimize its interior lighting, seating and overall comfort. Unlike most other club owners, Ballard chose not to inflate liquor prices during the evening when live entertainment was onstage.

Ballard's entrepreneurial spirit shone through when he appointed Marion Motley, the renowned Cleveland Browns running back, as the Chatterbox's assistant manager. Another unique feature of the bar was its twenty-one-inch television screen, the largest in any Cleveland tavern. Ballard's timing could not have been better: the Cleveland Indians were one of the top teams in the major leagues in the 1950s.

The Chatterbox played host to major touring acts such as Billie Holiday, Della Reese and Dinah Washington and had the finest house bands in Cleveland. Unfortunately, the club's operations came to an abrupt close in February 1959 when a fire that originated at the neighboring Ritzwood Hotel spread, destroying several adjoining businesses.

One vital source of news and information for the African American community was the Cleveland *Call and Post*. The publication regularly featured reviews, advertisements and listings of popular nightlife spots in Cleveland's Black community. It served as a crucial resource for residents and visitors alike, highlighting venues that not only offered entertainment but also provided a safe and inclusive environment during a time when segregation and racial discrimination were pervasive. In his "Year in Review" on December 30, 1944, Bob Williams observed that "the Negro Café came into its own during the year 1944," noting the rise of Black-owned and frequented venues that gained prominence that year.

Williams described the year as a high point for these establishments, as they introduced a level of sophistication and upscale service not common in barrooms or saloons catering to Black patrons. According to Williams, the top-rated venue was the Blue Grass Club at 2173 East Fifty-Fifth Street, while the Caravan, Celebrity, Ron-Day-Voo and El Morocco earned honorable mentions. These taverns he wrote, provided warmth, friendliness and good cheer when, more than ever, a fellow needed a friend.

The Blue Grass Club opened in August 1944 with much anticipation and fanfare. The club's spacious interior featured a fifty-foot bar with the longest mirror in town, an open kitchen, six fans to keep patrons cool and, most importantly, top-notch music. The club's house band was the popular and talented Queen and Two Jacks. The Blue Grass was a regular stop for touring musicians, including the great jazz artist Art Tatum. However, the

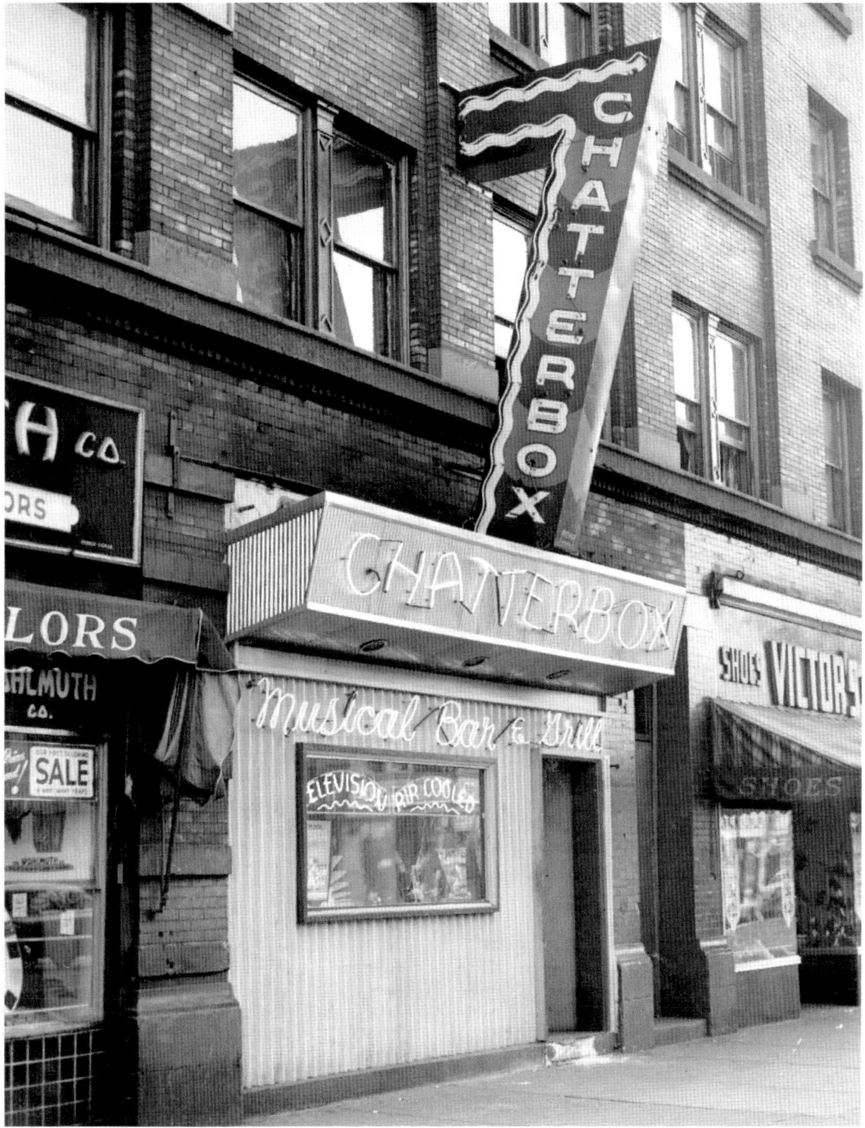

Chatterbox, 5123 Woodland Avenue, 1949. *Cleveland Press Collection, Cleveland State University, Michael Schwartz Library Special Collections.*

Blue Grass changed ownership after only a few years, and its popularity was short-lived. The new owner was forced to close for ninety days in 1949 due to liquor violations. With increasing competition, the Blue Grass lost its luster, and it went into liquidation the following year.

The Green Book's Cleveland Listings

Despite its brief existence, the Blue Grass Club represented the type of relatively upscale and welcoming environment for African American patrons that was highlighted in Victor Green's *Negro Motorist Green Book*. Published from 1936 to 1966, the *Green Book* served as a necessary guide for Black travelers navigating the segregated landscape of the United States. It listed hotels, restaurants, bars, service stations and other businesses across the country that were safely nondiscriminatory. Though the Blue Grass Club made the *Green Book* listings, the guidebook inexplicably never listed its correct address during its years of operation, 1944 to 1950.

A perennial listing in the *Green Book* from 1946 to 1955 was Cedar Gardens at 9706 Cedar Avenue. Opened in 1934 by White owner Jacob Hecht, this establishment initially advertised Chinese and American cuisine. However, Hecht brought in Ulysses S. "Sweets" Dearing from Pittsburgh, who later became a very successful restaurateur in Cleveland. Dearing shifted the menu to southern-style barbecue, and over the next several years, Cedar Gardens evolved into an immensely popular entertainment destination attracting national performers.

The Gardens featured a wide range of acts, even advertising the "Famous Detroit Red…the world's best looking, best dressed, and most entertaining female impersonators in the country." In 1941, new co-owner Joe Gould aimed to make the club more appealing to Black patrons. The *Call and Post* reported on May 17, 1941, that he would reduce prices to be more affordable, operate Cedar Gardens primarily as a "nightclub for negro patrons" and hire an all-Black staff to keep revenue circulating in the neighborhood. This establishment continued evolving through the decades as a lively venue. However, like many other nightclubs in the area, Cedar Gardens ultimately caught fire, and it closed in 1969 amid the turbulent unrest of that era. The property is now part of the Cleveland Clinic complex.

While many of the nightclubs listed in the *Green Book* featured high-level entertainment, Mike's Brown Derby at 4002 Woodland Avenue, which opened in the fall of 1945, catered more to the working-class crowd as a neighborhood bar. The *Green Book* first listed the Brown Derby in the late 1940s and continued listing the bar even after its sale in 1950. Though the establishment was integrated, the *Call and Post* reported that it had "TWO BARS—one for white and one for colored." The bar's clientele was estimated to be 85 percent Black; its White patrons mostly came from nearby factories. Black customers were served at the main bar, while the White crowd drank at what was dubbed the Midget Bar. Despite this segregated setup, Mike's Brown Derby was one of the only relatively integrated establishments available to both Black and White working-class patrons during that era.

For a more comprehensive understanding of the Northeast Ohio establishments listed in the *Green Book*, the Green Book Cleveland project is a valuable resource. Initiated by Dr. Mark Souther and his students at Cleveland State University, this project documents the full range of Black economic and leisure life in the region, including businesses such as restaurants, nightclubs, beauty shops, service stations and more.

Beyond the Green Book: Other Black Business Pioneers

In the late 1940s, Cafe Tia Juana was one of the hottest jazz clubs in Cleveland. Located at 1045 East 105th Street in Glenville, the establishment was founded in 1947 by Catherine and Arthur "Little Brother" Drake, taking over the space previously occupied by Solomon's Gold Bar—a venue listed in the *Green Book* as a safe place for African American patrons. Despite the ownership change, Cafe Tia Juana itself continued to be listed in the *Green Book* as Gold's Bar through the early 1950s.

Tia Juana's inception was a direct response to racial segregation in the city's nightlife scene: Catherine Drake was turned away from a segregated jazz club prior to opening her own venue as Cleveland's first female African American jazz club owner. With financing from her husband Little Brother Drake's numbers racket, she invested heavily in an extravagant interior featuring a bar shaped like a four-leaf clover and a revolving stage. The Drakes hosted top jazz talent like Dizzy Gillespie, Billie Holiday, Miles Davis and Charlie Parker, making Tia Juana a nationally recognized hot spot.

In 1954, the club eliminated cover and minimum charges and started innovative promotions like early morning "Monday Parties" at 5:30 a.m., featuring events like the "Bermuda Shorts Hop." However, Tia Juana was plagued by legal issues, battling a local councilman who wanted it closed as a public nuisance due to crime in the area, including a shooting outside the club. The club also suffered an IRS lien, and Little Brother Drake was imprisoned. Despite Cafe Tia Juana's attempts to evolve, the turbulent 1960s ultimately led to the club's demise in 1969, when the building at East 105th and Massie was demolished.

Just a few blocks away, at 9903 Cedar Avenue, thirty-four-year-old Fleet Slaughter had achieved a significant court victory. On January 24, 1953, the

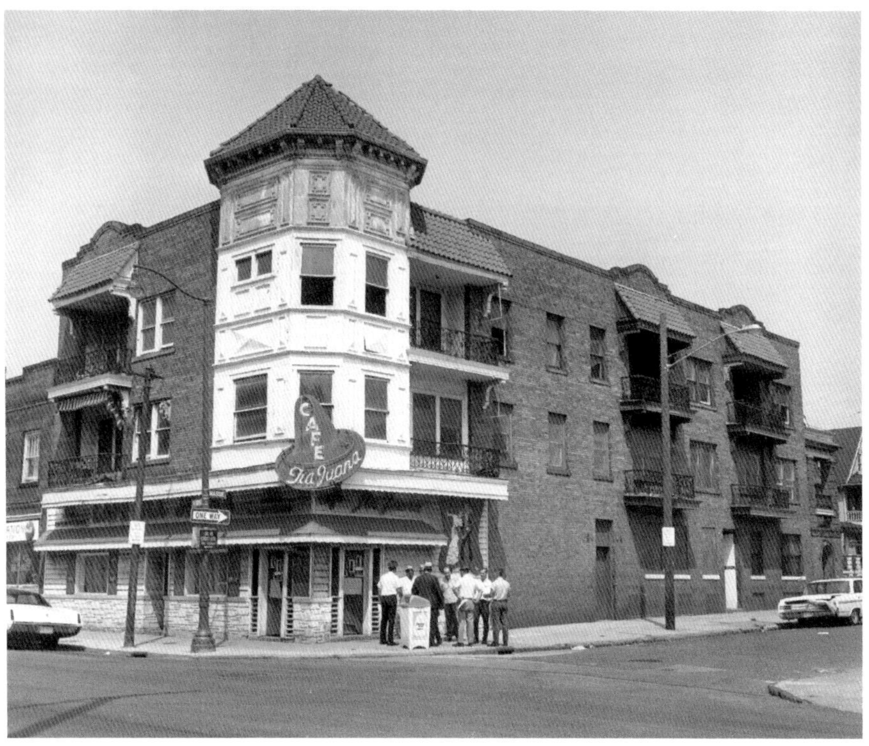

Club Tia Juana, 10405 East 105th Street, 1969. *Cleveland Public Library/Photograph Collection.*

Call and Post reported that a Franklin County judge ordered the state liquor board to grant Slaughter a D-5 liquor permit for his Manhattan Restaurant. Slaughter's lawyer highlighted that despite the presence of dozens of bars along Cedar Avenue, only four Black-owned establishments in the entire area had been granted this permit, which allowed the sale of all alcoholic beverages until 2:30 a.m.

Slaughter operated the Manhattan Restaurant with his wife, Beulah Norton Penn, who had owned it since 1946, before their marriage. A court ruling allowed Slaughter to open the Manhattan Tap Room within the restaurant, and a few years later, he expanded with the addition of the El Dorado Cocktail Lounge. The Tap Room quickly became one of the most popular lounges in the Black community along Cedar Avenue, which, at the time, had no other Black-owned bars with a D-5 license.

Slaughter was just getting started. He went on to become one of Cleveland's most prominent African American businessmen. In 1961, he opened the Lancer Steakhouse at 7701 Carnegie Avenue, which quickly became a renowned fine dining destination. The Lancer brought an upscale steakhouse experience to the city's Black community at a time when most restaurants remained segregated. The elegant establishment featured chandeliers, lush red carpeting and white tablecloth service. The Lancer attracted celebrities, athletes and entertainers, including regulars such as Mayor Carl Stokes, Congressman Louis Stokes and Jim Brown. Notable visitors like Martin Luther King Jr. also frequented the steakhouse whenever they visited Cleveland. Additionally, Slaughter opened the Lancer Motor Court behind the restaurant and bar. This venue not only served the Black community but also accommodated White individuals seeking to engage with the Black community for business, political strategy or social outreach.

Fleet Slaughter owned the Lancer until his death in 1975. Under his leadership, it became a celebrated establishment, embodying both success and integration. The venue continued to operate until 2009, when a devastating fire caused extensive damage, making rebuilding impossible.

Although the Lancer eventually reopened across the street, it never fully recaptured the allure and charm of the original. Nevertheless, its legacy endures as a testament to Slaughter's vision and the vital role it played in the community. Despite the challenges, the Lancer lives on in the memories of those who experienced its vibrant history.

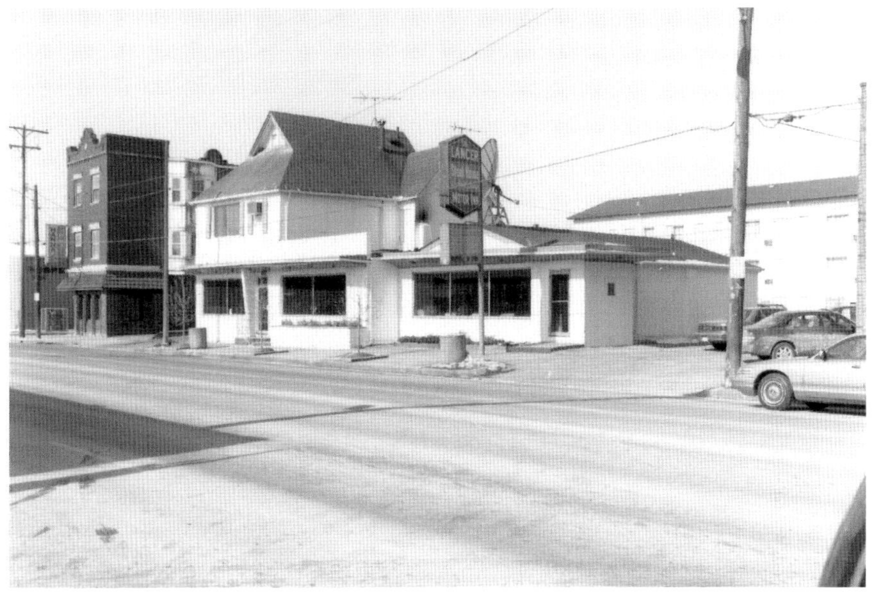

The Lancer Steakhouse with the motor court in the rear. *Cleveland Public Library/Photograph Collection.*

The unassuming storefront at 7800 Cedar has a complex, multilayered history intertwined with the city's underworld, its musical legacy and its recognition as a rock 'n' roll landmark. Its initial notoriety dates to August 1936, when a police raid on what was then a confectionery uncovered gambling slips, causing twenty people to flee through the back door or windows. Three years later, on October 12, 1939, the *Call and Post* announced the opening of the Corner Tavern at the same address. The new proprietors, Sam and Herman, eagerly invited everyone to "stop in and eat, drink and make merry." They regularly advertised happy hour specials, such as fifteen-cent mixed drinks, fostering a welcoming neighborhood tavern atmosphere.

In the 1940s, the Corner Tavern was owned by famed alto sax player and businessman Frank Handy. Handy also owned the Paradise Bar on Woodland Avenue. Both establishments were popular hot spots; Handy advertised them as "two places where your friends could be found in Cleveland." They served American and Chinese cuisine and featured local musical acts like saxophonist Caesar Dameron and the Four Jacks, who played the emerging "gentle jazz."

Despite its musical appeal, the venue also had ties to Cleveland's underground economy, particularly the city's prevalent "numbers games"—an illegal lottery system in which players placed small bets on daily number draws, hoping for a payout. These games were widely popular in working-class and Black communities, often operating out of taverns, barbershops and other small businesses.

Handy eventually turned state's witness against the Mayfield Road Mob, revealing that he had been earning $250 to $300 daily from his numbers racket before being pressured into handing over a share to the mobsters. Ownership of the tavern then passed to known rackets figure Joseph Allen. In July 1949, the *Plain Dealer* reported that $40,000 was stolen from the tavern's safe; police recovered $22,000 that someone had "dropped." In the aftermath of this mysterious robbery, eight officers faced charges for violating police department rules by returning the cash to Allen instead of logging it as evidence. Around the same time, Allen's home was the target of a mysterious firebombing.

In the late 1950s and early '60s, the Corner Tavern was under the ownership of boxing promoter and numbers runner Don King. The venue showcased jazz luminaries who defined the genre's modern sound, and King promoted concerts by artists like Marvin Gaye, the Spinners and James Brown.

However, after an IRS raid on both the tavern and King's home uncovered evidence of illegal gambling, the Corner Tavern's operations came to an abrupt halt in April 1965. Shortly after the raid, a large and unexplained fire engulfed the building.

The following year, in 1966, King was charged with murder after the beating death of a customer outside the Manhattan Tap Room. He was later convicted of manslaughter and sentenced to prison. After being paroled in 1971, King shifted his focus to boxing promotion, launching what would become a legendary career in the sport.

By 1967, the abandoned tavern was littered with code violations, prompting the City of Cleveland to order its demolition. The Corner Tavern's legacy was restored in 2002 when the Rock & Roll Hall of Fame recognized it as a historic landmark—only the fourth such designation in Cleveland—a testament to its significant contribution to the city's musical heritage.

Leo's Casino, located at 7500 Euclid Avenue, became a renowned music venue and nightclub in Cleveland during the 1960s and early 1970s. Its impact was so significant that the Rock & Roll Hall of Fame designated Leo's Casino a historic landmark in 1999, just two weeks before the passing of the original owner, Leo Frank.

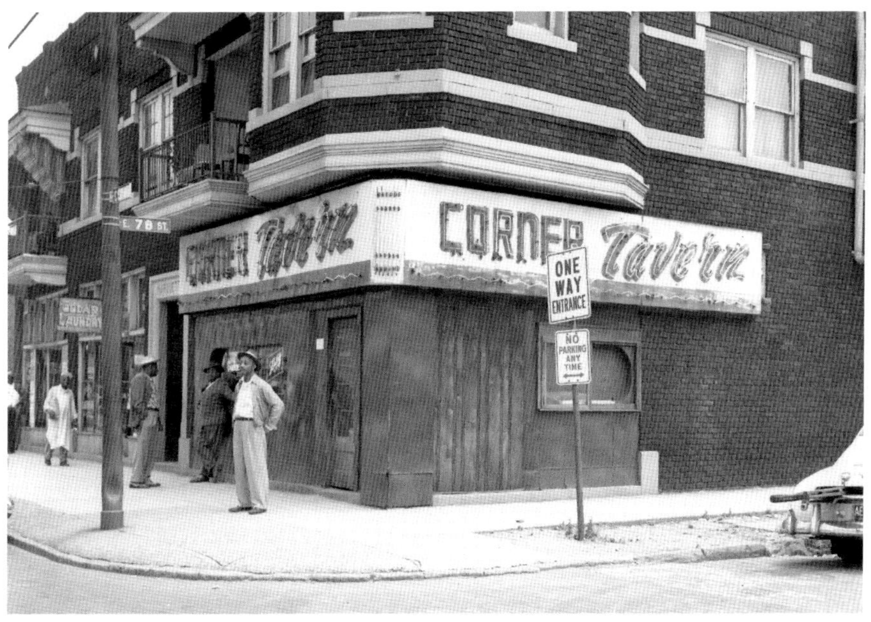

The Corner Tavern, Don King's tavern at 7800 Cedar Avenue, was acknowledged as a historic rock 'n' roll landmark. *Cleveland Public Library/Photograph Collection.*

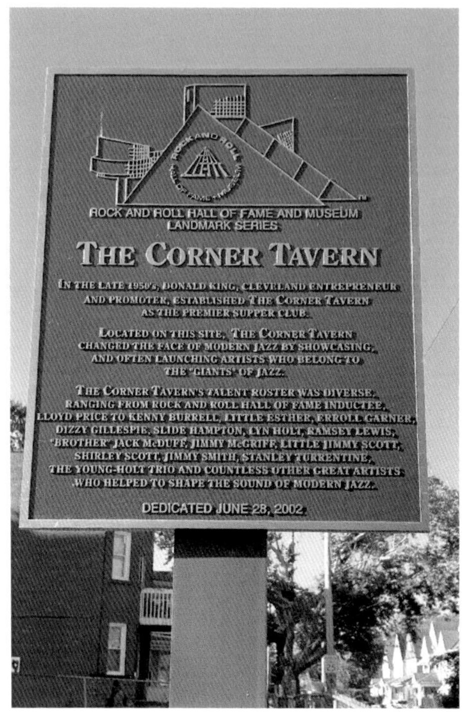

Left: Landmark designation of the Corner Tavern, 7800 Cedar Avenue, June 2024. *Author's collection.*

Below: City of Cleveland Violation File and Demolition Order, 7800 Cedar. *Courtesy of the City of Cleveland Archives.*

Opposite: The original Leo's Casino, 4809 Central Avenue, 1958. *Cleveland Public Library/Photograph Collection.*

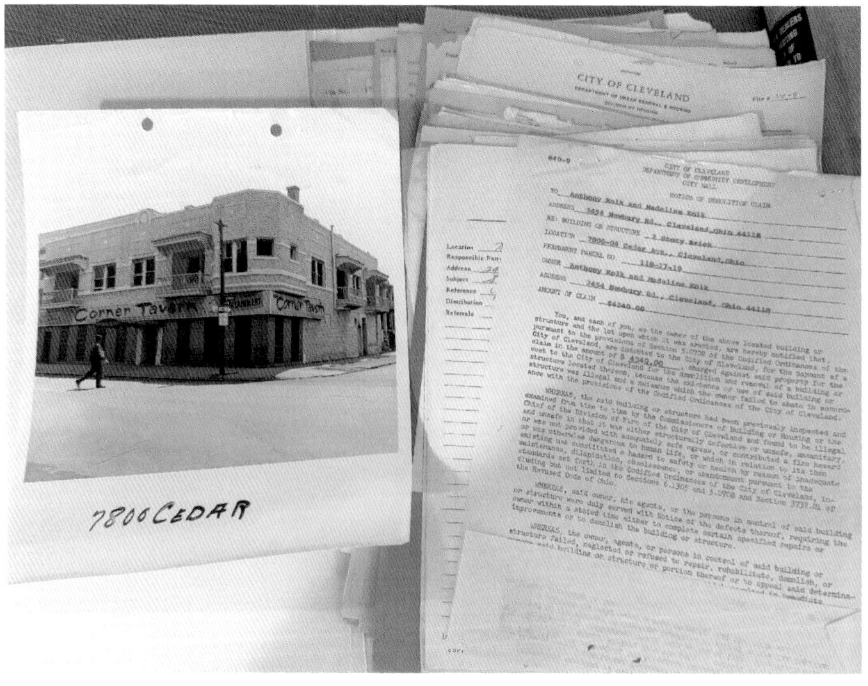

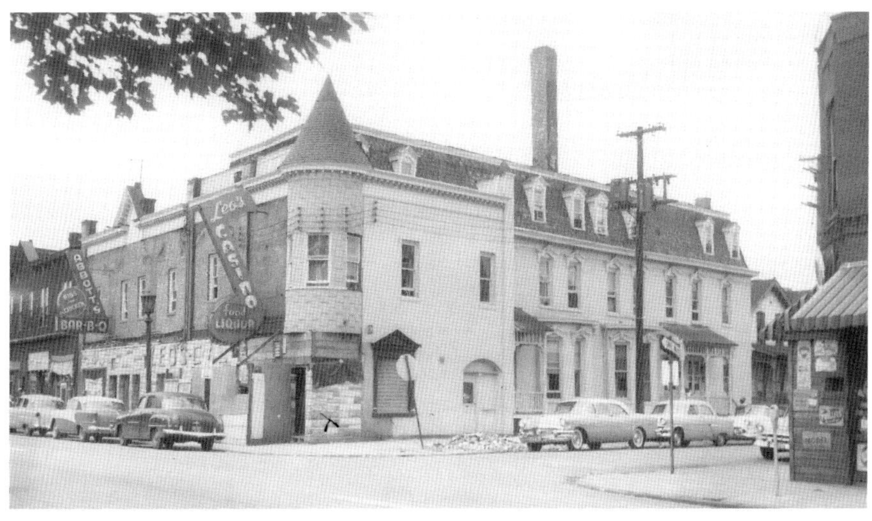

Frank's journey into the entertainment world began much earlier, when he opened the doors of Leo's Casino at 4817 Central Avenue back in 1952. Frank boasted his place was the "toast of the Gold Coast" (a nickname for Cleveland at the time) and advertised "no minimum, no cover." He was able to attract top talent, including Dizzy Gillespie and John Coltrane, through the 1950s. After ten years in business, the venue was destroyed by a fire, and in 1963, Frank partnered with Jules Berger to open the new Leo's Casino at 7500 Euclid Avenue. The club was known for welcoming all races, even during the racially turbulent 1960s. Leo's hosted activist and comedian Dick Gregory to headline a fundraising event for CORE (Congress of Racial Equality).

The Hough Riots in 1966 occurred near the club but didn't deter the mixed crowds who came to see the Supremes during that tumultuous time. After a brief closure, the club had an exciting reopening after the riots when it was able to attract Ray Charles. From the late 1960s to the very early 1970s, all the Motown greats performed at Leo's. A very partial list includes Smokey Robinson and the Miracles, Jackie Wilson, Marvin Gaye, Dionne Warwick, the Temptations, the Four Tops and Ike and Tina Turner. The club also hosted some of the earliest shows by future superstars Stevie Wonder and Aretha Franklin, before they achieved global fame. Otis Redding gave his final concert performance at Leo's, just one day before he died tragically in a plane crash in 1967. Beyond music legends, the venue provided an important launching pad for rising comedy talents like Richard Pryor, Flip Wilson and Redd Foxx.

Despite its trailblazing role, Leo's Casino could not survive the changing tides of the entertainment industry. With a capacity of around seven hundred, the club struggled to compete financially as the very acts it helped launch into the mainstream gained broader popularity. These rising stars could now command much larger paydays at bigger arenas that Leo's could not match. Facing this harsh economic reality, original owner Leo Frank sold his stake in the nightclub to his business partner Jules Berger in 1970. Just two years later, Berger was forced to make the difficult decision to permanently close the iconic club's doors. Though its original run was relatively brief, spanning just under a decade at its Euclid Avenue location, Leo's Casino left a permanent mark in Cleveland history. In June 1990, the *Call and Post* highlighted its impact in a two-article series titled "Roots of Black Entertainment: Yesterday and Today," emphasizing the role of Black entertainers in advancing racial integration. The article noted that "Flip Wilson, the Temptations, the Four Tops, Marvin Gaye, and the Supremes got more and better results with integration than any court could've ordered." The quote underscored how the success and visibility of Black artists at venues like Leo's Casino helped break down racial barriers in ways that legal rulings alone could not. By drawing integrated audiences, Black entertainers played a pivotal role in fostering change in Cleveland's racial landscape.

As we reflect on the significance of these East Side establishments, it is essential to also explore other parts of the city that catered to a different crowd—venues where the focus was on shots and beers, serving the local working class and creating their own unique cultural footprint. Let's now take a look at these neighborhood spots and their role in the nightlife of the city.

Chapter 6

Blue-Collar Brews

The East Side Taverns of Cleveland

After exploring downtown Cleveland and the vibrant African American music and tavern scene through Central-Cedar, Hough and Fairfax, our journey now leads us to Glenville. While we've already traveled down East 105th Street to discover some of its notable nightclubs, it's time to shift our focus to the neighborhood taverns that catered to the working class, where a shot and a beer were the drinks of choice.

The 1950s marked the beginning of a significant population decline in Cleveland, a trend that has persisted to the present day. While the city's Black population grew substantially, the overall population decreased by 4 percent, or over 37,000 residents, dropping to 876,000. Urban renewal projects, fueled by the Housing Act of 1949, aimed to revitalize blighted inner-city areas. However, these projects often displaced low-income residents, many of them African American families. The construction of freeways, 90 percent funded by the Federal Highway Act of 1956, further segregated cities. New highways sliced through neighborhoods, displacing residents and disrupting communities. Additionally, these freeways made commuting from the suburbs to downtown much quicker, which accelerated what became known as white flight.

The population decline became even more pronounced in the 1960s: a staggering 14 percent drop brought Cleveland's population down to 750,000. As the suburbs gained a reputation for safer and more modern living, their appeal continued to rise. This shift led many White residents to move out of the city center, leaving behind a more concentrated and under-resourced population in the urban core. Concurrently, the Black population grew to nearly 288,000, 38 percent of Cleveland's total population. The largest White ethnic groups remained those of Slavic origin (Poles, Slovaks, Czechs, Slovenians and Hungarians), followed by those of Italian and Irish descent. The city remained highly segregated, as evidenced by the 1972 *Minority Business and Professional Directory*, which listed seventy-three Black-owned bars, every single one located on the East Side of the Cuyahoga River.

Eastward Bound to Glenville

Glenville boasts a prominent history. It was annexed to Cleveland in 1904, and initially, it was a predominantly Jewish community: Jews were 90 percent of the population at its peak, in the 1940s. The area around East 105th Street, often referred to as the Jewish Downtown, was bustling with Jewish-owned stores, bakeries, kosher butchers and synagogues. Starting in the 1950s, as Jewish residents began moving to the suburbs, Glenville underwent a significant transformation, becoming a predominantly African American neighborhood. This demographic shift brought about a change in the social and cultural landscape of the area, including its taverns and nightlife.

As Glenville evolved, so did the concentration of bars and taverns around East 105th and Saint Clair. This compact area became a vibrant hub with seventeen bars catering to the local community. Establishments such as J&J African American Tavern, Jamaica Breeze and the Ebony Boy Bar emerged as popular spots for socializing after a hard day's work. Notably, Jamaica Breeze sponsored a young Chuck Thorpe on the PGA tour. On October 22, 1966, the *Call and Post* reported, "It is unprecedented—a first for the city of Cleveland, the first time any Cleveland Negro golfer has been so honored, and we are proud to participate." This sponsorship came only five years after Charlie Sifford broke the PGA color barrier.

Chuck Thorpe participated in sixty-one tournaments, achieving seven top ten finishes. His younger brother, Jim Thorpe, went on to win three PGA Tour events and earned $2 million in prize money during his career. Coincidentally, Charlie Sifford retired in Cleveland and served as the club professional at Sleepy Hollow, just down the road in Brecksville. These connections highlight the rich history and cultural significance of the Glenville neighborhood and its taverns.

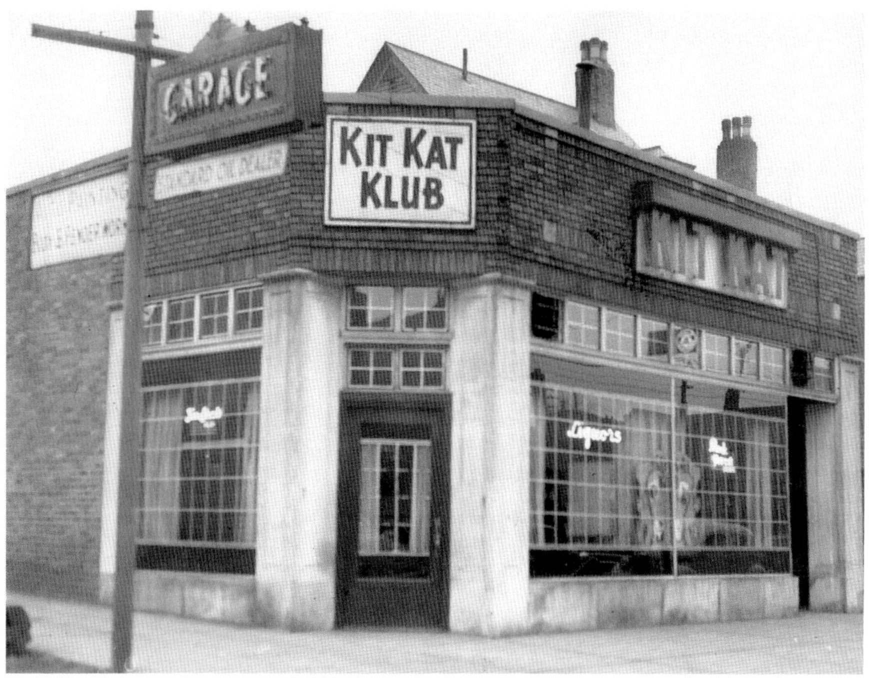

Kit Kat Club, 12376 Superior Avenue, Glenville, 1960s. *Cleveland Press Collection, Cleveland State University, Michael Schwartz Library Special Collections.*

Taverns became flashpoints during the 1960s on Cleveland's East Side, a period marked by simmering racial tensions that erupted into violence. This era reached a boiling point with two major events: the Hough Riots of 1966 and the Glenville shootout of 1968. These incidents were the result of long-standing issues between law enforcement and the African American community. The unrest during this period not only reshaped the physical landscape of these neighborhoods but also had profound and lasting effects on Cleveland's social and political dynamics.

The Hough Riots ignited on July 18, 1966, when the White owner of the Seventy-Niners Cafe at Hough Avenue and East Seventy-Ninth Street denied a Black takeout customer a glass of water. Frustrations boiled over, leading to clashes with police. What began as rock-throwing quickly escalated into vandalism and looting that swept through the surrounding area. The following night brought further unrest: fires erupted, and reports of sniper fire added to the chaos. On July 20, Mayor Ralph Locher called in the National Guard to restore order and mandated the closure of all bars citywide. Vandalism and arson continued until July 25. As the violence

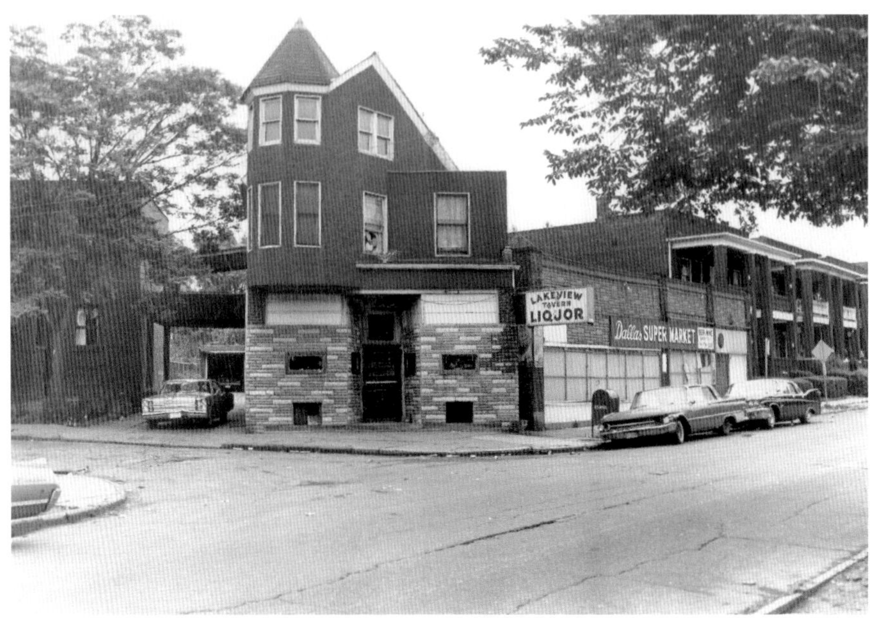

Lakeview Tavern, 1963, location of the Glenville riot in 1968. Fred Ahmed Evans' home is in the rear. *Cleveland Press Collection, Cleveland State University, Michael Schwartz Library Special Collections.*

finally subsided, businesses began to reopen. The scars of the Hough Riots would be a reminder of the racial divide for years to come. The Seventy-Niners Café has been demolished and remains a vacant lot.

Just two years later, tensions flared again just down the road in the Glenville shootout. This four-day conflict erupted on July 23, 1968, between Cleveland police and a Black nationalist group led by Fred Ahmed Evans. The incident began when Evans and his followers engaged in a firefight with police officers at Lakeview Road and Auburndale Avenue, just outside the Lakeview Tavern. The tavern, which was adjacent to Evans's home, served as a gathering place for his followers. The Glenville shootout triggered widespread rioting and looting, which resulted in the deaths of seven civilians and three police officers. To restore order, the National Guard was deployed, and the area was locked down again. These events highlight the deep racial divisions that plagued the entire city during the 1960s.

Heading North: Discovering the Superior and Saint Clair Avenue Tavern Scene

Continuing our nostalgic pub crawl, let's head about a mile north from Hough and the Central and Cedar area to explore the tavern scene along Superior and Saint Clair Avenues. These main thoroughfares traverse several distinct neighborhoods, including Goodrich/Kirkland, Superior/Saint Clair, Glenville and Collinwood. On our way, we'll pass Payne Avenue, which also boasts its own selection of taverns, as well as the old Central Police Department and Municipal Court. Payne Avenue taverns were often named after their owners, such as Glenn's, Jo-Ann's Nite Club, Frank's, George's, Mike's and Joe's, all conveniently located on Payne within a few miles of each other.

Across the street from the police station was Shaia's Tavern, a popular haunt for officers after a long shift. On February 24, 1964, the *Plain Dealer* reported an intriguing incident at Shaia's: several "shapely young women" came in for an "eye opener"—a morning drink to start the day—and then locked the porter in a back room and made off with a safe containing $4,500. Despite taking place right across the street from hundreds of police officers, the heist initially went unnoticed. Nevertheless, the culprits were tracked down and arrested later that same day.

Shaia's later transformed into the Campus Lounge and Bar, aiming to attract students from the newly established Cleveland State University. The Campus Lounge humorously proclaimed itself the "Garden Spot of Payne Avenue" due to a single plastic daffodil placed next to the cash register. When Sunday liquor licenses became available in Cleveland, the lounge became embroiled in a price war with the 2300 Club, located two blocks down on Payne Avenue. The 2300 Club offered a hot dog plate with cold sauerkraut for ten cents, prompting the Campus Lounge to counter with a hot dog plate including beans and hot sauerkraut for twenty-five cents. The 2300 Club seemed to come out on top when the Campus Lounge's drains became clogged with shreds of sauerkraut, highlighting the quirky and competitive nature of these neighborhood taverns.

Since we're near the Cleveland State campus, let's stop by Moe's on East Seventeenth Street just south of Payne. Over the years, Moe's has occupied several locations on the outskirts of downtown. It was originally named after its owner, Phillip Assad, nicknamed Moe. Phil's brother, Albert, took over the bar in 1960 and moved it to its current location in the late 1970s. The building itself has a fascinating history. Built as a rooming house in 1890, it has served as the Downtown Baptist Church, a punk and gay bar and

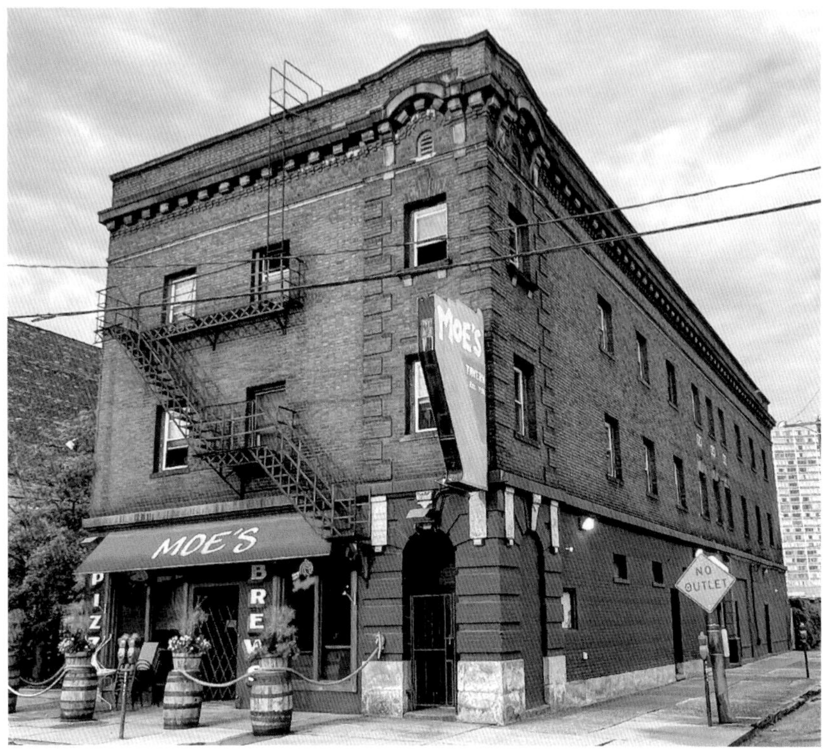

Moe's Tavern on East Seventeenth Street in August 2024. The building dates to 1890. *Author's photo.*

even a front for gangster Danny Greene's gambling operations, brothel and speakeasy. There are rumors that Moe's Tavern on *The Simpsons* was inspired by this bar, though that might just be another urban legend. Today, Moe's remains a vibrant bar, serving CSU students, visitors to Playhouse Square and local neighborhood residents.

Let's head less than a half mile north toward Saint Clair Avenue. This area, historically a heavy industrial and manufacturing zone, was home to twenty-three different nationalities in the early 1900s, including the first Croatian settlement. A little farther down Saint Clair, Lithuanians, Slovenians and Poles established their communities. Throughout the 1900s, Cleveland boasted the largest Slovene population in the United States. Today, Saint Clair Avenue continues to be a diverse area: it encompasses Cleveland's Asia Town, and the number of African American residents has increased substantially since the 1990s. This mix of cultures is reflected in the neighborhood taverns that served as social hubs for these communities.

St. Clair Avenue: East 40th to East Boulevard

East 40th	1964	1975
4001	Arko's Bar	
4017	Tomsic's Tavern	Tomsic's Tavern
4118	Edelweiss Hall	Little Europe Bar
4304	Eli's Tavern	
4428	Norbar Tavern	
4502	Lausin's Cafe	
4714	Friendly Tavern	Sally's Bar
4830	Deutsch's Tavern	Phil's Cafe
5238	Krizman's Tavern	Leo's Lounge
5301	Lil & John's Cafe	Bill's Tavern
5379	Pauline's Cafe	
5388	Marquette Cafe	
5393	Bertha's Cafe	Bertha's Cafe
5401	Julia's Cafe	Julia's Cafe
5501	Treer's Bar	
5705	Novak's Bar	
6010	Bozeglav Tavern	Bozeglav Tavern
6017	Kepic's Bar	Lupe's Lounge
6030	Tino's Bar	Tino's Bar
6201	Modic's Cafe	Beanie's Tavern
6400	Flaisman Cafe	Flaisman Cafe
6524	John's Cafe	John's Cafe
6616	Al & George's	Al & George's
6622	Sophie's Bar	

East 66th	1964	1975
6626		Jerry's Lounge
6702	Carol's Bar	
6723	Luzar's Bar	
6737	St. Clair Tavern	St. Clair Tavern
6911	Seaway Tavern	
6918	Maple Lanes	Maple Lanes
7006	Dee Kay Bar	
7011	Mick's Cafe	Jerris Inn
7114	Mihcic Cafe	Mihcic Cafe
7117	Satellite Bar	
7501	Leo's Cafe	Leo's Cafe
7508	Mell-O-Bar	Mell-O-Bar
7513	Kotnick's Bar	Kotnick's Bar
7601	S&L Cafe	S&L Cafe
7613	Jim's Grill & Bar	
7708	Ed's Cafe	
7810	Holiday Bar	
7822	Blossom Bar	Blossom Bar
7900	5th Wheel Tavern	
7920	Doo Drop Inn	
8012	Lonero's Bar	Lonero's Bar
8202	M&M Cafe	M&M Cafe

Source: City of Cleveland City Directory, 1964.

The Croatian Tavern: A Storied Legacy on Saint Clair Avenue

Our first stop is 3244 Saint Clair Avenue, the historic location of the Croatian Tavern, now known as Crobar. This iconic establishment has been serving the community since 1921, even operating during Prohibition. Throughout its long history, the tavern has been a steadfast presence in the neighborhood, accumulating countless stories and evolving with the times.

The Croatian Tavern quickly became popular among the working-class community, known for its tough, gritty patrons. In 1944, the tavern made headlines when robbers targeted the bar, aiming to steal patrons' freshly cashed paychecks. The blue-collar patrons fought back by throwing beer bottles, successfully thwarting the robbery.

A year later, another event showcased the resilience of the tavern's patrons. On July 5, 1945, the *Plain Dealer* reported that two young thugs targeted Stanley Malicki, a "lean, hard-muscled fellow," believing he had a lot of money because he'd been playing the jukebox. Malicki grabbed a fence picket and chased away the robbers, who were later apprehended.

In 1969, Joe Lasic took ownership of the Croatian Tavern. Under his management, the bar remained a community staple, even as the area

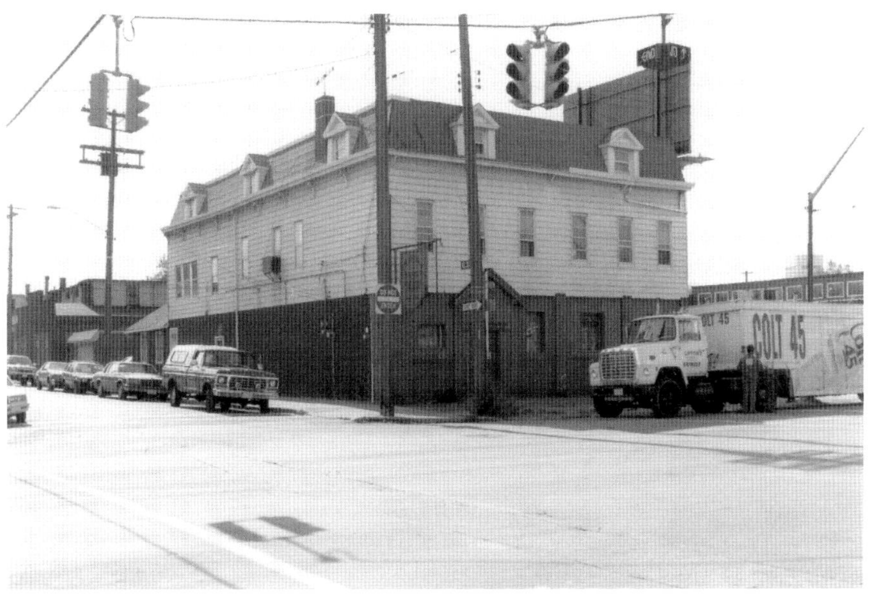

Crobar, 3244 Saint Clair Avenue, open since 1921. *Author's photo, August 2024.*

changed and many longtime customers moved to the suburbs. However, the late 1970s and early 1980s were a volatile time for ethnic and political tensions, particularly among Yugoslav expatriates in the United States.

In 1980, Lasic was the target of a murder-for-hire plot orchestrated in retaliation for his brother's past role as a Yugoslav policeman. His brother had reportedly been involved in suppressing anti-Yugoslav nationalist activities, making Joe a target for revenge. The Cleveland Police and the Bureau of Alcohol, Tobacco and Firearms received a tip from an informant known as "John the Albanian" about a $3,000 contract put out by a Croatian American terrorist group.

In a dramatic sting operation, an undercover agent posed as a Croatian nationalist hit man and staged Joe's murder, using ketchup as fake blood. Photographs were taken as proof, and the $3,000 payment was handed over to the agent. Gaines "Snake" Buttry eventually pled guilty, though his coconspirators were acquitted. Despite this harrowing experience, Joe Lasic continued serving shots and beer at the bar as the tavern endured another chapter in its history.

In 1992, Joe was persuaded by patrons to purchase the Olympic Triplecast so his Croatian customers could watch their national basketball team compete in the Olympics. The investment paid off: the bar was packed with fans watching thrilling games, including a comeback win over Spain and a narrow victory over the Russian Unified Team. Although Croatia lost to the United States Dream Team in the gold medal game, they proudly earned a silver medal. The team's star player, Toni Kukoč, went on to play in the NBA and was later inducted into the Basketball Hall of Fame.

For decades, the Croatian Tavern remained a cherished fixture in the neighborhood, evolving with the times while retaining its distinctive charm. After fifty-three years, Joe Lasic sold the tavern, and in 2021, it was rebranded as Crobar. Despite the changes, the tavern has preserved its authentic dive bar atmosphere while introducing modern touches, including live performances from top local and regional bands. More than a century after its opening, the bar still upholds its original spirit, continuing to serve as a beloved community landmark.

Leaving the Croatian Tavern, we continue our journey down Saint Clair Avenue to another iconic establishment just a few blocks away.

Jerman's Cafe: A Living Piece of Cleveland's History

Mitzi Jerman's Café—commonly known as both Mitzi's and Jerman's—located at 3840 Saint Clair Avenue, stands as a testament to Cleveland's rich ethnic history and enduring spirit. Often considered one of Cleveland's oldest bars, the tavern was established in 1908 by John Jerman and his wife, Frances. This neighborhood tavern has been a fixture in the community for over a century, weathering world wars, Prohibition and the ever-changing landscape of the city.

The tavern faced adversity early on. In 1910, it suffered its first robbery. One quiet afternoon, when Mrs. Jerman was alone at the bar, three men requested glasses of beer. As Mrs. Jerman stepped outside to retrieve the glasses from their buggy, parked in front of the tavern, one of the men pried open the cash register and stole their $220 bankroll.

The heart and soul of Jerman's Cafe for many decades was Mitzi Jerman, John's daughter. She was born above the tavern in 1914, and her life was inextricably linked to the establishment. Mitzi grew up in the apartment above the bar and learned the ins and outs of running a tavern during some of the United States' most tumultuous times. During Prohibition, the bar operated as a speakeasy, and young Mitzi was trained by her mother to keep an eye out for federal agents, easily identifiable by their white socks and black pants.

Mitzi eventually took over the family business and became synonymous with the tavern. An avid Cleveland Indians fan, she would hold court while the team played on the tavern's television, often educating patrons about the history of the neighborhood and recounting stories she had heard from factory workers who stopped in after their shifts.

Mitzi's dedication to the tavern was lifelong. Even after retiring, she continued to live above the bar; her children took over the day-to-day operations. Her presence remained a constant; she was often seen greeting visitors at the door, occasionally with freshly baked chocolate chip cookies, followed by her loyal dog, Roscoe. A March 17, 1995 *Plain Dealer* article noted, "Mitzi pours drinks with a chemist's concentration, setting out shot glasses and mixer glasses like test tubes." Mitzi lived to the remarkable age of ninety-two, having spent her entire life in the building that housed both her home and the family business.

Following Mitzi's passing, the tavern faced an uncertain future. It briefly closed after the deaths of Mitzi's daughter, Susan Myers, and her husband, George, who had been running the establishment. However,

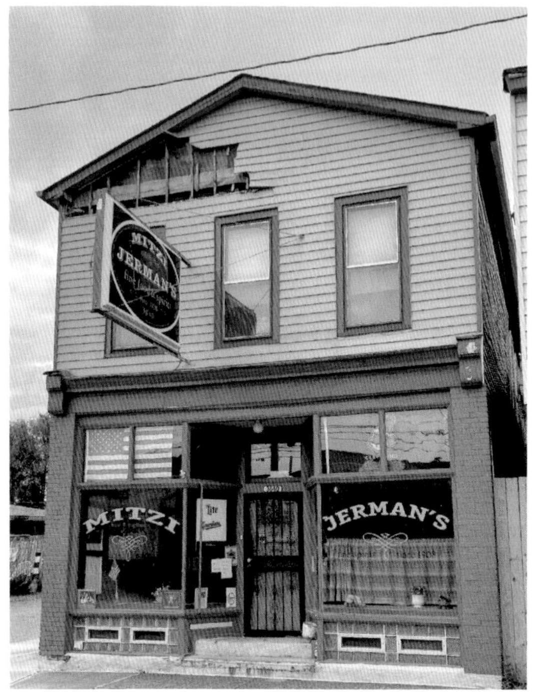

Left: Mitzi Jerman's Café, open over one hundred years. *Author's photo, August 2024.*

Below: Mitzi Jerman's Café, 3840 Saint Clair Avenue, 1951. *Cleveland Press Collection, Cleveland State University, Michael Schwartz Library Special Collections.*

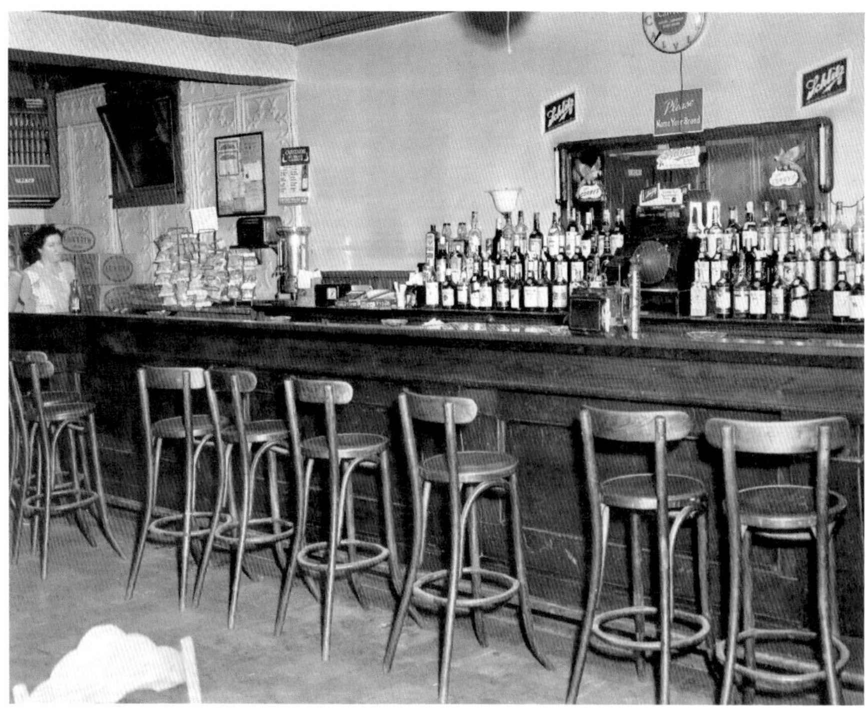

after a two-year pause, the legacy of Jerman's Cafe and its importance to the community have inspired efforts to reopen its doors, ensuring that this piece of Cleveland history continues to serve future generations.

Tavern Life in the Slovenian Neighborhood

The Slovenian neighborhood, spanning approximately forty blocks between East Fortieth Street and Ansel Road along Saint Clair and Superior Avenues, was the epicenter of tavern culture in mid-twentieth-century Cleveland. In this compact area, the 1964 city directory listed a staggering forty-one taverns on Saint Clair Avenue and eighteen on Superior Avenue. At the center of these forty blocks, at East Sixty-First off Saint Clair, stands Saint Vitus Roman Catholic Church, the spiritual and geographical heart of the community.

Just a block away from Saint Vitus was Modic's Bar, a quintessential example of the era's neighborhood taverns. Owned and operated by a husband-and-wife team, John and Carolina Modic, the bar first opened its doors in 1908. Tragically, John passed away during the 1918 pandemic. Undeterred, Carolina continued to run the bar with the help of her son, who eventually took over the business. She lived upstairs for the rest of her life, passing away in 1958. The bar remained under the management of her son until it was sold in 1967.

Many working-class bar owners faced increasing crime starting in the turbulent 1960s. At the intersection of East Seventy-Ninth and Saint Clair, three taverns—Cascade Lounge, Gordon Park Café and the Doo Drop Inn—were repeatedly robbed. Frank Nagode, who had owned the Gordon Park Café since 1953, was shot by robbers on two separate occasions. The first incident occurred in 1966 and the second in 1967, when he was involved in a gunfight and was shot five times. During the first shooting, the robber also fired at Frank's wife. In response to these events, Frank installed security doors and, like many tavern owners in the area, implemented an electronic buzzer to screen visitors before granting access.

Tragedy struck again on June 20, 1982, when Frank Nagode was awakened by a noise and confronted a twenty-year-old and a sixteen-year-old inside the bar, fatally shooting them. An editorial in the *Call and Post* on July 3, 1982, stated, "Everyone in the Gordon Park Café killings was a victim." Nagode sold the tavern one month later.

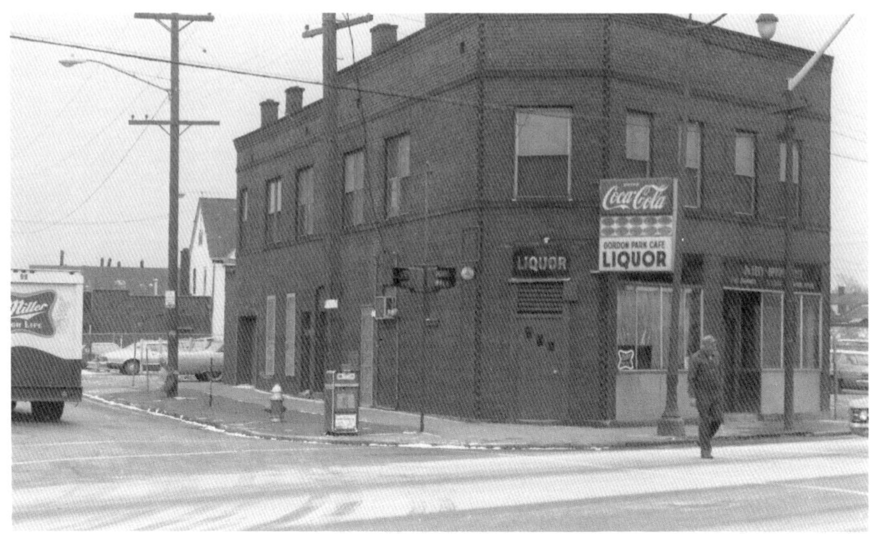

Gordon Park Café, 7901 Saint Clair, 1976. *Cleveland Public Library/Photograph Collection.*

As we continue our pub crawl, let's head east down Saint Clair Avenue to Collinwood. This expansive area encompasses North Collinwood, South Collinwood and Nottingham, stretching from the city of East Cleveland to the south all the way to the city of Euclid in the east. At the heart of this neighborhood lies its commercial hub, known as Five Points—a bustling intersection where East 152nd Street meets Saint Clair and Ivanhoe Avenues.

Welcome to Collinwood

Inspired by the film *Welcome to Collinwood*, starring George Clooney, which humorously portrays the misadventures of a group of small-time crooks in this Cleveland neighborhood, we dive into the real-life working-class essence of Collinwood. In the early twentieth century, this neighborhood was home to large Irish, Italian and Slovenian populations, attracted by the opportunities provided by the massive Collinwood rail yard and major employers such as the Fisher Body Plant, General Electric and Lincoln Electric. As these opportunities expanded in the 1950s and '60s, the area also drew Appalachians. Meanwhile, as eastern Europeans moved to the inner ring suburbs, African Americans began to settle in Collinwood, which, at that time, also experienced the volatile race issues characteristic of Cleveland's East Side during this period.

Five Points, the heart of Collinwood, boasted several notable taverns that became fixtures of the community. Stein's Café at 948 East 152nd, owned by Joseph Stein and A.J. Macher through the 1940s, demonstrated civic engagement by raising funds for the war effort, offering patrons World War II memorabilia in exchange for donations. These items were often sourced from the European front and served as tokens of appreciation for those contributing to the cause. By the 1970s, the establishment had transformed into the East 152nd Show Bar, which featured "go-go girls" and operated well into the 1980s. Nearby Turk's Tavern served the community until 1968, when it was advertised for sale as a "working man's bar" on the owner's retirement. Another longtime fixture was Hermit's Tavern, which opened shortly after Prohibition's end in the 1930s. Despite falling victim to a $5,000 robbery in 1937, it remained a neighborhood go-to tavern for decades. In 1963, Hermit's was put up for sale, touting a potential weekly income of $1,700 for prospective buyers.

East 185th Street was home to a cluster of notable taverns, each with its own rich history. The building at 779 East 185th, now housing an upscale restaurant called the Standard, has a storied past as a tavern. It began as Eddie's Café in the 1930s and then enjoyed a long run as Hank & Stan's Tavern, followed by stints as Orange Tree, Busters and then Quinn's through the 1990s before briefly becoming a barbershop. Just two blocks down stood the LaSalle Tavern; the Tech Tavern was one block further down at 882 East 185th.

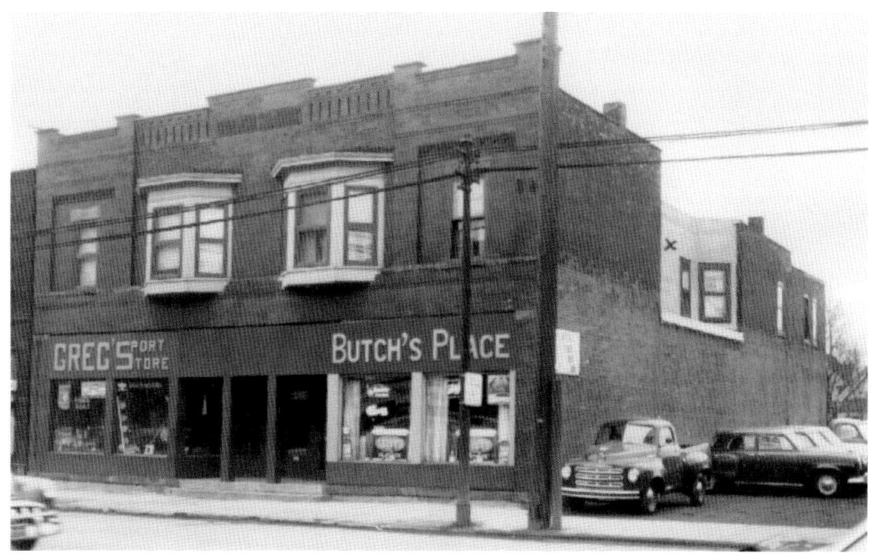

Butch's Place, 797 East 152nd, 1954. *Cleveland Public Library/Photograph Collection.*

The Tech Tavern, opened in 1940 by Joe and Rose Tekavcic, became a family affair, with the couple living in the apartment above the bar. After Joe's death in 1961, Rose continued operating the bar, but tragedy struck on August 28, 1964, when she was brutally beaten and robbed by three men while closing up. The robbers not only took the night's receipts but also broke into the safe in the living area. After Rose's passing in 1974, the establishment became Joseph's Tavern, but throughout the 1990s, it struggled with rising crime and deteriorating neighborhood conditions. These ongoing issues culminated in tragedy in 1997 when a young man celebrating his bachelor party was fatally stabbed outside the bar. Following numerous complaints about fights, zoning violations and after-hours liquor sales, the two brothers who owned Joseph's were pressured by the Ohio Liquor Commission to sell. In 1999, the property was transformed into Scotti's Italian Eatery, which remains a popular dining spot in the area to this day.

As we head south toward the Lakeland Freeway, let's stop at Fritz's Tavern at 991 East 185th Street. World War II veteran Fritz Hribar and his wife, Ruth, opened the tavern in 1951, and it remained a constant presence on East 185th for the next forty-seven years. In the early years, Fritz's Tavern faced scrutiny from law enforcement for allegedly serving minors. The situation became so severe that on September 12, 1957, the *Plain Dealer* quoted Fritz saying that if a patron looked young, he would need to see not only a driver's license but also a birth certificate. Fritz began carding even familiar customers in their thirties to avoid any risk of violations.

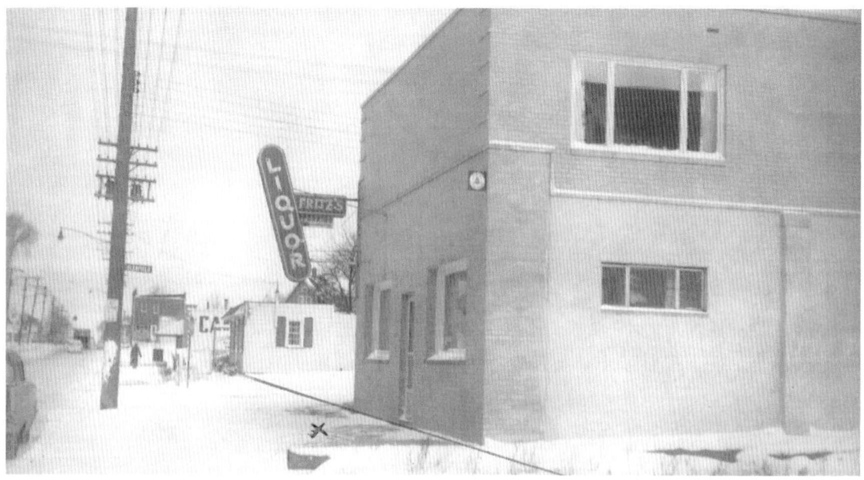

Fritz Liquor, 991 East 185th, 1959. *Cleveland Public Library/Photograph Collection.*

In 1961, Fritz was shot during a robbery as he returned to the bar from the bank with cash to cover his customers' paychecks. He quickly recovered, and the tavern continued to thrive as a popular spot for Friday fish fries and weekend polka bands. Over the years, Fritz generously sponsored many bowling and softball teams. The Hribar family lived above the bar until it was sold for $210,000 in 1998. The bar eventually became Bistro 185, which operated until 2018.

Our last stop is the Dugout Café, located across the street from Fritz's and adjacent to the freeway. Owned by Sam Nader, a World War II infantry veteran and member of the Greater Cleveland Slo-Pitch Hall of Fame, the tavern operated from the early 1940s to 1971. Sam took pride in teaching and developing young ballplayers and was a legend in the sandlots, serving as a longtime player, coach, and sponsor of some of Cleveland's best teams. In 1981, the property was purchased by Billy Dagg, who transformed it into Muldoon's, a popular sports bar that remains a favorite neighborhood spot located at the entrance ramp to I-90.

Exploring University Circle

As we continue our journey, let's make our way to University Circle. Despite its modest residential population, University Circle stands as an economic powerhouse, providing over thirty thousand jobs and drawing approximately 2.5 million visitors annually. This cultural and intellectual hub is home to prestigious institutions such as Case Western Reserve University, the iconic Severance Hall, world-class medical facilities, renowned museums and picturesque parks and gardens. Within this condensed neighborhood, there were several notable taverns that catered to a diverse clientele of working-class patrons and students. Our next destination brings us to one of the area's most celebrated establishments: the famous Euclid Tavern at 11629 Euclid Avenue.

The Euc, as it was affectionately known, opened its doors in 1909 and remained a fairly unassuming neighborhood tavern until the 1970s. Over the years, it attracted a diverse crowd of students and workers from the surrounding area. Its owners cultivated a welcoming atmosphere that drew local musicians playing various genres, including blues, jazz and alternative rock. The tavern's stage hosted several acts early in their careers, including notable performers like Chrissie Hynde and Green Day. A local favorite, Bill Miller—better known by his stage name, Mr. Stress—frequently played

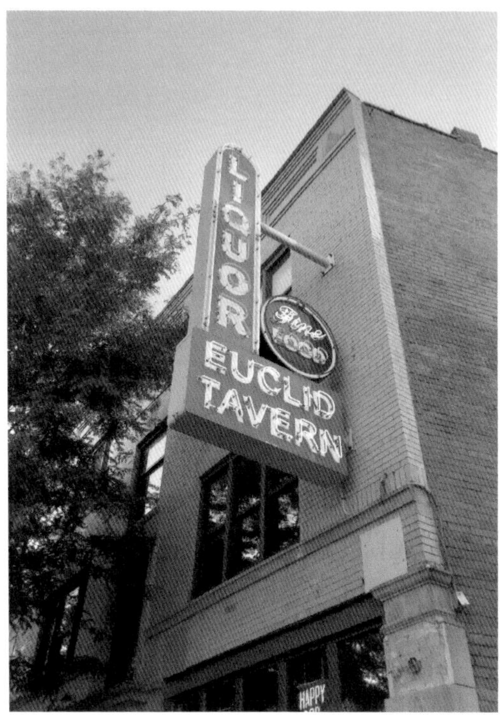

Left: Euclid Tavern, an iconic historical tavern at 11625 Euclid Avenue. The "Euc" gained national fame when it was featured in the 1987 movie *Light of Day*. *Courtesy of Wikipedia Commons, 2018.*

Below: Adele's Lounge, 11605 Euclid Avenue, home of the hipsters and a target of the authorities, 1965. *Cleveland Public Library/Photograph Collection.*

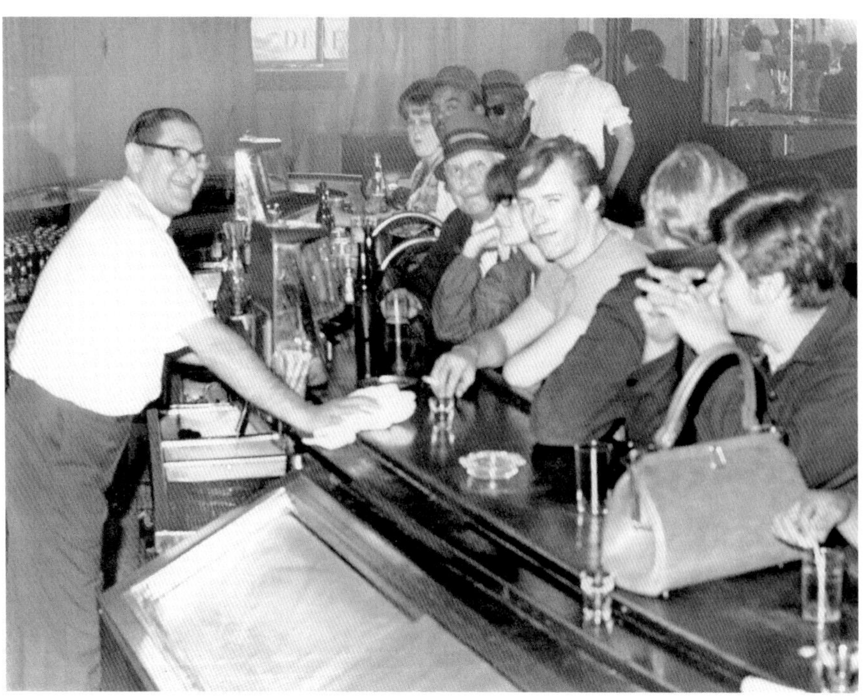

with his band, drawing large crowds to the Euc and other low-key bars in University Circle.

The bar gained national attention in 1987 when it was featured in the movie *Light of Day*, starring Michael J. Fox and Joan Jett. Director Paul Schrader had previously visited the bar and found its atmosphere perfect for his fictional band. Despite its brush with fame, the Euc remained true to its roots as a neighborhood tavern for decades, finally closing its doors in 2001.

Since then, there have been several attempts to revive the iconic establishment, including a four-year run as the Happy Dog from 2014 to 2018. Though the original Euclid Tavern is no more, its legacy lives on: today, the iconic "Euclid Tavern Fine Food and Liquor" sign illuminates Jason Aldean's bar in Nashville.

A few doors down from Euclid Tavern was Adele's Lounge at 11605 Euclid Avenue, a notable spot in Cleveland's 1960s countercultural scene. Adele's, which opened in 1954, quickly became known as a "hippie haunt" and a gathering place for a diverse group of patrons, including motorcycle gangs, poets like Allen Ginsberg, activists, revolutionaries, high school students and members of the LGBT+ community. The bar's physical appearance was typical of the area, with a long, narrow bar, wooden tables and chairs and dim lighting.

Adele's embrace of countercultural movements drew unwanted attention. The bar faced numerous allegations of drug use and underage drinking and was targeted continually by law enforcement throughout the 1960s. Despite these challenges, Adele's remained a beloved spot for its diverse community, even when the University Circle Police Department moved in right next door.

On September 12, 1967, the *Plain Dealer* reported that Cleveland's city council declared it was "going to war" with Adele's, since the bar catered to "many persons who show a total disregard for the safety, health, and welfare of the residents and travelers in the vicinity." This led to court battles and temporary closures during its final years. Ultimately, it wasn't the liquor commission or the local police that shut down Adele's. An arsonist set fire to the bar in February 1969, forcing it to close its doors. With that, we now leave the University Circle area, crossing Euclid Avenue and proceeding up Mayfield Hill to Little Italy.

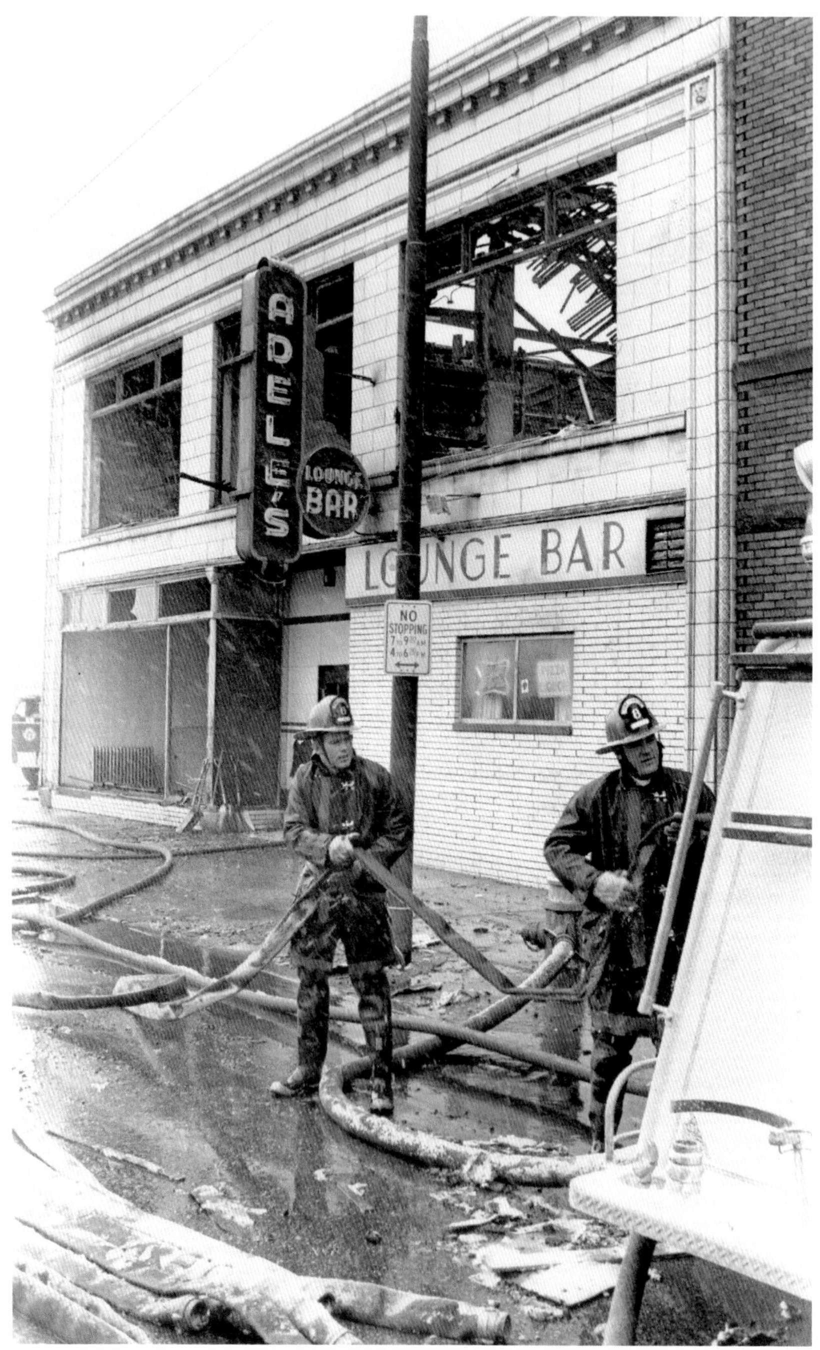

Fire at Adele's Lounge, home of the hipsters, 1969. *Cleveland Public Library/ Photograph Collection.*

Up the Hill to Little Italy

As previously mentioned in the chapter on Prohibition, Little Italy was the heart of the Mayfield Road Mob, one of the most notorious mafia organizations between New York and Chicago. While surrounding neighborhoods experienced a significant increase in their African American populations during the 1950s and '60s, Little Italy remained predominantly Italian. The tight-knit community maintained its cultural identity, traditions and businesses, creating a distinct enclave within the changing urban landscape. To this day, Little Italy has largely preserved its Italian character, continuing to host numerous Italian restaurants, bakeries and specialty shops that line Mayfield Road and Murray Hill.

No visit to Little Italy is complete without a stop at Guarino's on Mayfield Road. According to the restaurant's website, Guarino's opened in 1918 and is recognized as Cleveland's oldest restaurant. The establishment reportedly began as a poolroom and tavern. Vincent Guarino, an immigrant from Sicily, purchased the property from Vincent Campanella and, with his wife, Mary, transformed it into a beloved Cleveland institution that has endured for over a century.

The transition from tavern to restaurant began when Mary started cooking dinners for customers, and soon the food became the establishment's main draw. Like most tavern owners of the time, the Guarinos lived and raised their three children above the tavern and restaurant. Vincent's tenure at the helm of Guarino's was cut short when he passed away at the age of fifty-six while on a ship visiting Sicily in 1954. His son Sam took over the reins, continuing the family legacy until his own passing in 1987. At that point, close family friends stepped in to run the restaurant, maintaining many of the same dishes that had been served for nearly a century.

A block away at 12113 Mayfield, a typical storefront café evolved through the years into various taverns. Originally converted from a confectionery during Prohibition, it was the Mayfield Inn for decades. Tragedy struck on December 18, 1950, when a fire took the life of a porter who also lived above the bar. The tavern later became the Ramey Café, owned by Dominic "Ramey" Ramacciatti and his granddaughter Patricia DiBello. According to Ramey, his father, Michael, was the second immigrant to settle in Little Italy. Besides managing the tavern, Ramey served as the groundskeeper at Lakeview Cemetery for over sixty-five years, working until his late eighties and living to the age of ninety-three. Eventually, the bar transformed into Maxi's Bistro, which continues to thrive in the neighborhood.

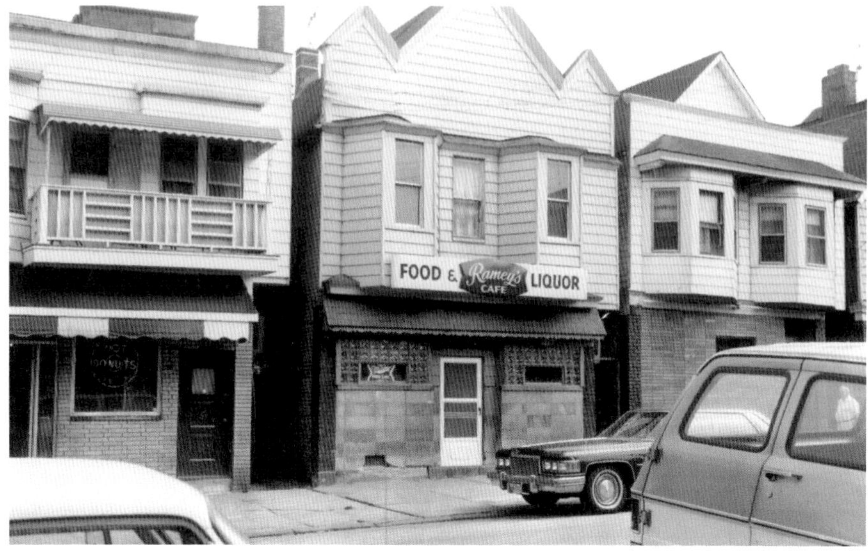

Ramey's Tavern, Little Italy, 1981. Today the tavern is Maxi's Bistro. *Cleveland Public Library/ Photograph Collection.*

In the early 1960s, the Murray Hill area faced significant challenges as crime and violence increased. On September 5, 1962, the *Plain Dealer* reported that conditions had deteriorated to such an extent that the Murray Hill Citizen's Committee demanded action from the local councilman. However, their pleas seemingly went unanswered.

Just two months later, on November 9, a gang of fifteen to twenty youths stormed the Library Tavern, at 2151 Murray Hill Road, demanded the women at the bar leave and proceeded to vandalize the establishment. Despite the severity of the incident, the tavern's proprietor chose not to prosecute the offenders. Unfortunately, the situation worsened, and two years later, a similar but more destructive event occurred. A gang of about twenty-five individuals armed with baseball bats entered the tavern, smashed windows, stole one hundred dollars from the cash register and assaulted the owner and several patrons.

In an effort to curb the violence, the tavern was eventually converted into a private club. However, trouble continued to plague the building. In 1973, the FBI and Cleveland police raided the club during a dice game, confiscating gambling equipment. Affidavits filed by the FBI stated that over $300,000 a week was gambled at the location; each roll of the dice involved bets between $50 and $1,000. A few years after the raid, the club was converted into an art gallery, a role it continues to play to this day.

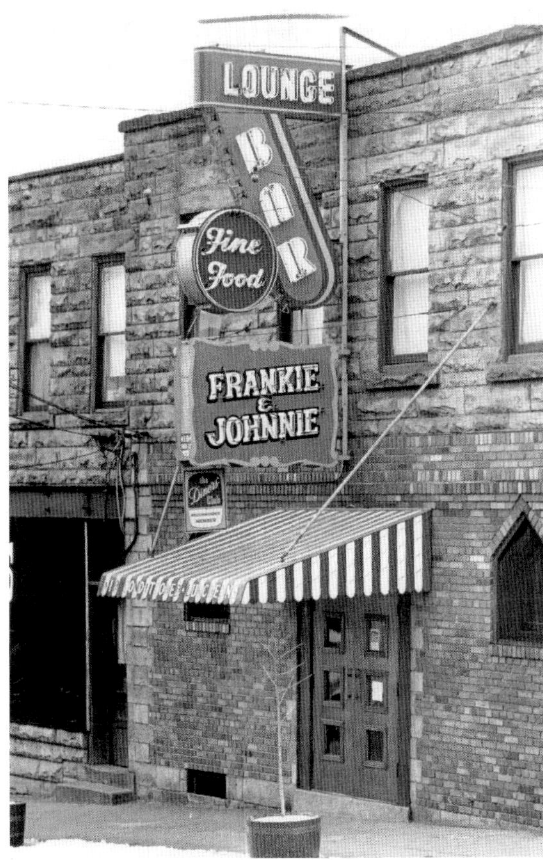

Left: Frankie and Johnnie Bar & Lounge, 12511 Mayfield Road, February 1964. In 1965, the establishment moved to Chardon and became La Camelia Restaurant. *Cleveland Press Collection, Cleveland State University, Michael Schwartz Library Special Collection, photographer Tom Tomsic.*

Below: Nick's Inn, Murray Hill, 1962. *Cleveland Press Collection, Cleveland State University, Michael Schwartz Library Special Collections.*

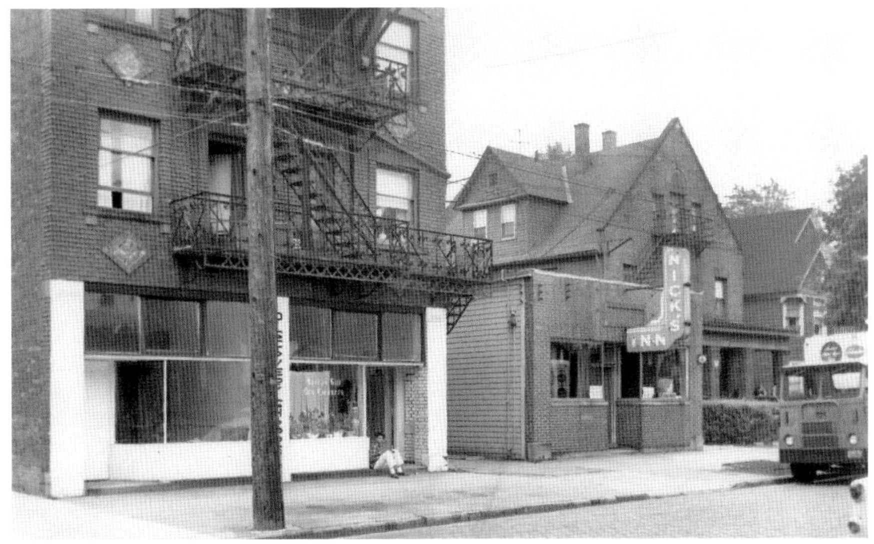

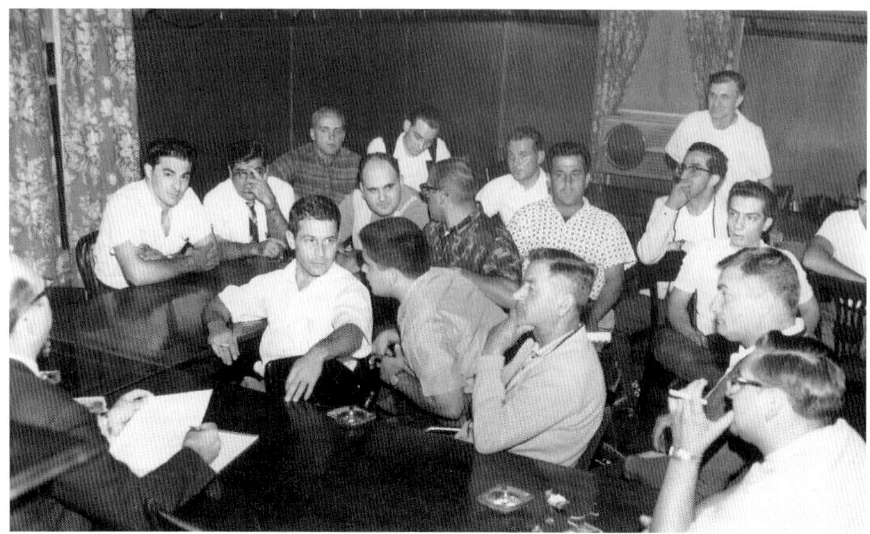

Nick's Inn, Murray Hill, 1962. Today, this stretch of Murray is dotted with art galleries. *Cleveland Press Collection, Cleveland State University, Michael Schwartz Library Special Collections.*

Nick's Inn and the Cellar also transitioned through the years into art galleries. Nick's first became the Zodiac Bar in 1970 and then evolved into the Algebra Teahouse. Meanwhile, the Cellar was put up for sale in 1969 and reopened in 1971 as Cynthia Gale's Earth Prayers, a ceremonial art gallery. Today, Murray Hill Road continues to be filled with art studios along the street. As we leave the vibrant, artistic community of Murray Hill, our journey takes us to the neighborhoods of Kinsman, Buckeye and Woodhill, which are collectively recognized as a Statistical Planning Area by the Cleveland City Planning Commission.

Southward Bound: Buckeye-Woodhill, Shaker Square, Kinsman

Heading south on Martin Luther King Jr. Drive, we arrive at the Buckeye-Woodhill and Shaker Square neighborhoods. The Buckeye area was once home to the largest population of Hungarians in the United States. Between 1870 and 1920, Hungarian immigrants were recruited by steel mill officials and manufacturing plant representatives. In Budapest, wages were a meager fifteen cents a day, while Cleveland's mills offered a staggering one dollar a day, a powerful incentive for a brighter future.

By 1900, nearly ten thousand Hungarians resided in Cleveland. By 1920, this number had surged to over forty-three thousand, and Hungarians comprised 20 percent of the city's foreign-born population and owned three hundred businesses. Hungarians worked in factories such as Van Dorn Iron Works, Cleveland Bronze and Standard Foundry. The area saw another surge in Hungarian immigration after World War II and then again in the late 1950s, for political reasons, as refugees fled the 1956 Hungarian Revolution.

Like many White ethnic neighborhoods, Buckeye experienced integration and racial tensions during the 1960s. The demographics of the neighborhood, once a thriving Hungarian enclave, began to shift. This change is poignantly captured in a February 18, 1971 *Plain Dealer* article by renowned Hungarian Clevelander Joe Eszterhas. Writing about Buckeye, he observed, "There are more German shepherds here now than Hungarians." This statement reflects not just the demographic changes but also the underlying tensions that arose as the neighborhood became more diverse.

These tensions, along with other social and economic factors, contributed to a decline in the Buckeye area's traditional businesses, including its taverns. According to a 1974 study by Cleveland Ethnic Heritage Studies at Cleveland State University titled "Selected Ethnic Communities of Cleveland: A Socio-Economic Study," the number of saloons in Buckeye remained relatively stable from 1925 to 1960, with around twenty taverns. However, after 1960, the number of taverns declined significantly: only eight remained by 1973.

Our journey begins at the Academy Tavern on Larchmere Boulevard, near the Cleveland-Shaker Heights border. Just a stone's throw from Shaker Square (the nation's second-oldest shopping center, established in 1929), the Academy Tavern has a rich history. It opened its doors in 1939 under its current name, quickly becoming a popular spot. Before that, in 1938, the location was home to the Wagon Wheel Café, which unfortunately faced a dramatic robbery when a gang targeted the bar, robbing fifteen patrons and several waitresses. Despite this rocky start, the transition to the Academy Tavern in 1939 marked a new chapter, leading to the thriving establishment we know today. Throughout the 1970s, it was common for reporters to find patrons glued to the televisions, eagerly discussing breaking political news. A 1981 Plain Dealer review captured the tavern's essence perfectly: "Far from fancy…appeals to people of all ages. The Academy Tavern's charm lies in its welcoming atmosphere, attracting a diverse clientele—Clevelanders and suburbanites alike, young and old, well-heeled and not so well-heeled.

Here, good conversation and hearty food remain the cornerstones of a truly enduring establishment."

Let's head south to 11100 Buckeye Road, the center of the Hungarian community. Here, the Frog Town Café thrived for decades. Owned by World War I veteran Joe Pavilonis and his wife, Mary, since 1929, the café remained a local landmark until 1965, twelve years after Joe's passing. In April 1949, the Frog Town Café made headlines when Mary refused service to two young patrons. The pair waited until closing and then robbed Mary and assaulted a customer who wouldn't comply with their demands.

In 1966, the establishment underwent a major transformation, becoming the Vanity Fair Lounge. The Vanity Fair boasted an impressive lineup of entertainers, including Tommy Edwards, the first African American to reach No. 1 on the Billboard Hot 100 with his hit "It's All in the Game." Other entertainers included the Ink Spots and the Four Coins. Sadly, the lounge was plagued by fire, suffering three incidents before arson finally destroyed it in March 1967.

Continuing our journey down Buckeye Road, we remain immersed in the Hungarian community, where entertainment was deeply woven into the fabric of neighborhood taverns and restaurants. Just beyond the short-lived Vanity Fair Lounge, Hungarian music, drink and dining came together to create a lively social scene. The Gypsy Cellar, a renowned establishment, opened its doors in 1955 at 11123 Buckeye Road. Owned by Joseph Rabb, a violinist celebrated for his performances before presidents at the White House, the Gypsy Cellar attracted a star-studded clientele. Zsa Zsa Gabor, Myrna Loy and Robert Goulet were just a few of the celebrities who were drawn to the lively atmosphere created by Rabb's music.

Rabb led a small orchestra featuring a piano and a cimbalom (a distinctive Hungarian instrument with strings stretched across a flat soundboard that produces a twangy sound). The Gypsy Cellar became a destination spot for celebrating special occasions. Sadly, its famed run ended on July 1, 1972; the mayor of Cleveland, Ralph Perk, even made an appearance to mark its closing.

If the Gypsy Cellar was booked, Settler's Tavern offered a similar experience. Initially established at 11701 Buckeye Road in the 1940s, it relocated to 12906 Buckeye Road in the late 1950s. Owned by Peggy and Jim Orosz, Settler's Tavern featured Hungarian music and many of the same talented entertainers. Unfortunately, the tavern permanently closed its doors in November 1982. Its contents were auctioned off, and the building was demolished to make way for a fast-food restaurant.

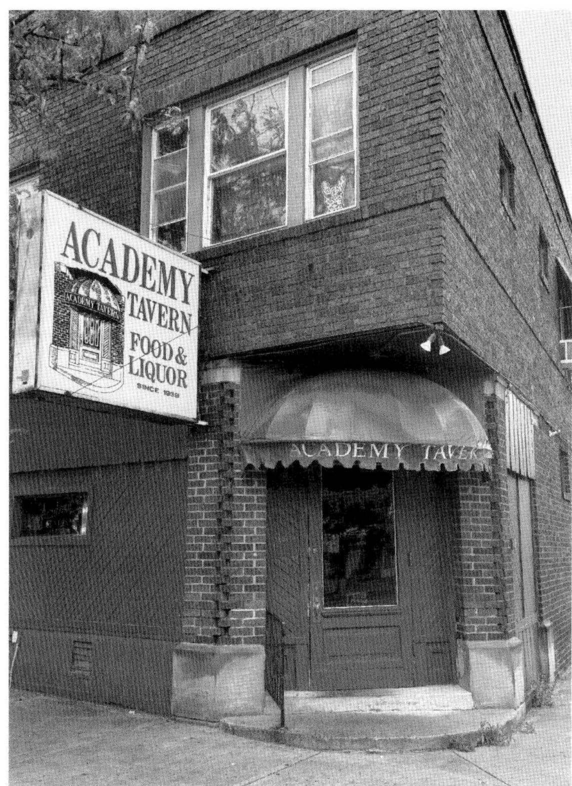

Left: The Academy Tavern, on Larchmere Boulevard since 1939, September 2024. *Author's photo.*

Below: The Gypsy Cellar, 11123 Buckeye Road, a destination spot for celebrations. *Cleveland Public Library/Photograph Collection.*

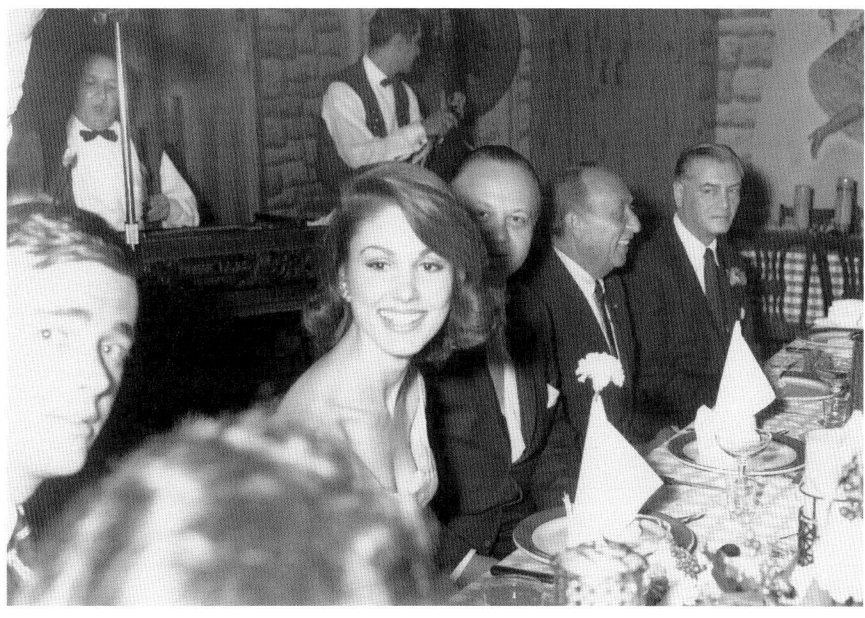

If you wanted to make a quick stop, Mike Boros Café at 12302 Buckeye was a popular choice. This storefront café was owned by Mike Boros, who operated taverns on Buckeye from 1935 to 1975. Boros, a Hungarian immigrant who came to Cleveland in 1916, was also a talented violinist and cimbalom player. After Mike passed away in 1980, his son took over the café. The bar continued to operate and advertised fine dining and entertainment in the *Plain Dealer* until 1990. Today, the location is home to a coffee shop owned by the Meeting Place Church.

Other notable bars near East 116th and Buckeye in the mid-1960s included Lal Cafe (later known as Joe's Place), Ruskin's, Laudis, Major's and Ganim's Cafe.

Now, let's move to lower Buckeye, near East Ninety-Third where several bars were located close to each other. This area bristled with taverns, many clustered within a few blocks of each other. One such establishment, at 9115 Buckeye, underwent a series of name changes throughout the years: Barakony Café in 1941, Plank's Café in 1964 and, finally, Cliff's Bar by 1969. Tragedy struck Cliff's Bar in April 1969 when owner Clifford Hatchett and off-duty patrolman Kenneth Houser were murdered during a robbery. A barmaid and a customer were also wounded. By 1971, the bar had been renamed the Red Ball Saloon, but incidents of violence continued at the location. That year, a customer cleaning his shotgun accidentally shot and killed a 103-year-old regular patron, James Polk. By 1973, the establishment had become Joe's Things Lounge, and advertisements in the *Plain Dealer* classifieds throughout the mid-70s reveal a constant search for barmaids and "go-go girls."

Within a couple blocks were Farkas Café, Mausers Café and Roma's, which later became Spark's Bar. Mausers was a long-standing neighborhood bar dating to the 1930s and remained open through most of the 1960s. Unfortunately, Mausers was plagued by robberies in the 1950s. In 1952, four armed men stole over $1,100 from the bar. In December 1956, a sixteen-year-old and two adults stole over $7,300 and assaulted the owner, Adolph Mauser, striking him on the head with a gun. The money was eventually recovered, and the juvenile was sent to prison, where he was stabbed to death in 1959. A year later, Mausers was robbed again, and a sixty-year-old woman was killed during the holdup.

Let's continue south down Woodhill Avenue, which becomes East Ninety-Third Street at Kinsman Road. In the 1920s, Kinsman was a thriving, affordable neighborhood that attracted a wave of Jewish immigrants. Fueled by plentiful jobs and easy access to public transportation, the area evolved

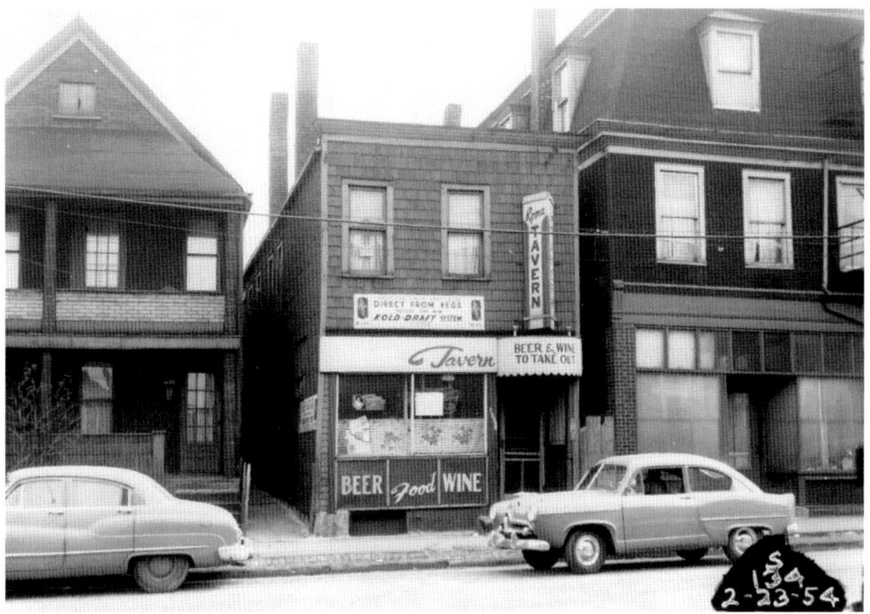

Roma Tavern, 2655 East Eighty-Ninth Street, in 1954. *Cleveland Public Library/Photograph Collection.*

into a diverse community with a mix of Jewish, Italian and eastern European residents. However, after World War II, Kinsman experienced a period of significant change. The neighborhood's demographics shifted dramatically as African Americans migrated north during the Second Great Migration. Simultaneously, urban renewal projects in downtown Cleveland displaced many African American families, who settled in Kinsman.

Our first stop is at Penkala's Tavern at 3284 East Ninety-Third, which later became Ed's Bar in the 1960s and Kipp's in the 1970s. The establishment was opened in 1927 by Hungarian immigrant John Penkala, who rented the storefront and upstairs apartment for ninety-five dollars a month. John operated the bar for thirty-two years until his death in 1959. In August 1975, this quiet neighborhood watering hole experienced a brazen robbery attempt that was thwarted by the owners, James and Dorothy Zebbs. The would-be robber brandished a .38 caliber revolver, and James engaged in a struggle with the intruder, who fired a shot, narrowly missing the couple. Meanwhile, Dorothy retrieved a shotgun from the back room and, as the assailant fled, managed to wound him. Her memorable quote to the *Plain Dealer*, "I hope word gets around that this isn't the place to rob," captured the tough, no-nonsense attitude of many Cleveland bar owners of the era.

Just a block away from the Zebbs's establishment stood Barto's Café at 3344 East Ninety-Third Street, directly across from the Hell's Angels Clubhouse at 3355 East Ninety-Third. On February 28, 1968, a tragic incident unfolded that shook the neighborhood. A group of ten to twelve bikers at the bar instigated a fight with several patrons, two of whom were killed: James Tillett, a thirty-eight-year-old White truck driver, who was beaten to death, and Roosevelt Brown, also thirty-eight, a Black factory worker, who was shot and killed. Renowned *Cleveland Plain Dealer* reporter Joe Eszterhas investigated the incident, interviewing members of a rival gang known as God's Children. They suggested that the all-White Hell's Angels were actually looking for their integrated gang and attacked when they saw a Black man in Barto's. The aftermath saw nine Angels initially indicted for first degree murder; however, many of the charges were later reduced, and eight Angels ultimately served prison time.

The taverns along East Ninety-Third Street, from Barto's Café to the Bluestone, Square Bar, Lucek's, Jack's Bar and Tom & Vi's, represented just a fraction of the thirteen establishments that dotted the stretch from

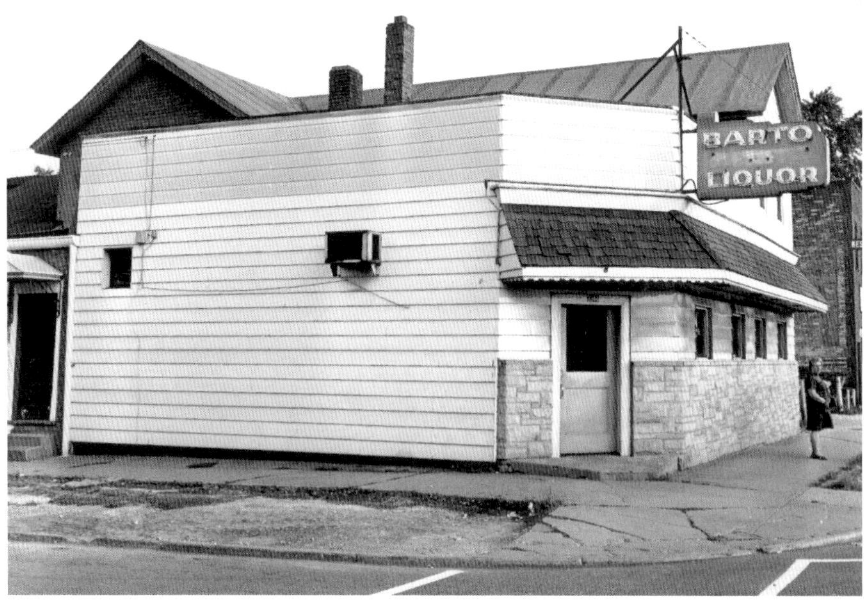

Barto's Café on East Ninety-Third, location of double murder involving the Hells Angels on February 28, 1968. *Cleveland State University, Michael Schwartz Library Special Collections, Cleveland Press Collection, photographer Herman Seid.*

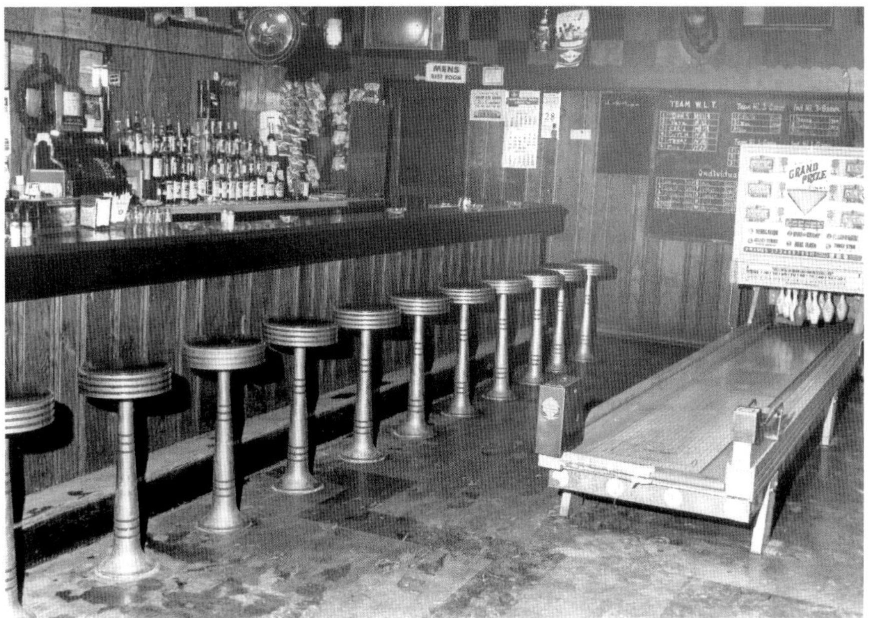

Barto's Café, scene of a double murder by the Hell's Angels in February 1968. *Cleveland Press Collection, Cleveland State University, Michael Schwartz Library Special Collections, photographer Clayton Knipper.*

Kinsman to Harvard in the 1960s. Each bar had its own character and clientele, reflecting the working-class roots of the neighborhood. However, as White residents migrated out of the area and racial tensions grew, these establishments often became flashpoints for the conflicts simmering beneath the surface of Cleveland's changing urban landscape.

Beyond the Core: Transformation in Mount Pleasant and Union Miles

As we venture eastward from the bustling taverns of East Ninety-Third Street, we enter the neighborhoods of Mount Pleasant and Union Miles. Developed primarily in the 1920s and '30s, Mount Pleasant and Union Miles initially attracted upwardly mobile families seeking spacious homes and tree-lined streets away from the city's industrial core. However, as with many Cleveland neighborhoods, the post–World War II era brought significant demographic shifts and economic challenges that would reshape the character of these communities.

Traveling south on East 116th Street, we pass through Mount Pleasant and into the Union Miles area. At 3880 East 116th Street stood the Pinwheel Cocktail Lounge, a beloved East Side destination for music and dining from the 1940s to the early 1970s. This two-room tavern, with one room dedicated to the bar and the other to entertainment, hosted top performers including Ruby Carter and Detroit recording star Emanuel Laskey. In March 1973, tragedy struck when a twenty-one-year-old army veteran, attempting to interrupt a robbery in progress, was shot and killed. The following month, the bar faced legal troubles when Warner Bros. unexpectedly sued for copyright infringement, alleging that unauthorized songs had been performed at the establishment. While the specific songs weren't identified, the lawsuit raised questions about why Warner Bros. had singled out this particular venue. In subsequent years, the venue underwent several transformations, becoming A Place to Play and later, in the 1980s, the My Spot Lounge and the Elegance Lounge. Today, the small storefront has been repurposed as the Union Hill Mission Church.

As we continue our journey, let's travel about a mile away from the Pinwheel along Miles Avenue. On our way, we'll pass 11607 Miles, home to Tyler's Bar from the 1940s until the 1960s, when it became Miles Bar. While we won't linger at Tyler's, it's worth noting a peculiar incident reported by the *Plain Dealer* on July 7, 1941, when a "quart full of stench fluid" was thrown at the bar.

Continuing, we arrive at 12711 Miles Avenue. In the 1960s, the establishment housed a VFW hall, which served as a gathering place for veterans and community events, including elections (it functioned as a polling place). However, the early 1970s saw a dramatic shift when it reopened as the B&W Lounge. The establishment quickly gained notoriety. The *Plain Dealer* reported in late 1971 that the owner and barmaid had been accused of selling heroin and cocaine, highlighting the drug issues plaguing the East Side of Cleveland at the time. The bar's troubles continued into February 1972, when it suffered extensive damage from an explosion caused by four or five sticks of dynamite detonated after closing time, at three o'clock in the morning. In an apparent attempt at reinvention, the venue rebranded as the Golden Cocktail Lounge in 1973, pledging to bring in top-tier entertainment. True to its word, the bar hosted renowned acts such as the Ohio Players, Ed Kendricks and Albert King, joining the excellent live music scene in the area. However, by the late 1970s—mirroring the fate of the Pinwheel Lounge—the building found new purpose as the Sacrificial Missionary Baptist Church, marking yet another transition from nightlife to spiritual life in the area.

As we cross over to East 131st Street, we reach the eastern edge of the Mount Pleasant and Union Miles neighborhood. This thoroughfare was a popular locale for taverns, boasting five establishments within less than a mile of the intersection with Miles Avenue. However, the volatile 1960s and '70s brought trouble to most of these venues. A tragic incident occurred in June 1973 at the J&S Café at 3695 East 131st: off-duty policeman Grover Collins Jr. was slain while attempting to break up a disturbance. The tavern later rebranded as Riley's Bar and Grille, also operating as a beverage store. Trouble continued to plague the location; a would-be robber was killed by a clerk in 1980.

Just a few doors down, at 3744 East 131st, stood the Gay Corner Café, a neighborhood staple since the 1950s. This establishment was also not immune to violence. In June 1970, owner Antonin Simek found himself at the center of a tragic incident. After Simek denied entry to a fifteen-year-old, he claimed, the youth threatened him and threw a bottle through the tavern's window. In response, Simek fired three shots, killing the ninth-grader. He was subsequently charged with murder and ultimately found guilty of manslaughter.

Before we leave the neighborhood, let's conclude our journey on a brighter note with a visit to the African Wine Cellar at 13824 Harvard

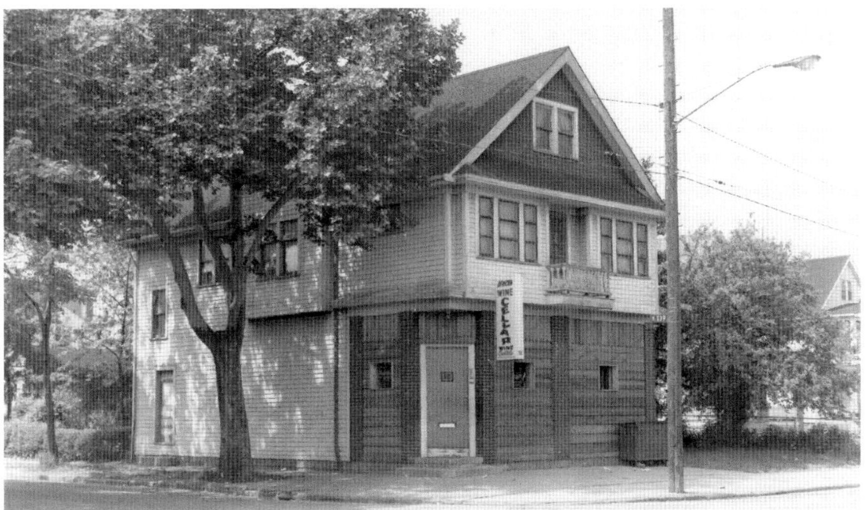

The Wine Cellar at 13824 Harvard in 1978, today an upscale beauty salon. *Cleveland Public Library/Photograph Collection.*

Avenue. This location has a rich history dating to the 1930s, when it was the home and business of Stanley Powierksi, who ran a remodeling and paint business while also selling wine. In 1937, Powierksi faced a minor legal hiccup when he was cited for selling whiskey with only a wine license.

Following Powierksi's passing, the property—which comprised a store and a six-room suite—changed hands. It eventually transformed into the African Wine Cellar, adopting the catchy motto "Do your thing where it's done the best." Unlike some of its more turbulent counterparts in the area, this establishment led a quiet neighborhood existence until its closure in the mid-1970s. The building's story didn't end there, however. In the years since, it has housed a spiritual reader and a day care; it's now an upscale beauty and hairstyling studio.

Let's continue our journey eastward along Harvard Avenue. Our path leads us to Lee Road, the bustling center of our next destinations: the Lee-Harvard and Lee-Seville neighborhoods. These areas developed later than Mount Pleasant and tell their own unique story of Cleveland's expansion and evolution.

Lee-Harvard and Lee-Seville: Pioneers of African American Suburbia

As we cross Lee Road, we enter the heart of the Lee-Harvard and Lee-Seville neighborhoods. The area emerged from the small enclave of Miles Heights Village in the 1920s and became a pioneering community for Black residents seeking suburban-style living. Following World War II, a wave of modest brick homes drew in Black middle-class families who had previously been excluded from suburban opportunities. By the 1970s, the area boasted vibrant diversity, with residents ranging from factory workers to municipal judges. While Lee-Harvard and Lee-Seville have faced challenges, such as population decline and school closures, they've retained their core character as stable, middle-class neighborhoods. Remarkably, many original residents still call Lee-Seville home after five decades, a testament to the enduring strength of this community.

As we explore the vibrant history of Lee-Harvard and Lee-Seville, let's focus on a building that encapsulates the area's evolution and its role as a social and cultural hub. Our first stop is 17324 Harvard Avenue, a large structure that has worn many hats over the decades. This building stands as a microcosm of the area's rich history and cultural dynamism. Since the

1950s, it has hosted a variety of establishments, each reflecting the changing tastes and needs of the community. The late 1960s ushered in a new era with the popular Heat Wave Supper Club. Its grand opening in 1968 featured none other than Patti LaBelle and the Bluebelles, signaling the venue's commitment to showcasing top-tier talent. This trend continued when prominent Cleveland restaurateur U.S. Dearing took over in September 1969, opening a party center so noteworthy that Mayor Carl Stokes attended its grand opening.

As the 1970s progressed, the space evolved into the Juva De' Club, becoming a popular gathering spot for young Black professionals. This incarnation of the venue mirrored the neighborhood's growth as a hub for Cleveland's African American middle class. Over the next two decades, the club adapted to changing musical tastes, transitioning from jazz to disco and eventually to rap by 1990.

Continuing our journey through the Lee-Harvard neighborhood, we come to 4170 Lee Road, an address that has a fascinating history, having transitioned from a place of mourning to one of celebration and community gathering. In the 1930s, 4170 Lee Road was home to Stastny's Funeral Home, serving the neighborhood's final farewells. However, as times changed, so did the building's purpose. In a striking transformation, the property was marketed for lease as a beer parlor, shifting from a place of mourning to one of lively social gatherings.

From there, it became the Kirby Tavern, which operated until 1966, when Bobbi and June Harris opened the Sir-Rah House. The name, cleverly derived from *Harris* spelled backward, reflected the owners' personal touch. They invested over $150,000 to transform the neighborhood bar into an upscale dining and entertainment venue, attracting patrons from across the area. The popular Bud LaBianco's LaQuintette served as the house band, and the establishment sponsored jazz sessions every Saturday. After a brief closure for remodeling, the venue reopened as the New Sir-Rah House, quickly reclaiming its loyal patrons. Over the following decades, the location continued to evolve. In 1997, it became the Blue Note Lounge before reverting to the Sir-Rah Lounge House in the mid-2000s. The 2010s brought further changes: The Rated M Lounge relocated from Public Square to this historic spot in 2013, followed by Carter's Pub and Lounge and the Sway Lounge.

Before we conclude our journey through this vibrant neighborhood, let's take a moment to acknowledge some of the other notable taverns that once called Lee Road home. Across from the Sir-Rah stood Jud's Tavern at 4145

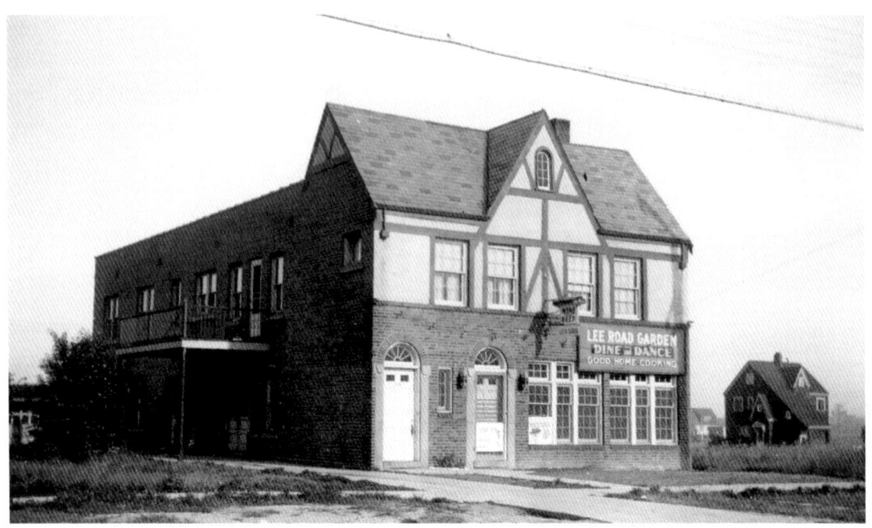

View of 4170 Lee Road: from funeral home to the Sir-Rah Lounge and Carter's Pub and Grill. *Cleveland Public Library/Photograph Collection.*

Lee, a fixture of the 1960s. In an interesting twist, this location temporarily housed an office of the Ohio Bureau of Employment Services in the 1970s before returning to its roots as Pat's Lounge in the late 1980s.

Further down, at 4254 Lee Road, stood the Caprice Lounge, popular during the 1970s and early 1980s. Known for its lively atmosphere, the Caprice was also the site of a tragic incident in November 1979, when a patron, upset that his girlfriend was asked to dance, fatally shot a man on the dance floor. The building's story didn't end there; it later became Wedding Pals, a shop offering wedding photography and services. By 2014, it had been acquired by Zion Chapel Missionary Baptist Church, along with several other properties, including 4268 Lee Road, which had housed the Lee Road Tavern in the 1960s.

It's time to head west on Harvard and transition from the mid-century suburban dreams of Lee-Harvard to the older, more densely populated urban neighborhood of Slavic Village. Founded in the mid-nineteenth century, this Polish neighborhood has weathered significant changes over the years. Once bustling with the activities of eastern European immigrants, it now tells its own stories of transformation, resilience and revival.

Chapter 7

Flanking the Furnaces

Tavern Culture in Slavic Village and Tremont

While we previously explored the North Broadway area during the post-Prohibition tavern scene, our focus now shifts to the heart of Slavic Village, particularly the historic Warszawa district. This area, named for its predominantly Polish immigrant population, who settled here in 1870, became a microcosm of eastern European culture in Cleveland. Centered on Fleet Avenue and Broadway, Slavic Village actually encompassed two distinct ethnic enclaves: the Czech-dominated Karlin and the Polish Warszawa. The area's proximity to Cleveland's Industrial Valley made it an ideal home for factory workers, and the neighborhood flourished into the 1950s. The neighborhood faced decline during the 1960s with the flight of second-generation residents to the suburbs.

The intersection of Broadway and East Fifty-Fifth Street formed the bustling heart of a major business district, while Fleet Avenue and East Seventy-First were lined with a diverse array of mom-and-pop establishments. Butcher shops, bakeries and various small businesses thrived, catering to the daily needs of the neighborhood's residents. Perhaps most notably, Slavic Village was home to an impressive number of taverns—so many, in fact, that their stories could fill an entire volume on their own. Let's transport ourselves back to the streets of Warszawa and Karlin in the 1960s, when local taverns were as integral to the neighborhood's fabric as churches and factories.

Fleet Avenue Taverns: The Hub of Slavic Village

Our journey begins on Fleet Avenue, once home to a remarkable concentration of taverns. In the 1960s, an impressive ten bars lined the half-mile stretch from East Forty-Ninth Street to just past East Sixty-Fifth. Many of these establishments trace their origins back to the 1910s, when liquor licenses were first issued to most of these addresses, reflecting the neighborhood's deeply rooted drinking culture.

At Fleet's western edge, where it now meets the I-77 off-ramp, stood a notable establishment at 4902 Fleet. This building, owned for decades by the Jira Brothers, had a rich history dating to the early 1900s. It exemplified the multifaceted nature of early twentieth-century businesses, housing not only a tavern but also a realty company and men's furnishings store. In the 1940s, it transformed into the Parkview Inn before becoming Krejci's Tavern in the 1950s. Krejci's was a neighborhood fixture, serving patrons for several decades until 1974, when the bar fixtures and equipment were finally auctioned off, marking the end of an era.

Building on our tour along Fleet Avenue, we encounter another long-standing establishment a few doors away at 5007 Fleet. Originally owned by the Jira family, this location began its life as a grocery store before transforming into Jelinek's tavern. The bar's deep roots in the community are evidenced by its remarkable fifty-year commitment to sponsoring local softball and bowling teams, a tradition documented in the *Plain Dealer* from the 1920s through 1971. Jelinek's evolution mirrored the changing face of the neighborhood. In the 1970s, it became known as Sophie's; it was the Erie House through the 1980s and 1990s; then it was converted into a restaurant, Dopo Domani. This establishment eventually closed its doors; however, the building itself stands to this day.

Continuing eastward along Fleet Avenue, we encounter a series of establishments that reflect the character of the neighborhood. At 5109 Fleet, we note the building's evolution from Chet's Bar in the 1950s to the Beacon Bar, which served patrons from the 1960s until 1983. Just one block over was the Park Café at 5212 Fleet. Initially, this location was the Washington Park moving picture theater, which sold for the considerable sum of $3,250 in 1914. It remained a popular theater until the Great Depression, after which it was converted into a beer parlor. The venue operated as the Park Café for decades and eventually became the Roll Call Lounge, which closed in 2024.

Our next stop is 5406 Fleet, home to the JB Tavern in the 1960s and '70s. It began as a Republican Club in 1910 before becoming Kindel's

Bowling Alley. By the 1930s, it had transformed into Budny's Hall, and in the 1940s, it evolved into the Modern Corner Tavern. By the 1960s, it had become J.B. Hall and Tavern, a name it carried into the 1970s. The 1980s brought yet another change with JR's Tavern, which became renowned for its lively polka music.

The story took a dramatic turn in the late 1980s, when the establishment, then known as My Baby Jams Night Club, tragically burned down in April 1989 and was demolished the same day. For years, the lot stood empty, serving as a stark reminder of the neighborhood's challenges. However, even this vacant space found new life when "guerrilla gardener" Sam Tylicki began planting vegetables on the city-owned property. Ultimately this fertile soil caught the attention of the Cleveland Botanical Garden Green Corps. Today, the site continues to serve the community as the Green Corps Slavic Village Learning Farm.

Let's cross over East Fifty-Fifth to the Fleet Café. This old-school tavern obtained its first liquor license way back in 1913. The bar survived Prohibition, and in 1943, federal tax agents seized twenty-five cases of whiskey—likely due to violations from unstamped liquor or licensing issues. Despite this setback, the tavern experienced a turn of good fortune. In

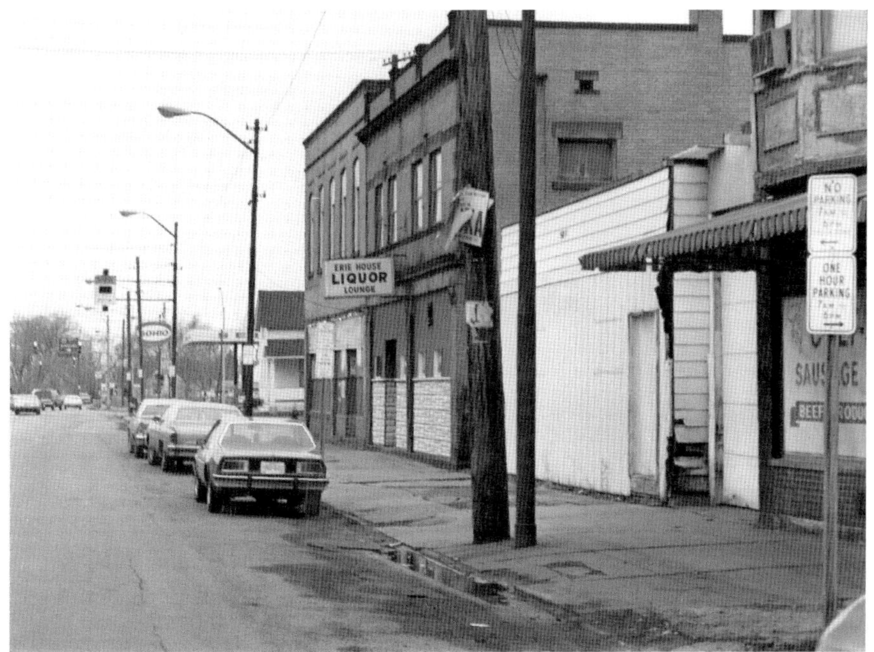

Facing east at East Fiftieth and Fleet in 1982. *Cleveland Public Library/Photograph Collection.*

1958, an upstairs resident, Carolyn Tenerowiez, who was the queen of the Polish Legion of Veterans, had the honor of leading the parade for the 167th anniversary of the Polish constitution. Even luckier was Vincent Skladany, who purchased a lottery ticket at the bar while celebrating a night out with his wife on October 28, 1976, and won $100,000. Today, the site is a vacant lot, but its legacy lives on in the memories of the community.

As we approach the intersection of East Sixty-Fifth Street and Fleet Avenue, we encounter a cluster of four notable taverns: Backiel's, Casey's, Jack & Al's and John & Eddie's. Let's focus our attention on Backiel's, located at 6006 Fleet Avenue, for our next stop.

The story of Backiel's begins in 1917, when Adolph Backiel purchased the property. By 1940, his son Chester, then twenty-four years old, had taken over the tavern's operations. Chester wasn't just known for running the family business; the *Plain Dealer* also recognized him as one of Cleveland's finest bowlers. For over six decades, the Backiel family maintained ownership and operation of the tavern, creating a lasting legacy in the neighborhood. In 1978, the Klafczynski family stepped in, purchasing what was then known as a classic "shot and beer" tavern. They rebranded it as the Fleetwood Inn, which was truly a family affair: three generations of Klafczynskis lived and worked at the tavern. Under the Klafczynski family's ownership, the Fleetwood Inn became an integral part of the community, sponsoring softball teams in the Southeast League.

Slavic Village Taverns, 1964 and 1975

Fleet Avenue	**1964**	**1975**
4902	Krejci's Tavern	
5007	Jelinek Cafe	Jelinek Cafe
5109	Beacon Bar	
5212	Park Cafe	
5302	Karlin Club	Karlin Club
5406	JB Tavern	JB Tavern
5505	Fleet Cafe	
5606	Palace's Cafe	Palace's Cafe
6006	Backiel's Cafe	Backiel's Cafe

Fleet Avenue	**1964**	**1975**
6009	Polish Legion	Polish Legion
6305	Casey's Tavern	
6312	Jack & Al's	Musarra Cafe
6519	John & Eddie's	John & Eddie's

East 65th	**1964**	**1975**
3614	Karb's	Karb's
3656	Martha's Tavern	
3664	Lemon's Cafe	
3824	Double X Bar	Double X Bar
3876	Red Rose Bar	Red Rose Bar

Lansing	**1964**	**1975**
6416	Lansing Tavern	Lansing Tavern
6501	Union of Poles	Union of Poles

Aetna	**1964**	**1975**
7032	Grodek's Tavern	Grodek's Tavern
7303	Aetna Cafe	
7417		Jolly Tee
7700	F&R Cafe	
7803	Kozy Korner Cafe	White Mountain Club
8001	El Conga Club	El Conga Club
8101	Mary's Bar	Southern Inn
9102	Lake Erie Tavern	Lake Erie Tavern

Union	**1964**	**1975**
7018	Ohio Cocktail Bar	Ohio Cocktail Bar
7214	B&G Tavern	B&G Tavern
7731	Zabak's Bar	Zabak's Bar
8813	Sip's Cafe	

Harvard	1964	1975
5211	Brown's Tavern	Brown's Tavern
5504	Ozzie's Tavern	Ozzie's Tavern
5612	A&A Tavern	
5721	Harvard Grove Tavern	Knights of Columbus
6602	Sixty-Six Tavern	Sixty-Six Tavern
7528	Holiday Lounge	Holiday Lounge
7613	New Swan Cafe	New Swan Cafe

East 71st	1964	1975
3795	Polish Village	Polish Village
3856	Bottoms Up Cafe	Bottoms Up Cafe
3876	Orzech's Tavern	Orzech's Tavern
3909	Rudy's Bar	Rudy's Bar
3919	Lenny's Tavern	
3924	Huters Tavern	Huters Tavern
3942	Perk's Bar	Tigers Tavern
3998	Eleanor's Tavern	
4050	K&S Tavern	
4061	F&I Bar	Jed's Tavern
4069	Sunrise Cafe	Sunrise Cafe
4070	Marceline Tavern	Marceline Tavern
4097	Night Hawk Cafe	Night Hawk Cafe
4106	Pinewood Cafe	Pinewood Cafe
4131	Polonaise Lounge	Golden Mule
4136	Victory Tavern	Victory Tavern
4166	Kay's Cafe	Lamp Lite Inn
4233	Ray's Cafe	Joe's Inn
4341	Casey's Tavern	
4368	Paul's Tavern	

Broadway	**1967**	**1975**
4030	Steel Inn	Steel Inn
4108	Lottie's Cafe	Lottie's Cafe
4641	Finn Cafe	Finn Cafe
4927	Chief's Tavern	Chief's Tavern
4939	Bohemian Hall	Bohemian Hall
5210	Jolly Time's Cafe	
5400	Mayflower Lounge	Mayflower Lounge
5450	Lennie's Bar	Zevie's Bar
5470	Hub Cafe	Hub Cafe
5623		BC's Tavern
5824	Sheraton Lounge	
6120	Toot's Bar	
6224	Tramend Lounge	Tramend Lounge
6446	Jaybee's Bar	
7018	Grand Tavern	
7146	Polish Falcon Hall	Polish Falcon Hall
7314	Jolly Tee Tavern	Jolly Tee Tavern
7663	George's Cafe	EMS Cafe
7771	Butch's Tavern	Butch's Tavern
8128	Babe's Bar	Babe's Bar
8417	Newburgh Inn	

Source: City of Cleveland Directories 1964 and 1975.

East Seventy-First Street: The Tavern Corridor

Leaving Fleet Avenue behind, we now head to East Seventy-First, where an astounding eighteen taverns once lined a one-mile stretch starting at Fleet and heading south to the border with Cuyahoga Heights. This vibrant corridor was a bustling hub of social activity, offering a wide array of establishments for locals to gather, relax and enjoy the community spirit. Let's explore some of the notable taverns that made East Seventy-First a cornerstone of neighborhood life.

Let's pass the Polish Village and make a quick stop at Orzech's Tavern at 3876 East Seventy-First. Stan Orzech began operating the bar on his return from World War II. Stan was a notable local athlete and a prominent basketball and football referee for decades. He leased the tavern in 1983 and passed away at an award banquet the following year. As we continue, we'll pass Rudy's Tavern and Perk's Bar, which later became Tom's Bar and, eventually, Tiger's Tavern in 1970. We'll also pass Eleanor's Tavern. We now enter the epicenter of taverns, with twelve bars in the next half mile.

As we continue our journey along East Seventy-First Street, crossing Harvard Avenue, we pass by the K&S Tavern and F&I Bar, which later became known as the Happy Hangover. Our next stop brings us to 4069 East Seventy-First Street, home of the Sunrise Café. The owner, Steve Lesiak, originally opened the tavern on Lansing Avenue before relocating to this address. It was a popular neighborhood tavern from the 1950s through the 1970s. In later years, the establishment transformed into Ewa's Family Restaurant, which became a neighborhood staple for over two decades.

Directly across the street stands a building with a rich and varied past. It originally opened in 1910 as Guss Oscar's Saloon and underwent several transformations over the years. In the early 1920s, it became Metzal's Bowling Alleys and then transitioned to Nig and Scotty's Alleys in the 1930s. After World War II, it was reborn as Marceline's Recreation, hosting several professional bowling tournaments. The establishment's later incarnations included the Amazing Grace Church in the 1990s and, finally, Reptile Corner Pet Shop. Today, the building stands vacant, a silent witness to the neighborhood's evolving story.

A short distance away at 4097 East Seventy-First Street, we find a building that began its life as Pyramid Savings and Loan in the early 1920s. From the late 1930s into the 1970s, it was home to the Nite Hawk Café, a long-standing fixture in the community. At 4106 East Seventy-First, the Pinewood Tavern building has its own tale to tell. Originally a confectionery in the 1920s, the establishment became the site of a tragic incident in 1930 when a potential customer caused a disturbance. After the customer refused to leave, the proprietor fired a shotgun, killing the man. By the 1940s, it had become Zizeneski's Café, and in 1950, it transformed into the Pinewood Inn. The Pinewood was a proud sponsor of local softball teams for decades. More recently, it's housed Becker's Donuts and, later, M&M Bakery.

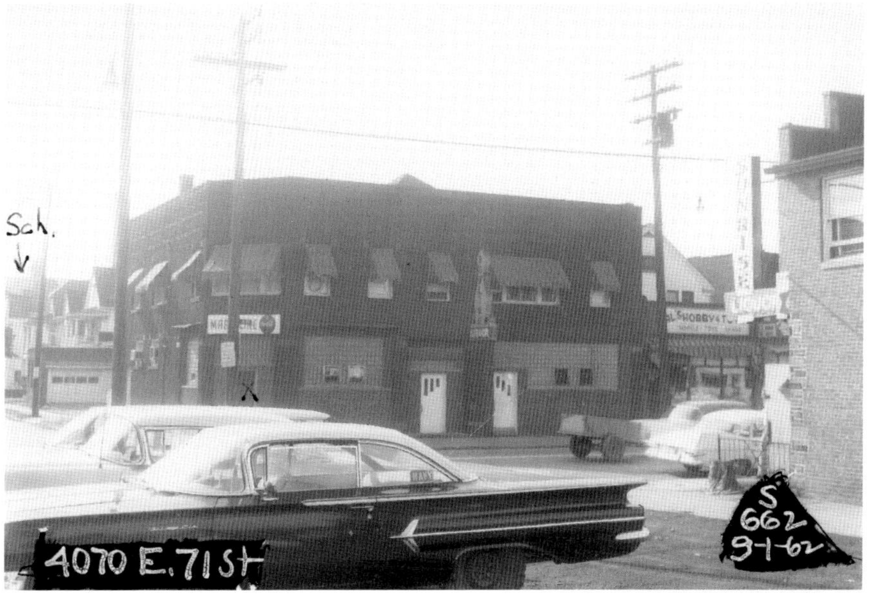

Marceline's Bowling Alley and Liquor with Sunrise Café across the street, 1962. *Cleveland Public Library/Photograph Collection.*

Our next stop brings us to 4131 East Seventy-First, a location with a particularly colorful history. Initially Konrad's Furniture, by the early 1940s, it had become the Clover Café. This establishment was no stranger to controversy, from a New Year's Eve brawl in 1943 to a shootout during a robbery in 1947. In the 1950s, it was known as the Polonaise Lounge and continued to make headlines. A peculiar incident in 1959 involved a mason jar of sweet-smelling liquid being thrown through the plate glass window, a mystery that was never solved. The 1960s saw the bar reinvented as the Golden Mule, complete with go-go dancers. Throughout the early and mid-1970s, the establishment faced legal troubles, including arrests for nudity. In 1975, firefighters responding to a call at the club discovered a hidden closed-circuit television system connected to a receiver in a locker room, adding another layer of intrigue to the building's storied past.

Before we conclude our exploration of East Seventy-First Street, let's make two final stops at a pair of establishments that were integral to the local community: the Victory and Casey's Tavern. Both of these long-standing businesses were known for their enthusiastic support of local sports, sponsoring teams in bowling, softball and touch football leagues.

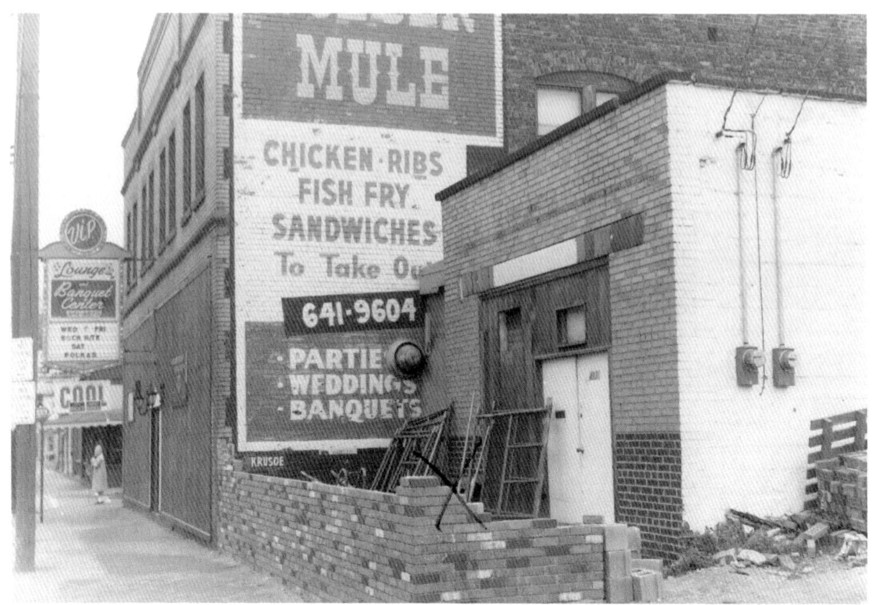

The Golden Mule, 4131 East Seventy-First, in 1970. *Cleveland Public Library/Photograph Collection.*

The Victory Grill at 4136 East Seventy-First has a colorful history. Paul Zgrabik owned and lived in in it from 1942 until his death in 1955. In 1947, the Victory was the scene of a dramatic incident involving a thirty-five-year-old East Side resident who managed to hold three detectives at bay with what he later claimed was a toy pistol. During the encounter, a detective fired three shots at the man but missed. Interestingly, months later, the man's conscience got the better of him, and he turned himself in to police. The Victory Grill showed its resilience in the winter of 1973 when it survived a significant fire. Despite near-zero-degree weather, seventeen dedicated firefighters battled the blaze for over two hours, managing to save the establishment.

Our final stop on East Seventy-First is Casey's Tavern. Not to be confused with the Casey's on Fleet Avenue, this Casey's was owned by Cazimer Wozniak for many years. It was both a bar and a restaurant and was particularly popular for its Friday fish fries.

Beyond Fleet and Seventy-First: Uncovering More of Slavic Village's Hidden Watering Holes

As we venture beyond Fleet Avenue and East Seventy-First, we discover that Slavic Village's tapestry of taverns extends far and wide. The neighborhood's streets—Union, Harvard, Aetna and more—are dotted with local watering holes, each with its own story to tell. Let's turn our attention to Lansing Avenue and East Sixty-Fifth Street, where a concentration of bars once thrived.

In the 1960s, the intersection of Lansing and East Sixty-Fifth offered an impressive array of drinking establishments. While some, like the Double X Bar at 3824 East Sixty-Fifth, changed their names over the years, others maintained their identity for decades. The Red Rose, for instance, kept its moniker from before 1940 until it became Mr.'s in the 2000s. This bustling corner also boasted the Lansing Tavern and the Union of Poles.

Our final stop brings us to a true Slavic Village institution: Karb's Tavern at 3614 East Sixty-Fifth Street. Situated across from Morgana Park, where many tavern-sponsored softball teams competed in the Southeast Tavern League, Karb's was more than just a bar: it was a cultural hub. For over forty

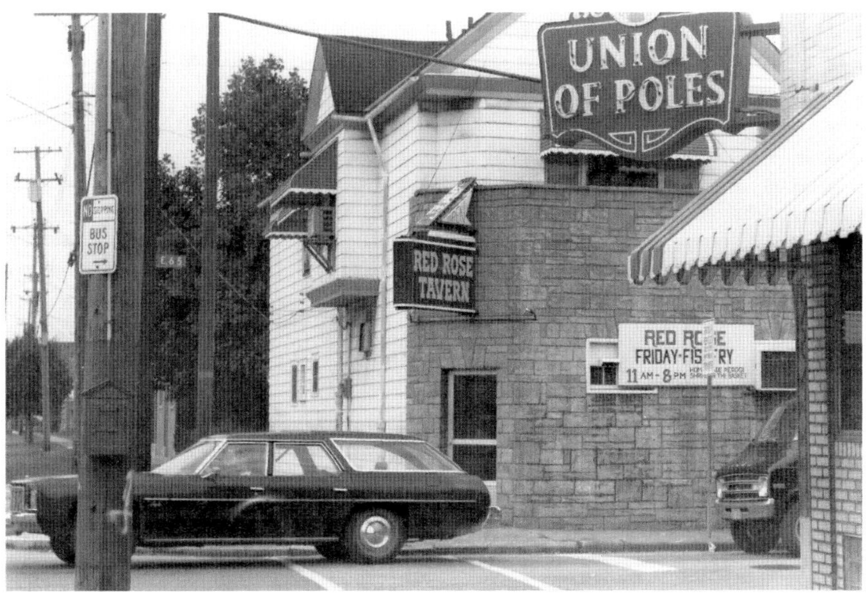

The corner of East Sixty-Fifth and Lansing, 1978. *Cleveland Public Library/Photograph Collection.*

years, Gerald "Hook" Tucholski ran this popular tavern and polka venue, passing the torch to his son John on his death in 2000.

Karb's history is as colorful as its patrons. On New Year's Eve 1966, excitement of a different kind erupted when a bomb was discovered in the basement; thankfully, it was dismantled before detonation. The following year, the bar caught the attention of local law enforcement for selling illegal raffle tickets in exchange for whiskey. But it wasn't all controversy; Karb's was also a place of celebration. In 1978, the tavern erupted in joy when Polish Cardinal Karol Wojtyla was selected as Pope John Paul II, the first Polish pontiff. Tucholski was quoted in the *Plain Dealer*: "All the old-time Polish people were hugging and kissing today." The connection ran deep, as the new Pope had previously celebrated mass across the street at Saint Stanislaus.

Karb's was particularly renowned for its weekend polka music. A 1995 *Plain Dealer* article captured it perfectly: "This stripped-down Slavic Village bar hops on the weekend, which is a good reason to go during the week. You want fancy? You want yuppie? You want hoity-toity? Go elsewhere." The bar's legacy continued until 2007, when it was sold and became MJ's Café; later, in 2022, it transformed into the current People's Bar and Grill.

As we conclude our journey through Slavic Village's vibrant tavern scene, we're left with a profound appreciation for the role these establishments played in the community's social fabric. From Fleet Avenue to East Seventy-First, from Lansing to East Sixty-Fifth, each bar and tavern we've explored tells a unique story of Cleveland's rich immigrant history, its industrial past and the enduring spirit of its people.

A Hop Across the River: Cleveland's Original Southside, Tremont

As we hop across the Cuyahoga River, we find ourselves in Tremont, an area historically known to its residents as Cleveland's Southside. The area began as part of Brooklyn Township and was briefly even known as University Heights due to the short-lived Cleveland University. Tremont's story is one of waves of immigration and constant evolution. From the initial nineteenth-century influx of Irish and German families to later arrivals from Eastern Europe, including Polish, Slovak, Ukrainian and Rusyn communities, each group left its mark. Greek and Syrian immigrants followed, and African American and Appalachian families joined during the post–World War II era.

The neighborhood's landscape tells this story of diversity through its historical landmarks, particularly its churches. The density of religious buildings in this relatively small area is remarkable. Each ethnic group established its own place of worship, resulting in a striking variety of architectural styles and denominations in proximity to each other. Many of the churches are over one hundred years old and still active, with renewed congregations.

Beyond churches, other ethnic landmarks dot the landscape. Reception halls, community centers and cultural institutions like Lemko Hall (which was featured in the movie *The Deer Hunter*), the Polish Library Home and the Ukrainian National Home were vital to preserving Tremont's immigrant heritage. Even the street names—Professor, Literary, College and University—evoke memories of the area's brief stint as a college town, adding another layer to Tremont's rich historical past.

While Tremont faced challenges in the mid-twentieth century, including population decline and the disruptive construction of Interstate 71, it has experienced a revival since the early 2000s. Today, Tremont balances its rich historical identity with a new wave of residents attracted to its taverns, restaurants and proximity to downtown. Let's begin our Tremont tour at what is arguably its oldest continuously open tavern, Hotz Cafe.

Timeless Taps: Hotz Cafe, Tremont's Living History

Nestled on the corner of Starkweather Avenue and West Tenth in Tremont, Hotz Cafe stands as a living monument to Cleveland's resilient spirit. While the first liquor license for this location was granted to Louis Moells in 1913, it wasn't until 1919 that John Hotz Sr., a Rusyn immigrant, opened the doors to what would become Cleveland's oldest continuously operating tavern.

John Hotz Sr., who arrived in the United States in 1905, founded the café with the vision of creating a haven for his fellow countrymen and local laborers. Little did he know that his humble establishment would weather the storms of Prohibition, the Great Depression and the decline of Cleveland's industrial era to become a cherished local institution.

During Prohibition, Hotz Cafe operated as a speakeasy, attracting not just local steelworkers but also some of the biggest names in baseball. Legend has it that Ty Cobb, Lou Gehrig and even the great Babe Ruth frequented the tavern. Its reputation grew, and it became a discrete meeting

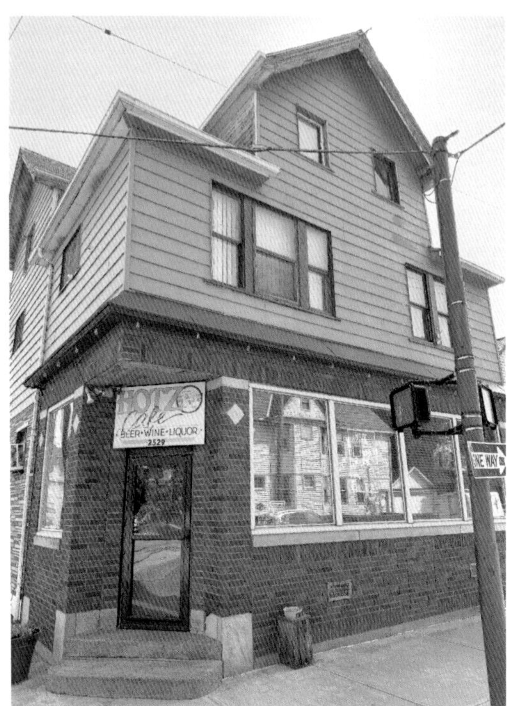

Left: Hotz Café, since 1919: still operating in the family. *Author's photo, September 2024. Courtesy of John Hotz.*

Below: Hanging at the bar in Hotz Café in the 1930s. *Author's photo, September 2024. Courtesy of John Hotz.*

Opposite: One of only five twenty-four-foot shuffleboards in the United States, from the 1930s, at Hotz Café. *Photo by author, September 2024. Courtesy of John Hotz.*

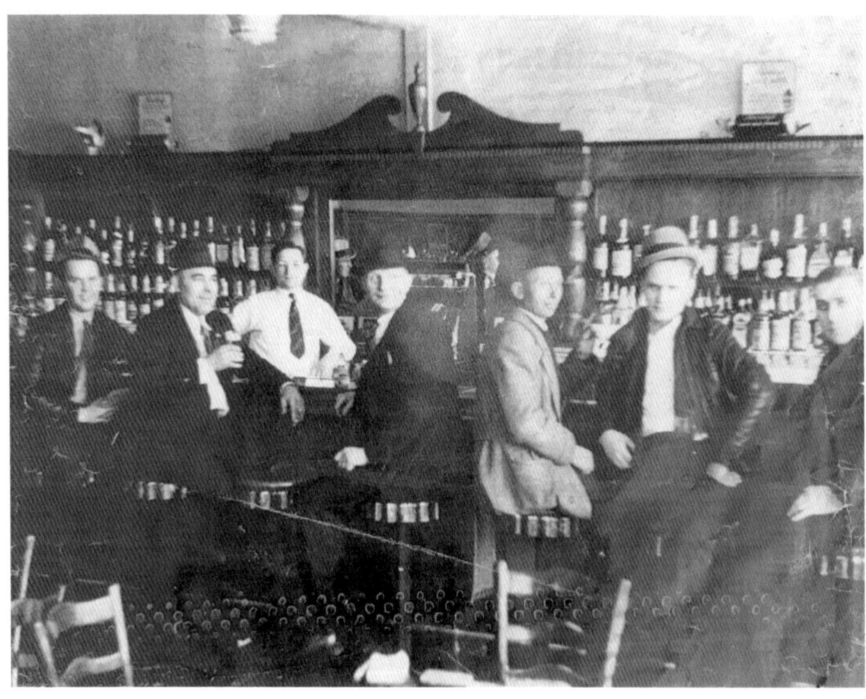

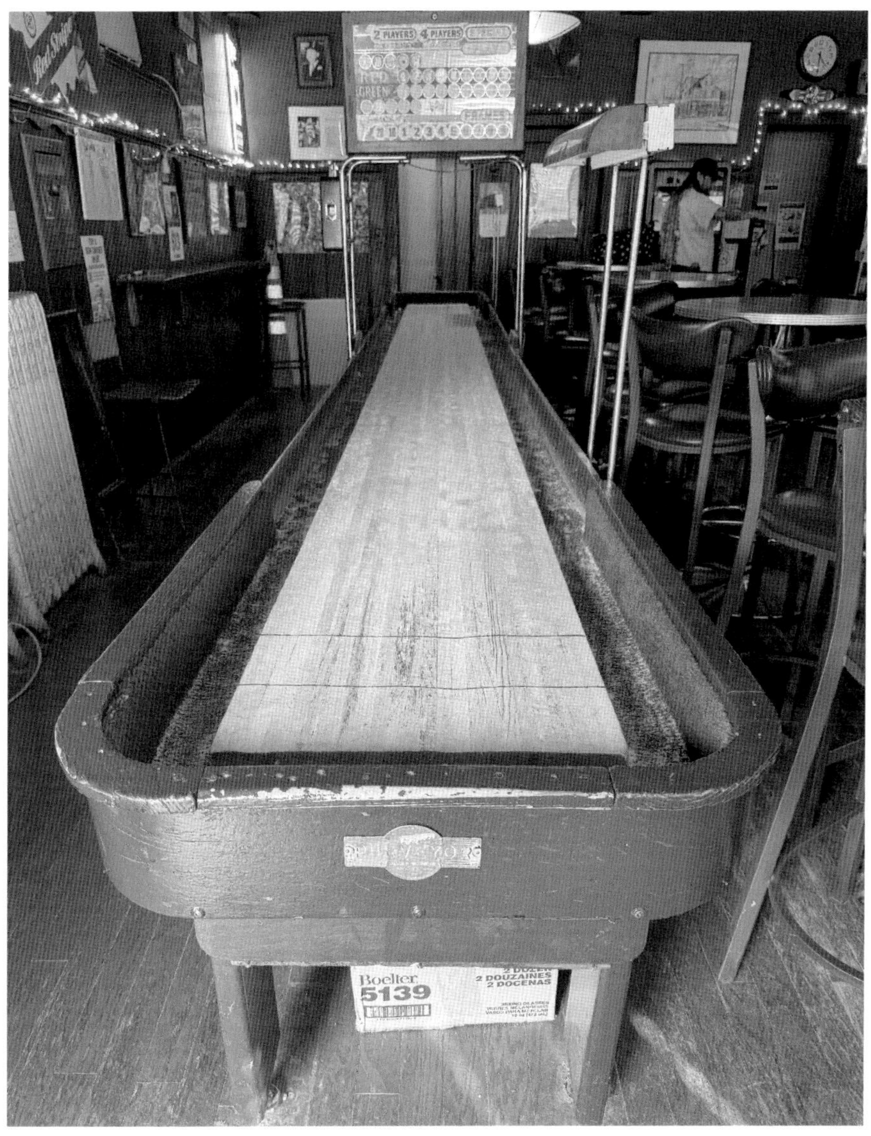

place for politicians, judges and law enforcement officials. Even Eliot Ness, Cleveland's safety director from 1935 to 1940, was known to stop there in between his efforts hunting for the infamous Torso Murderer—a serial killer who terrorized the city in the 1930s by dismembering victims and leaving their remains scattered throughout the area.

After World War II, the business expanded as John's sons, Andrew and Mike, joined the family enterprise. The postwar era saw Hotz Cafe continue

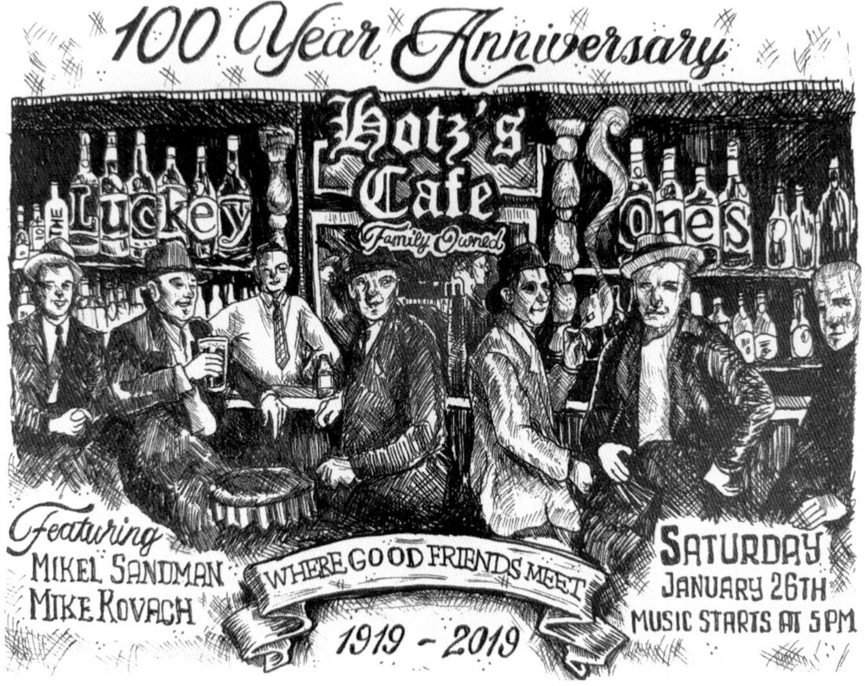

Hotz Café's "100 Year Anniversary" drawing re-creating the 1930s photo above the bar. *Photo by author, September 2024. Courtesy of John Hotz.*

in its role as a sanctuary for steel mill workers and laborers, a place where they could unwind after a long shift or pass the time before clocking in.

As Tremont faced challenges with the closing of area steel mills and population decline, Hotz Cafe remained a constant. Today, with the fourth generation of the Hotz family involved in the business, the tavern continues to serve as a hub of community life.

Step inside Hotz Cafe, and you'll find yourself transported through time. The original bar and soda pop–style barstools still stand, while a twenty-four-foot-long shuffleboard game invites friendly competition. Nostalgic photos and vintage decor line the walls, telling the story of a neighborhood and a family business that have weathered tremendous change. As noted in an article by Regina Brett in the *Plain Dealer* on December 8, 2001, Hotz Cafe is more than just a bar—it's a keeper of memories. Brett captures the essence of the place: "Open the door and the memories spill out of a barstool." She describes how patrons can "take a seat at a barstool from 1919 that looks like a giant bottle cap and order a shot of liquor from the rich cherry-wood shelves." Brett's article paints a vivid picture of the café's enduring role in the community, describing how it was a place where "steelworkers cashed their checks…for generations."

While the neighborhood around it has changed, Hotz Cafe remains a constant. It's a place where the past and present mingle, where newcomers to Tremont can connect with the area's rich history and where longtime residents can reminisce about the neighborhood's evolution.

From Dempsey's Oasis to Prosperity: The Dual Legacy of a Tremont Tavern

Just a few blocks down from Hotz Cafe, at 1109 Starkweather Avenue, stands another Tremont tavern with a colorful history: Prosperity Social Club. This beloved tavern, situated in the epicenter of Tremont and directly across from Lincoln Park, has been an integral part of the neighborhood for over eighty-five years.

The story begins in 1938, when Stanley Dembowski, a Polish immigrant and World War I veteran, opened the establishment as Dempsey's Night Club—a name initially chosen to appeal to women customers. It later rebranded as Dempsey's Oasis to attract a broader clientele.

The name Dempsey wasn't chosen at random. It was Stanley's nickname, acquired after a fateful $500 bet on Jack Dempsey to defeat Gene Tunney in their 1926 boxing match. Despite Dempsey's loss, the nickname stuck. When asked about the Oasis part, Stanley explained years later that it was added because "that is where thirsty people go to drink."

Dempsey's Oasis quickly became more than just a watering hole. It was a gathering place for a diverse clientele—from Tremont residents and workers from the nearby steel mills to downtown businesspeople and health care professionals from Metro General Hospital. The Dembowski family, who lived next door to the tavern, became integral members of the community, actively involved in local charity work.

The tavern's community involvement extended beyond local causes. A *Plain Dealer* article from February 11, 1982, highlighted Stanley's support for the Polish Solidarity movement. During Solidarity Week, he offered "Polish revenge"—kielbasa and kraut washed down with Krakus, a Polish beer. This tradition of serving Polish favorites—along with an incredible fish fry—continues to this day.

In 2005, Bonnie Flinner breathed new life into the tavern, renaming it Prosperity Social Club. She carefully preserved the establishment's original

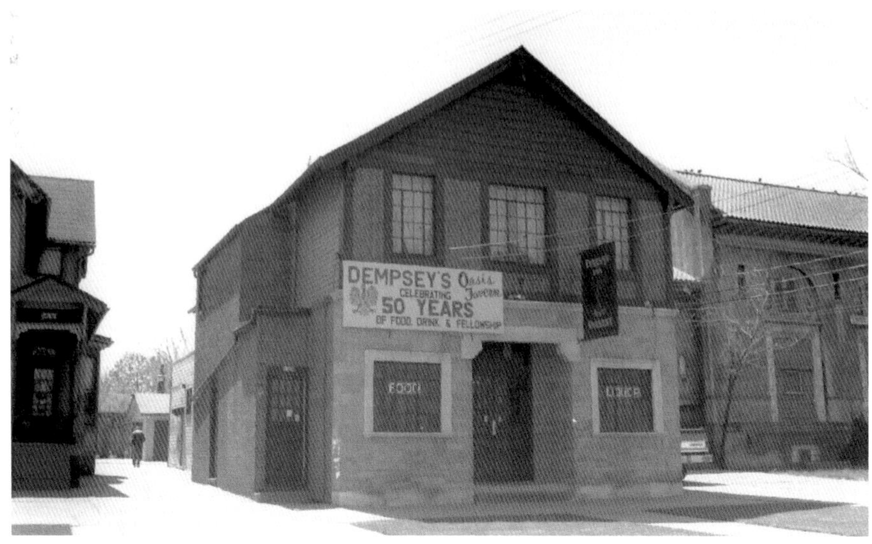

Dempsey's Oasis, 1960s. *Courtesy Tremont History Project.*

character, including its distinctive chestnut walls, walnut bar and vintage beer memorabilia. An old-fashioned bowling machine stood as a cherished relic of the past until just a few years ago. Flinner honored the tavern's Polish working-class roots by introducing Old World Wednesdays, featuring stuffed cabbage and noodles, and continuing the annual celebration of Dyngus Day. After sixteen successful years at the helm, Bonnie sold the tavern in 2021 to Will Hollingsworth, another local patron and owner of the Spotted Owl Bar. Today, Prosperity Social Club stands as a testament to Tremont's rich history and ongoing evolution, seamlessly blending the neighborhood's past with its vibrant present.

Tremont's Tavern Transformations: Old Haunts, New Flavors

As you wander throughout Tremont, you'll discover popular destinations that once housed neighborhood taverns, each with its own rich history. At 777 Starkweather stands Lucky's Café, formerly the site of Tymoc's Café. The Tymoc family's connection to this location dates to 1927, when they purchased the property; Walter Tymoc resided there until the 1980s.

Around the corner on Professor Avenue, the building that once housed the Valley View Café, owned by Barbara Hotz for thirty-one years until her death in 1969, has seen several transformations. After operating as the Valley View until the 2000s, it became Istanbul Grill and then Dervish Turkish Grill before settling into its current incarnation as Tandul Indian restaurant.

The Literary Tavern, another popular spot, has a tavern history dating to the 1930s. The building itself is one of the oldest in Tremont, dating to the Civil War era. In fact, it was a notable neighborhood bakery in the early 1900s.

Its early days were marred by tragedy when Joe Jamitowski, a Polish Lodge president, was robbed and murdered in front of the bar. In the 1950s, it became Joe & Helen's Café, which also fell victim to a dramatic robbery in which silk stocking–clad thieves made their getaway in a tractor-trailer. In the 1970s, it was rebranded as Friendly's Café, which catered to local blue-collar workers. According to the *Plain Dealer*, one intriguing legend surrounding the bar involves Robert De Niro. During the filming of *The Deer Hunter*, De Niro reportedly became a regular, drinking Rolling Rock and conversing with local Vietnam veterans to help develop his character. The story goes that he was so enamored with the bar that he asked to keep his barstool when filming ended.

In 1990, the tavern became the Literary Café. Known affectionately as the Lit, the bar hosted poetry readings and book clubs and served as a venue for selling local art. In February 2016, the *Plain Dealer* reported that the bar was listed for sale for $499,000, which included its coveted liquor license, a two-bedroom apartment and a beautiful backyard garden. The Café remains a very popular destination in the heart of Tremont.

Before we leave the neighborhood, a visit to Tremont's southern edge offers us a chance to tour the famous Christmas Story house. Directly across the street from this iconic home, the Rowley Inn provides the final stop on our Tremont tavern tour. The Rowley Inn, established in 1906, is a historic bar nestled in a residential neighborhood just a few blocks from the now-demolished Clark Avenue Bridge. It quickly became a popular stop for workers from the nearby mills and factories, both before and after their shifts. The inn was also a generous supporter of local sandlot baseball teams. Its fame reached new heights in 1983 during the filming of the Christmas classic *A Christmas Story*. The tavern served as the makeup and wardrobe department and was a natural spot for the crew to unwind after a long day of filming. Today, the Rowley Inn remains a beloved destination for both visitors and locals, continuing to serve outstanding food and maintain its historic charm.

As we leave the Rowley Inn, our Tremont tavern tour concludes just a few blocks away, at the Clark Bar. In 2013, *Cleveland Scene* recognized this

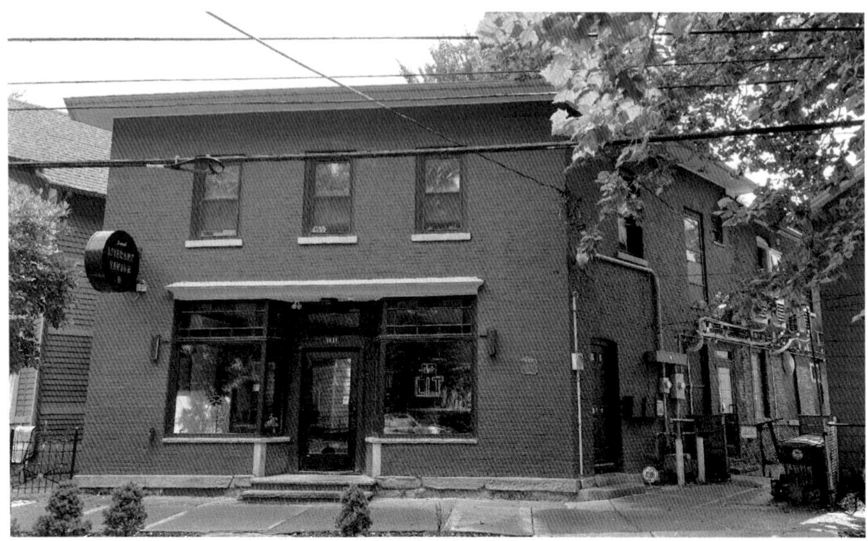

Above: Literary Tavern, 1031 Literary Road, Tremont. *Author's photo, August 2024.*

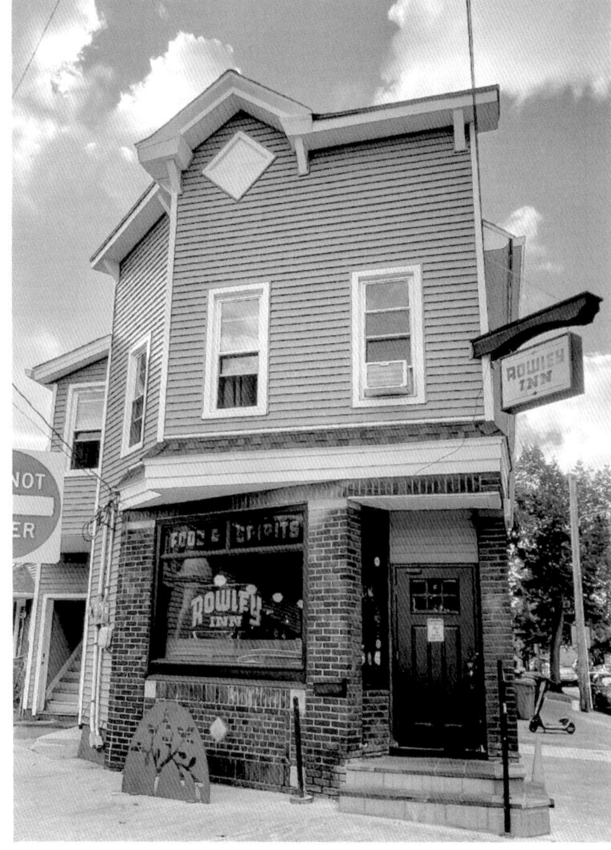

Right: Rowley Inn, across the street from the Christmas Story home. *Author's photo, 2024.*

establishment as one of the top five dive bars in Cleveland, offering a vivid description of its unique atmosphere: "One of the last strongholds of Tremont in the '80s is the Clark Bar. Walking in, you are greeted with as much suspicion and hesitation as a door-to-door salesman. But once you take your first shot of Kamchatka vodka, you will be welcomed as an honorary Clark Bar-er."

The bar's resilience was put to the test in 2014 when an unwelcome guest—a stolen jeep—crashed through the front patio, sending a patron to the hospital. However, true to the spirit of this tight-knit community, customers rallied around the establishment. A temporary front entrance was quickly set up, allowing the tavern to maintain its tradition of staying open seven days a week, a practice it proudly continues to this day.

Chapter 8

West Side Story

From Old World to New Brews

While the East Side is home to cultural institutions centered on University Circle, the West Side is characterized by its working-class ethnic neighborhoods. The West Side has been shaped by waves of immigration, from Irish and German settlers in the nineteenth century to later influxes of eastern Europeans, Hispanics and, starting in the 1950s, Appalachians. This cultural diversity is reflected in the area's architecture, cuisine and, of course, its taverns. From century-old bars that have witnessed the city's industrial boom and decline to trendy craft breweries breathing new life into old buildings, the west side's drinking establishments tell the stories of neighborhoods that honor their past while embracing the future. Since our last stop was near Clark Avenue, let's continue west to the Clark-Fulton and Stockyards neighborhoods.

Clark-Fulton's Liquid Landmarks: A Journey Through Local Taverns

On Cleveland's Near West Side lies Clark-Fulton, a compact working-class neighborhood. Spanning roughly one square mile, it's the most densely populated area in Cleveland, though estimates of its population vary considerably, ranging from six thousand to ten thousand. This is in stark contrast to the 1940s, when the neighborhood's population, primarily central and eastern Europeans, exceeded twenty-one thousand.

The neighborhood's demographic landscape has evolved significantly since the 1960s, when Puerto Rican families began settling in the area. By 2020, Hispanics were the majority of Clark-Fulton's population, with Whites making up about one-third and African Americans less than one-quarter. This demographic shift occurred against a backdrop of significant urban changes. The construction of I-71 and I-90 in the 1960s, while not directly carving through Clark-Fulton, effectively isolated the neighborhood on three sides. This isolation, compounded by the demolition of the Clark Avenue Bridge, severely limited access to surrounding communities. Consequently, new construction was suppressed and population decline accelerated, reshaping the neighborhood's physical and social landscape.

Despite its compact size, the Clark-Fulton area once boasted a remarkable concentration of taverns along its main thoroughfares: West Twenty-Fifth Street, Clark Avenue and Fulton Road. As we continue our journey westward on Clark Avenue, we encounter a stretch that historically hosted no fewer than twelve taverns at various times.

At the corner of Clark and West Twenty-Fifth Street stands the Honecker Building, which opened in 1888 and housed Cleveland's oldest pharmacy. In the mid-1940s, this historic structure took on a new identity when Art Cavar established the Merrie-Arts Anchor Bar, decorated in a nautical motif. Cavar hoped to replicate the success of his recently sold Merrie-Arts establishment in Lakewood. However, the bar was short-lived. The space later transformed into Belkin's Men Shop and now serves the community as the Heart to Heart Enrichment Center.

Just a few blocks south of Clark Avenue lies Dickey's Recreation and Cocktail Lounge, a neighborhood institution that served as both a bowling alley and a popular watering hole for decades. The building's history dates to 1915, and it has housed various recreational facilities over the years. In 1926, it was advertised as a bowling alley, with nine lanes for sale. It later operated as Wildwood Recreation in 1936 and Gimbel Recreation in 1940.

Dickey's Recreation and Cocktail Lounge opened in 1945 when George Dickey's parents purchased the establishment. The venue has remained under family ownership through the decades. George, who started working there as a pin boy at age fourteen, dedicated his entire career to the business until his passing at the age of ninety in 2022.

Continuing our journey along West Twenty-Fifth Street, we encounter a series of establishments that reflect the area's evolving nightlife scene. Two doors south of Dickey's, at 3295 West Twenty-Fifth, stood the Rainbow

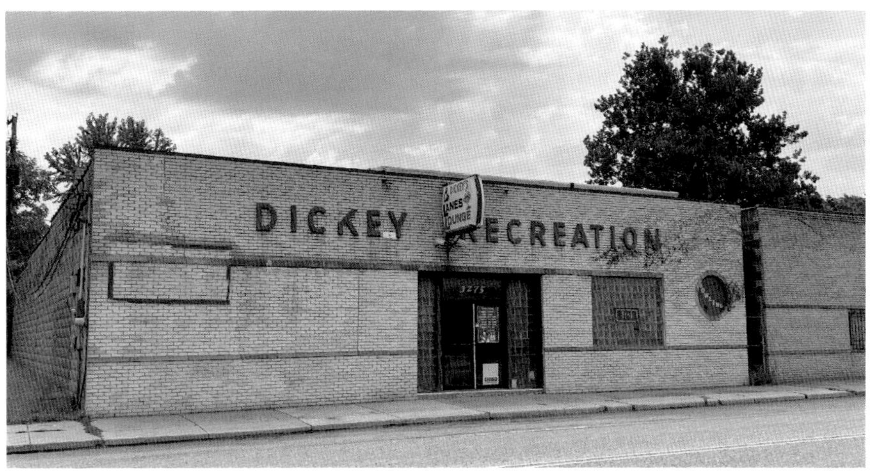

Dickey's Recreation on West Twenty-Fifth, since 1945. *Author's photo, August 2024.*

Gardens Bar in the 1940s, which became the Can Can Bar in the 1960s. Tragically, in 1967, a patron lost his life playing Russian roulette in the bar.

A few doors north of Dickey's stood an older tavern, originally operated by the Carje family as far back to as the 1920s. This establishment narrowly escaped destruction in 1940 when a car crashed into the front of the building. By the 1960s, it had transformed into the Comet Bar, advertising go-go girls and promising patrons a place "where the action is." However, the Comet's history took a dark turn in 1976 when its part owner was shot to death in the bar following an argument about firing a go-go dancer. The space later reinvented itself as Niko's, offering salsa dancing; through the late 1990s and 2000s, it was the popular Monroe's Cabaret. For those seeking alternatives when Monroe's was busy, Latin dance music could also be found at nearby El Caribeno and Players on West Twenty-Fifth Street. In a 1996 interview, Players owner Ron Davis described his efforts to cater to a diverse crowd by adding hip-hop to the rotation of salsa music. Davis aimed to create a "no race club," attracting patrons of all nationalities.

As we leave West Twenty-Fifth Street in the 1960s and make our way toward Fulton Road, it's worth noting the prevalence of first-name establishments on the street: Pete's, Steve's, Wally's and Marie's. These taverns, along with the Seymour Café, La Cue Billiards and Lounge, Erin Café and JH Tavern, all competed for customers in this densely populated neighborhood.

As we make our way to Fulton Road, we pass by 3258 West Thirty-Second Street, home to a century-old building that has been a tavern and entertainment venue since the end of Prohibition. Originally opened as

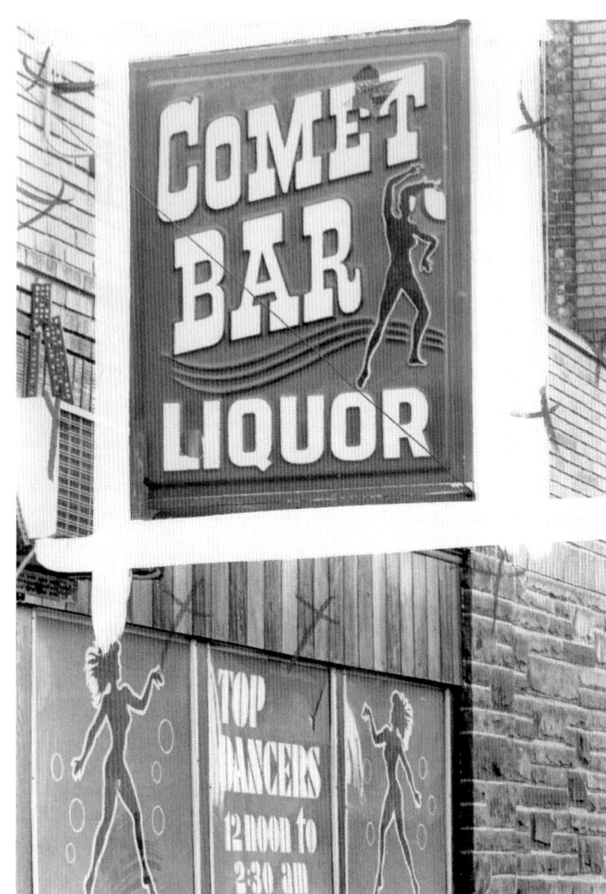

Left: Comet Bar on West Twenty-Fifth, 1970s. *Cleveland Press Collection, Cleveland State University, Michael Schwartz Library Special Collection.*

Below: Dunlap Tavern, tucked into a residential neighborhood at 3258 West Thirty-Second. The exterior has been renovated, but the original Dunlap sign remains. *Author's photo, August 2024.*

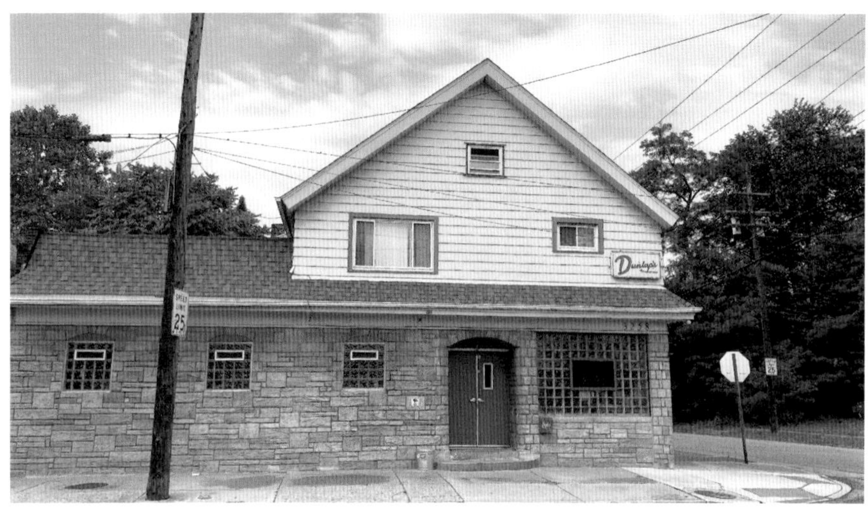

Pacino's Wonder Bar by Sicilian immigrant Sam Pacino, the establishment quickly became known for Rose Pacino's excellent spaghetti and Italian sausage. The bar hosted various entertainers, including local talent Kay Ballard before her Broadway fame, and even featured female impersonators from Chicago in the late 1930s.

Over the decades, the tavern has undergone several transformations while maintaining its character as a neighborhood gathering spot. Today, the tavern is Dunlap's Corner Bar, owned by Nick White and his partner Jason Mattern, who are preserving the classic tavern atmosphere while making necessary improvements. They've restored the original mahogany bar, added a brass foot rail and installed a new draft beer system. Dunlap's continues to offer live performances on the original stage for musicians and comedians.

As we explore the area near the intersection of Clark Avenue and Fulton Road, we encounter several notable taverns and restaurants. At 3164 Fulton Road stands the famous Johnny's Bar and Restaurant, a Cleveland institution. While its massive neon sign prominently displays "Johnny's Bar," this establishment has earned a reputation as one of Cleveland's finest dining venues. The building's history dates to the 1920s, when it opened as Louise's Garden, but it has operated as Johnny's since 1952.

In the 1960s, this two-block section of Fulton offered several options for a night out. You could choose from Danny's, Villa Tavern or Dennie's Bar, just a couple of blocks south. Dennie's underwent several transformations over the years. It became the BKS Bar in the late 1960s and then evolved into the popular Bottom Line Saloon. More recently, it operated as the District before becoming Benny's Sports Grille, known for its late-night Latin entertainment and excellent food.

As we cross the invisible boundary into the Stockyards, we'll continue our journey along tavern-rich Clark Avenue, uncovering the bars and taverns that have served as social anchors for both neighborhoods.

Stockyards: Where Beef and Brews Built Community

The Stockyards neighborhood derives its name from the Cleveland Union Stockyards Co., which moved to 3200 West Sixty-Fifth Street in 1893 after a landslide destroyed its original site. At its peak in the 1920s, the stockyards were one of the largest meat-processing centers in the United States. The complex sprawled across more than sixty acres in the neighborhood. While the Stockyards were busy processing livestock, the Pilsener Brewing Co. operated on West Sixty-Fifth from 1892 to 1963. The brewing company employed three hundred workers churning out enough suds to fill 375,000 barrels. Demographically, the Stockyards area has seen significant shifts. Initially populated mainly by Hungarians and Czechs in the early twentieth century, it has become increasingly diverse since the 1980s. The Latino population has grown substantially, and African American residents, virtually absent until the 1980s, now make up a significant portion of the community.

As we cross the invisible border into the Stockyards neighborhood, we encounter a stretch of Clark Avenue rich with tavern history. In the 1960s, K's Café at 4519 Clark stood just a stone's throw from Bunny's Tavern at 4310 Clark. The building that housed Bunny's has a particularly fascinating past and future. Before becoming Bunny's, this large structure was the Sokol Hall, a centerpiece of the local Bohemian community. Situated next to the Cleveland Fire House, it hosted numerous significant social and political events. In the 1970s, the building became Mesker's Tavern, which operated until the early 1980s, when its eighty-year-old owner fell ill and was forced to sell. The tavern's history then took a dramatic turn as it transformed into a series of gentlemen's clubs throughout the 1980s and beyond. It cycled through various incarnations, including Little Caesar's, the Unicorn Lounge, Mickey's Lounge, Jimi's T Bar, Bad Boyz Club, Romeo's Show Bar, Million Dollar Club and Dreamer's Gentlemen's Club.

Departing Clark Avenue toward the Stockyards' southern end, we encounter Sachsenheim Hall at 7001 Denison, a century-old cornerstone of the community. Erected in 1910 by Transylvanian German immigrants, the hall—*sachsenheim* means "home of the Saxons"—became a cultural hub for Cleveland's German population. A gathering place for everything from traditional dances and political meetings to social events and community celebrations, the Sachsenheim was the heart of the neighborhood. Expanded over the years to include a ballroom and bowling alleys, the hall catered to a wide audience, hosting weddings and other local events. Through the decades, the hall underwent significant expansions, adding a ballroom and bowling alleys. The renovations allowed the Sachsenheim to open its doors wider to the Stockyards neighborhood, accommodating local weddings, showers and other events. In November 1971, the hall caught fire during an event attended by over one hundred children. Fortunately, no one was injured, and the damage was quickly repaired in time for the holiday season. The hall has adapted to changing times, now

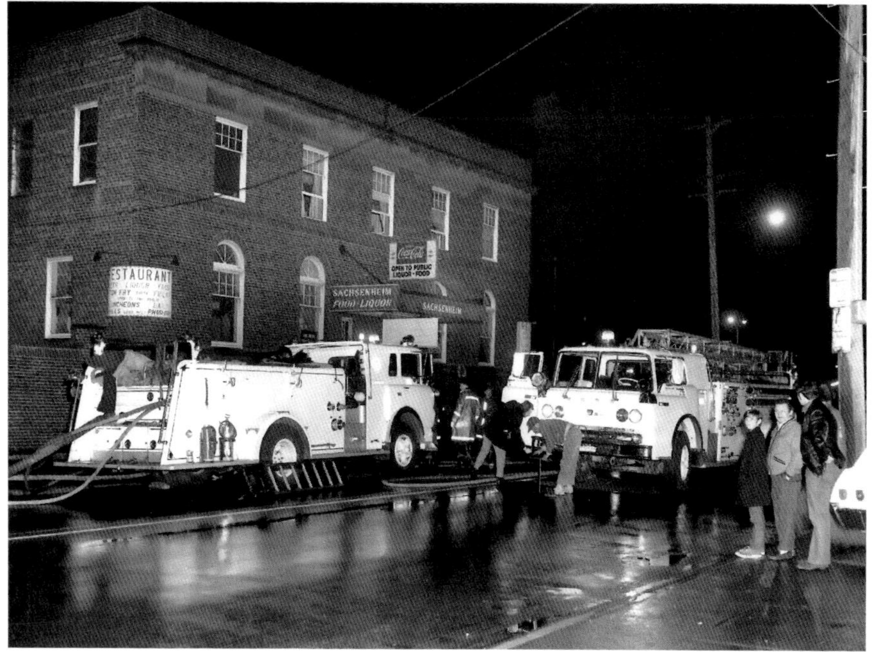

Fire at the historic Sachsenheim Hall, a pillar of the West Side community, 1971. *Cleveland Public Library/Photograph Collection.*

hosting events like Taco Tuesdays, while still maintaining its connection to its Transylvanian Saxon and German roots.

Continuing our journey along Denison Avenue, we encounter Verba's Café at 6410 Denison. Despite enduring several armed robberies, John and Marie Verba served their community for forty-three years. Marie, affectionately known as the Halupki Queen for her renowned Slovak stuffed cabbage rolls, nourished countless factory and packing plant workers. The Verbas were pillars of the community, sponsoring sports teams, hosting celebrations and offering hospitality to those in need. Marie continued operating the tavern after John's death in 1973, finally closing its doors in 1976.

As we leave the Stockyards and head toward Brooklyn-Centre, we see that Denison Avenue continues to feature a variety of neighborhood taverns. Along the way, we pass by Dick's Café, Stoyko's Bar and Carl's Corner Bar, which was known as Andy's Bar in the 1940s and '50s. Our journey along this stretch ends at a single building that has housed several incarnations of neighborhood bars over the years. At 4804 Denison, there was once the Blue Haven Café, which later became Jean's Top of the Line and, in the 2000s, Quigley's Café.

South of the Stockyards: Brooklyn Centre and Old Brooklyn's Bar Trail

As we venture into Brooklyn Centre and Old Brooklyn, we encounter two neighboring communities with rich histories and distinct identities. Both areas were once part of rural Brooklyn Township, settled by the pioneers from the Connecticut Land Company in the early 1800s.

In 2020, Brooklyn Centre's population was diverse, with 61.1 percent White residents, 21.1 percent African American and a significant Hispanic and Latino population, at 37.8 percent. The neighborhood also included smaller Asian and mixed-race communities. As of 2019, over 17 percent of Brooklyn Centre residents were foreign-born, primarily from Latin America.

Old Brooklyn was once a pioneer in greenhouse agriculture; the Schaaf Road area led Midwest cultivation in the late 1800s. By the 1920s, the neighborhood was a national leader in greenhouse vegetable production. This industry declined in the 1960s due to urban development in the area. The neighborhood experienced significant commercial growth between 1920 and 1960, and numerous taverns emerged along Pearl, Broadview and State Roads. Residential construction flourished from the early twentieth century to the 1950s and experienced a resurgence in the 1980s and '90s.

As we enter Brooklyn Centre on Denison Avenue, our first stop is at the Ugly Broad Tavern at 3908 Denison. This building, which housed a paint store in the 1920s, began its life as a tavern in 1947 when it became Kelly's Tavern. The establishment faced challenges through the 1960s; its license was repeatedly put up for sale, culminating in a foreclosure in 1971. It briefly resurfaced as the Pub Tavern before adopting its current provocative moniker in 1974.

The Ugly Broad's name has become a defining feature of the neighborhood. In order to attract customers, a patron jokingly suggested the name, and it stuck, drawing curious visitors from miles around. The name has been a source of both attraction and controversy over the years. In 1994, owner Sherry Perry attempted to gauge community sentiment about the name through a survey. Despite some concerns, particularly from older residents, the name remained unchanged. A 1994 *Plain Dealer* article described the bar as a vintage West Side dive with a circular pool table, pinball machines and a long bar where you could almost see your reflection. The walls are adorned with photos of John Wayne and the bar's namesake "Ugly Broad"—a cartoon of a woman in a bikini who's in dire need of dental work and a shave. The Ugly Broad continues to operate with its original name, drawing

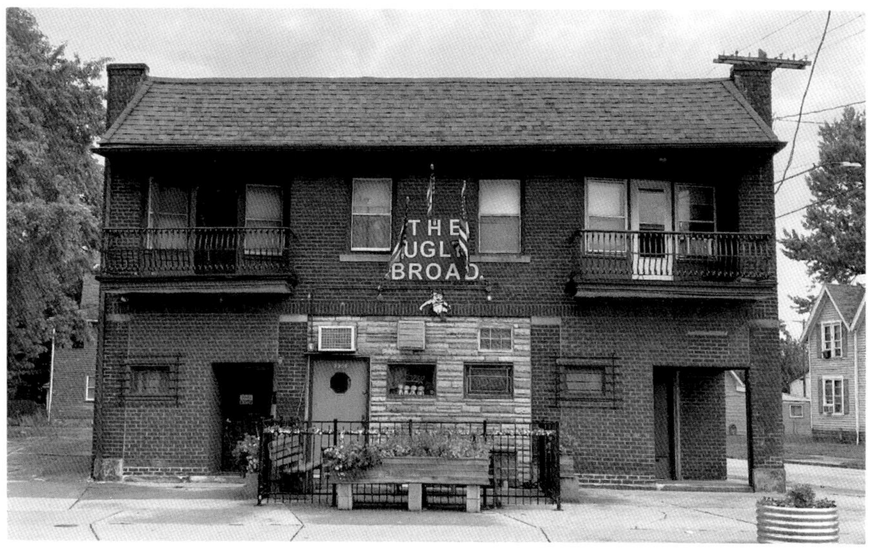

Despite calls to change its name, this tavern remains the Ugly Broad, at 3908 Denison. *Author's photo, August 2024.*

curious patrons and causing drivers on Denison Avenue to do a double take as they pass by.

As we leave the Ugly Broad behind and head toward the heart of Old Brooklyn, we'll travel south on West Twenty-Fifth, which becomes Pearl Road, and then turn onto Broadview Road. This stretch was once filled with neighborhood bars, including the White Rose, By Way Inn and Al's Place (known as Chuck's Place in the 1950s).

Our journey brings us to the Broadview Tavern at 2218 Broadview Road, a building with a chameleon-like history. Originally an A&P grocery store in the 1920s, it was later converted into a tavern. After its stint as the Broadview Tavern, the space underwent numerous transformations: it served as a flea market, the Rare Moments Lounge and even Cleveland's first Ethiopian restaurant, Lucy's Ethiopian Restaurant and Bar (later Lucy's Seafood and Steakhouse). The building's eclectic history continued with incarnations such as Club New York, Casablanca and Shenanigans.

Further down at 2100 Broadview Road, we encounter the former Wedge Inn. This building, constructed in 1900, has been a neighborhood fixture for over a century. For decades, the Wedge Inn was known for sponsoring sandlot baseball teams; however, its later years were marred by controversy. A *Plain Dealer* report from October 11, 2009, detailed how the bar was shut down after police discovered it was operating as an illegal strip club without the proper permits. The closure followed complaints of underage drinking, illegal alcohol sales and prostitution. In an unexpected turn of events, William Kaplysh, a retired Cleveland firefighter, was arrested for holding a party in the closed establishment, adding a final dramatic chapter to the Wedge Inn's long history.

As we move to State Road, we encounter a stretch that once boasted ten bars in just over one mile, from Pearl to Brookpark Road. On our way to the prominent Hillcrest Tavern and Gray Wolf Tavern, we pass several noteworthy establishments.

The Silver Dollar Bar near the bus terminal at 4331 State Road is a reminder of frontier-era saloons. Its name, common among early American taverns, originates from customers' habit of banging silver dollars on wooden bars to attract bartenders' attention. This neighborhood fixture later became the Lime Tree Inn in the 1990s.

A block away stood the Brooklyn Tavern, not to be confused with the long-standing Old Brooklyn Tavern on Pearl Road. We also pass the Tumble Inn, which later became Paula's Starlite and then the State Tavern. The State Tavern gained notoriety in 1973 when a tragic incident occurred. According to a newspaper report, the tavern owner shot and fatally wounded one man and injured another after they allegedly ignored his requests to quiet down during a disturbance. The incident resulted in the owner's arrest.

In the 1980s, the location transformed into Calhoun's Lounge, offering exotic dancers. The owner, James Calhoun, found himself in the spotlight again but for different reasons. In 2003, Calhoun's property became the subject of the U.S. Marshals Service's first online auction of forfeited assets in Northeast Ohio history. The property was Calhoun's floral shop; however, it also was a meeting place for drug dealers and a storage facility for cocaine.

As we continue our journey down State Road, we arrive at 4555 State Road, home to one of Old Brooklyn's most storied establishments: the Hillcrest Tavern. This location has witnessed nearly a century of Cleveland's social history, evolving from a Prohibition-era speakeasy into a renowned neighborhood bar. Originally a bootlegging operation owned by the notorious Morris "Mushy" Wexler in the 1920s, the site became known as the Hillcrest Tavern in the 1960s. It was during this period that the tavern gained national recognition, not for its drinks but for its world-class softball team. The Hillcrest Express, formed by Dave Neale, dominated tournaments throughout the 1970s, including world championships, bringing fame to both the tavern and Cleveland's softball scene.

In 1987, the establishment was rebranded as Wexler's Tavern, ushering in a new chapter of its colorful history. It was during this era that the tavern became the center of an intriguing mystery. In a story that made headlines across the country, the owner at the time, Lou Gentile, claimed to have discovered what appeared to be human remains hidden in the walls during renovations. This led to wild speculation about a possible connection to the disappearance of Jimmy Hoffa, though no concrete evidence was ever found. While the story gained the tavern publicity, the bones were not human. Today, the building operates as Bar 17, a neighborhood tavern and restaurant serving Latin cuisine.

Continuing our journey down State Road, we come to the Gray Wolf Tavern at 4761 State Road, a Cleveland landmark that for over forty years was renowned for serving up what many argued was the best fish fry and pierogis in the city. The story of the Gray Wolf begins in the post-Prohibition era, though its early history and original name remain a mystery. In 1955, brothers John and Joe Darwal opened the Gray Wolf, which quickly became a neighborhood institution that would endure for decades.

The Darwal family's influence on the tavern scene extended beyond the Gray Wolf. Their mother, Anna "Grandma" Darwal, was a legendary figure in Cleveland's tavern culture. According to her obituary, Anna and her husband, Charles, were Ukrainian immigrants and began in the tavern business on the Near West Side, operating the White Rose and the Golden Oak before their sons took over the Gray Wolf. On busy Fridays, the tavern would serve hundreds of patrons, and lines formed out the door even on bitter winter evenings.

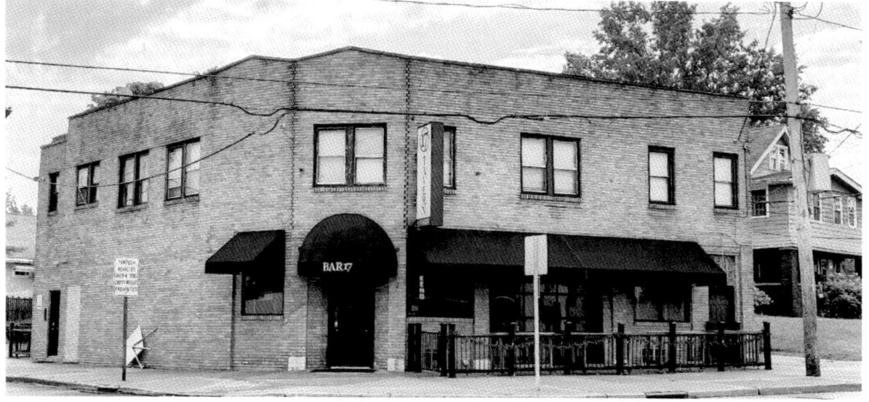

Bar 17, previously the Hilcrest Tavern, 4555 State Road: a tavern since Prohibition and home to the world champions Hilcrest Express Softball Team in the 1970s. *Author's photo, August 2024.*

The tavern's atmosphere was part of its charm. Described as "plain, almost to the point of drabness" in one newspaper article, it represented "a triumph of substance over style." The Gray Wolf also regularly hosted the George Stone Singers, a nationally renowned ensemble of crooners who would stop by after their weekly rehearsals in a nearby church hall. They performed show tunes over beers up until the tavern's closing in the 2000s. The closure marked the end of an era for Old Brooklyn, but the memories of its legendary pierogis and fish fries live on. Cleat's in North Royalton obtained the recipe and, to this day, advertises that it serves the original Gray Wolf fish fry!

Let's cut across State Road over to Pearl Road. In a tight cluster between 4370 and 4512 Pearl, there were four taverns operating in the 1960s. At 4370 Pearl stands the still-popular Pearl Road Tavern. This location originally housed a Chrysler dealership and then an Oldsmobile dealership before becoming the Mayflower Café after Prohibition. The tavern underwent several name changes: it was the Sapphire Inn in the 1950s, Mancuso's in the 1960s and Andy's Tavern in the 1970s. Throughout the 1950s and '60s, employment ads for this establishment were published almost daily, seeking "responsible and attractive barmaids between 25–35 years old." Interestingly, by the 1970s, the age range for potential employees had expanded to include women up to forty years old.

Other notable taverns in this stretch included Chuck's Tavern at 4426 Pearl (known as Mike's in the 1950s), Novak's at 4512 Pearl and the CCC Tavern at 4465 Pearl. The CCC Tavern was particularly well known for its avid sponsorship of softball teams, a tradition it maintained for over forty years.

Our next stops in Old Brooklyn take us to Memphis Avenue. As we pass by the Hanych Lounge and what was the Cameo Lounge in the late 1960s, we arrive at the Memphis Plaza Lounge. This tavern, located at 5303 Memphis Avenue, maintained its name from the 1950s through the 2000s, a testament to its enduring presence in the neighborhood.

The Memphis Plaza Lounge gained national notoriety as the inspiration for the Warsaw Tavern on *The Drew Carey Show*. Drew Carey grew up in Old Brooklyn and featured this local bar in his popular sitcom. The bar's interior, as described in the *Plain Dealer* on December 24, 1999, was a compact space of roughly 1,200 square feet, featuring a mini jukebox, bustling pool tables and an intimate atmosphere that made it a favorite among area residents. The lounge's decor reflected its local roots and connection to Carey's show. An autographed photo of Drew Carey hung on the wall, though the neon "Warsaw Tavern" sign had been taken down. The bar was described as a "shot and beer and game of pool" establishment.

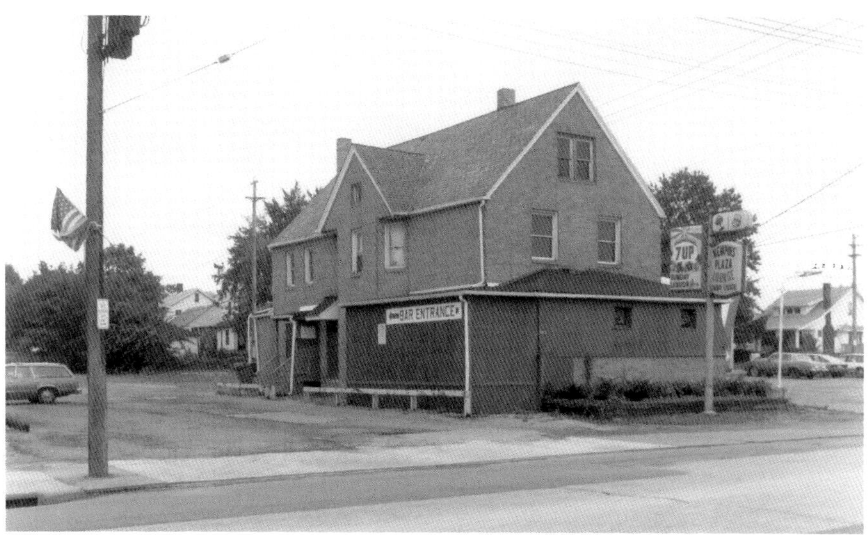

Memphis Plaza Lounge, 5303 Memphis, 1992. This bar was the inspiration for the Warsaw Tavern on *The Drew Carey Show*. *Cleveland Public Library/Photograph Collection.*

The Lounge became a point of curiosity for out-of-town visitors wondering whether the Warsaw Tavern from the show really existed. While the bar wasn't overtly "Drew-centric," its connection to Carey and its location in his old neighborhood made it a unique piece of Cleveland pop culture. After years of operating under its original name, the bar transformed into Murphy's Law Irish Pub in the early 2000s.

As we conclude our tour of Old Brooklyn, we pass by one final notable establishment: the Trio Tavern. This resilient institution has roots dating to the 1930s, when Andrew Skintek first opened it as a tavern. Despite facing numerous armed robberies over a fifteen-year period, Skintek persevered. In 1951, the establishment was rechristened the Trio Tavern, a name it proudly carried into the 2000s before evolving into the Memphis Station.

Our journey now takes us westward along Memphis Avenue, which eventually becomes West 117th Street. As we cross this boundary, we enter West Park, a historical area on Cleveland's West Side that was an independent municipality before being annexed by Cleveland in 1923. West Park covers twelve and a half square miles and is traditionally divided into four neighborhoods: Jefferson, Bellaire-Puritas, Kamm's Corners and Hopkins.

WEST SIDE STORIES: THE TAVERNS OF WEST PARK

As we drive north on West 117th Street, we enter the Jefferson neighborhood, part of the larger West Park area. The neighborhood offers a unique glimpse into Cleveland's westward expansion and development. Jefferson, originally part of Rockport Township in the early 1800s, remained largely rural throughout much of the nineteenth century, dominated by farms and greenhouse operations. The area began to develop when the suburb of West Park was established in 1900, carved out from Rockport Township.

Jefferson's growth accelerated dramatically following its annexation by Cleveland. The population surged from just 1,430 in 1910 to over 17,000 by 1930, driven by retail and residential development. Unlike many Cleveland neighborhoods, Jefferson has maintained a relatively stable population over the decades. It's a multicultural community of about 16,000 residents with a diverse demographic makeup, including a substantial Irish community; growing Hispanic and Latino and African-American populations; and a significant immigrant presence from the Middle East, Latin America, Romania and Southeast Asia.

On our drive, we pass Walter's Bar, later known as Squire's Inn, before heading west on Lorain Avenue, the hub of activity in the Jefferson neighborhood. In 1964, this bustling stretch boasted eleven taverns between West 117th and West 150th Street, many of which frequently changed ownership, reflecting the evolving social landscape of the late 1960s. We pass by Mehling's Tavern, which underwent several transformations over the decades. It became the Kent Lounge in the 1970s, followed by the Bacardi Lounge during the 1980s and the Dry Dock in the early 2000s.

One establishment that has stood the test of time is the Pride of Erin at 12228 Lorain. The bar was purchased by John Campbell in 1982, marking the beginning of its transformation into one of Cleveland's best-loved Irish pubs. John, a native of County Mayo, Ireland, infused the pub with an authentic Irish atmosphere and the Irish dedication to the game of darts. As Frank Pratt, a member of the Darter Hall of Fame, noted, the pub is "widely regarded as the dean of Cleveland darters."

The bar's interior reflects its Irish heritage: walls lined with dartboards against a green background evoke the fields of Ireland. The bar is famous for its perfectly poured pints of Guinness. As bartender Jimmy Coleman proudly states, "We've got good Guinness, and it's poured right." The bar serves a signature "half and half"—an Imperial pint glass filled just above halfway with Harp and topped off with Guinness, creating a definitive and resolute line between the two.

The Pride of Erin's commitment to quality and community has not gone unnoticed. In 2017, Jimmy Campbell was voted the best bartender in Cleveland in a Cleveland.com survey, garnering an impressive 48 percent of eleven thousand votes. This recognition speaks volumes about the pub's enduring popularity and the strong connections it has forged with its patrons over the years.

Today, the Pride of Erin continues to serve as a beloved fixture in the neighborhood. It stands as a testament to the enduring appeal of a well-run, community-focused tavern, bridging the gap between old-world charm and modern-day Cleveland.

A few blocks west, we encounter Vicki's Tavern, an establishment with a remarkable history. It was owned by Victoria Ibrahim, a pioneering woman in Cleveland's bar industry. Ibrahim's career began after Prohibition when

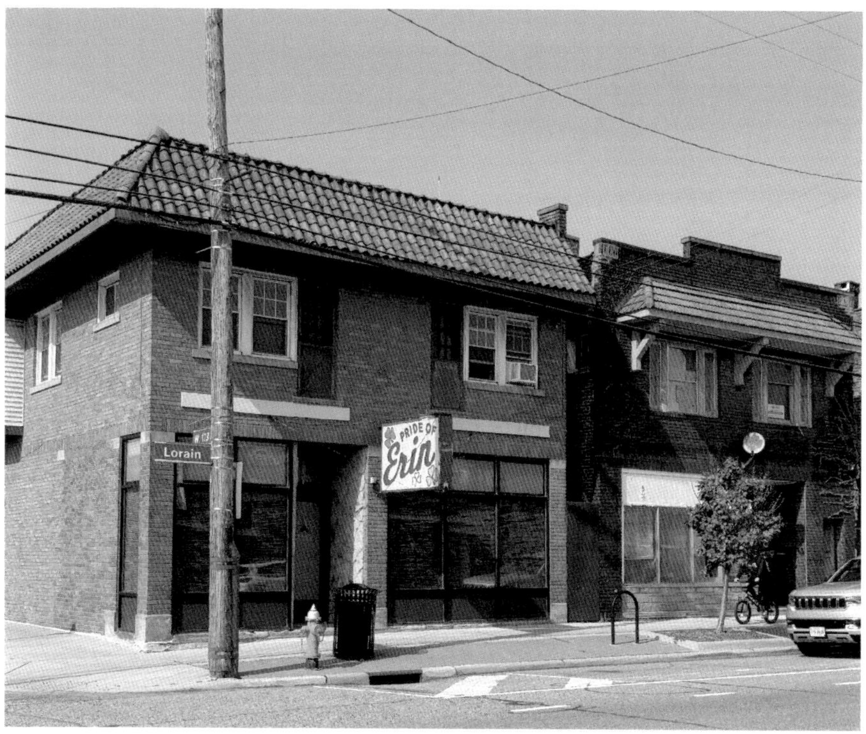

The popular Irish pub the Pride of Erin at West 123rd and Lorain. *Author's photo, September 2023.*

she opened Honey's Cafe, at a time when female bar owners were a rarity. In the 1940s, she owned Club 5000 at West Fiftieth and Lorain Avenue; in the 1950s, she established Vicki's Tavern on Lorain Avenue, which remained a neighborhood fixture for over twenty years.

After Ibrahim's tenure, the location continued to evolve, becoming the Boardwalk Lounge and, later, Cherrie's Lounge, which featured go-go dancers. The small brick building remains standing and has housed several establishments over the last decade, including Junior's Pub, Villaforte's Social Lounge (a gay bar) and Azure's Social Lounge. This progression from woman-owned neighborhood bar to entertainment venue with go-go dancers and then to a gay bar illustrates the changing social norms and business models in Cleveland's tavern scene over the decades.

In the 1960s, the stretch of Lorain from West 130th to West 150th Street was home to several bars, including Herzog's, Zemba's Cafe, Mayer's Cafe (later Charlie's), Nolan's, B&E Cafe and the Zephyr. Let's focus on Zemba's at 13334 Lorain Avenue. This building has a varied history, starting as a shoe repair store in the 1930s before becoming a candy store.

In the early 1980s, the location transformed into the highly popular Irish bar the Blarney Stone when the McGowan family from County Mayo took over. The Blarney Stone quickly established itself as more than just an Irish-themed establishment. As one review put it, "What's your poison, Guinness or Bud? This old-school joint serves both—and the people who drink them." It wasn't an "Irish theme park" but rather a genuine corner bar with a lively spirit, known for its perfect pour of Guinness and enthusiastic St. Patrick's Day celebrations.

The bar's journey continued with further transformations. In 2012, it became the Frosty Beaver Saloon, later evolving into the Flerish Wine and Grill. Looking ahead to 2025 there are plans to reopen the space as Bad Medicine, advertised as a "listening bar" that will combine music, cocktails and food.

Further down Lorain Avenue, we encounter the Normandy Tavern at 13999 Lorain, a location with a rich and sometimes tumultuous history dating to the end of Prohibition. In its early years, the establishment faced several tragedies. In 1934, a patron was shot in the neck and killed. Four years later, in 1938, the owner and patrons were robbed at gunpoint. Tragedy struck again in 1941 when the owner, Christian Waldenmaier, died of pneumonia at the young age of fifty-seven.

Over the decades, the bar underwent several transformations. It operated as the West 140th Cafe for a time before becoming the Normandy Tavern.

In 1995, it briefly rebranded as the Haus of Blues, billed as Cleveland's only German blues bar, an intriguing but short-lived concept. After just a few years, it reverted to the Normandy Tavern.

A November 30, 2018 review in the *Plain Dealer* paints a vivid picture of its character: "Let's get it straight: This is as dive-y a bar as you'll find in town. The drinks are dirt-cheap—$1.75 bottles and $2 mixed drinks. The milieu? Well, the joint is gritty but just right with an old, well-worn bowling machine and all sorts of union bumper stickers on the wall." This description fits the working-class spirit that has defined many of Cleveland's neighborhood bars over the years.

As we cross the invisible border between Jefferson and the Kamm's Corner neighborhood, we encounter the site of the former Zephyr Bar at 14737 Lorain Avenue. This location has a rich history dating to 1926, when the building was constructed as the Marquard Building, housing the Marquard Sash and Door Manufacturing Company. This company, with roots stretching back to the Civil War era, held the distinction of being Cleveland's oldest residential builder.

The building's transformation into the Zephyr Bar in the 1940s marked the beginning of its long tenure as a neighborhood tavern. Following the Zephyr's closure, the space evolved into the Honky Tonk Saloon, offering nightly country western music and adding a new flavor to the area's nightlife.

In 2011, the establishment became Cowan's Tavern, quickly developing a devoted base of patrons. The tavern became such an integral part of the community that several regulars chose to have their memorial services and celebrations of life held there, a testament to the strong bonds formed within its walls.

Despite strong opposition from local preservationists and longtime patrons, the building was demolished in 2022 to make way for new development at the corner of West 150th and Lorain. This controversial decision marked the end of an era for this historic site, reflecting the ongoing tension between preservation and progress in Cleveland's evolving neighborhoods.

As we leave behind the memories of the Zephyr Bar and its successors, we enter Kamm's Corner, a neighborhood with its own unique tavern history.

Kamm's Corner: Where History and Hops Intersect

As we enter Kamm's Corner, we find ourselves in a unique Cleveland neighborhood where the tavern scene has bucked the trend. While many areas of the city have seen a decline in neighborhood bars, Kamm's Corner has maintained, and in some ways expanded, its local tavern culture. Named after Oswald Kamm, a Swiss immigrant who established a general store and post office at the intersection of Lorain Avenue and Rocky River Drive in 1875, Kamm's Corner has evolved into a lively suburban-like neighborhood within Cleveland's city limits. Its population, 14,061 in 1940, reached its peak of 26,750 in 1970 before settling to about 23,000 as of this writing. Kamm's Corner has maintained its appeal, particularly among young professionals, including Cleveland firefighters and police officers, for its abundance of owner-occupied homes and, of course, its thriving bar and restaurant scene.

Kamm's Corner boasts the highest concentration of Irish Americans in both Cleveland and Cuyahoga County, a heritage vividly reflected in many of its pubs and taverns. This rich cultural identity is celebrated annually through the Hooley on Kamm's Corner, a vibrant festival that has become a cornerstone event for the neighborhood. The Hooley, derived from the Irish word for "party" or "celebration," transforms the streets into a lively showcase of Irish culture, featuring traditional music, dance, food and, of course, plenty of Guinness on draft.

This thriving tavern culture is not without its challenges and controversies. Over the years, Kamm's Corner has seen its share of debates over gaming machines, changing regulations and the balance between maintaining a neighborhood feel and attracting visitors from across the city. From traditional Irish pubs that honor the area's heritage to modern sports bars and eclectic lounges, Kamm's Corner offers a microcosm of Cleveland's drinking culture. The neighborhood has become known for its pub crawls, where patrons can experience a variety of atmospheres and offerings within a short walking distance.

Our journey leads us westward along Lorain Avenue toward Rocky River Drive, the very intersection where Oswald Kamm established his general store nearly 150 years ago. The first stop on our route is Irish 32—a relatively new name for a location with a rich tavern history. The space was home to the Golden Anchor Bar in 1970, later becoming Jami's Restaurant and Lounge in the 1980s. By the 1990s, it was as Bartley; it went on to operate as West Park Village Tavern for many years. Though Irish 32 carried on the Irish tavern legacy in more recent years, it has since closed, leaving behind another chapter in the location's history.

Just down the street at 15813 Lorain, we find A Bar, an establishment with a history stretching back to the 1920s, when the storefront originally served as a barbershop. In 1935, it was transformed into Far-Mor Café, a beloved local pub owned for many years by Michael Farry, who was honored as Irishman of the Year by the Shamrock Club in 1997. Sadly, Farry passed away unexpectedly in 1998. In 2008, the bar was featured in a *Plain Dealer* article due to its involvement in a legal dispute concerning the use of gas cards as prizes in the controversial Tic-Tac-Fruit game. The bar, along with other local establishments, faced scrutiny as state authorities questioned the legality of offering such prizes. After years of serving the community as the Far-Mor Café, the bar was rebranded as A Bar in 2017.

Our third stop takes us to Throwback Sports Bar at 16612 Lorain, where the motto "Let the old times roll" perfectly captures the spirit of this location's rich history. While Throwback has been a neighborhood staple for at least fifteen years, the space has hosted a variety of bars since the 1970s. In the mid-2000s, it was known as Price's Pub, and before that, it was Graven's Lounge, Rusty Nail Saloon, Mularkey's and the Choir Loft. The location's longest-running incarnation was the Castlebar, from 1986 to 2003, a name that pays homage to the area's strong Irish heritage.

A large cluster of pubs can be found around West 170th Street, each with its own unique history. One such establishment is Back Stage Bar, which has undergone several transformations since the 1920s. Initially a candy store, it later became a grocery store before evolving into a tavern and restaurant. Known as Arcade Tavern and popular for its karaoke, it rebranded as Back Stage Bar in 2008 and continues to operate under this name today.

Directly across the street stands Smedley's, a neighborhood fixture from 2001 until its closure in 2024. In a report for the *Plain Dealer's Friday Magazine* on July 20, 2012, John Petkovic described Smedley's as a time capsule, taking patrons "back to the days when classic rock ruled and people partied like it was the 1970s." Further capturing the neighborhood bar atmosphere, *The Scene Magazine* featured an interview with Smedley's owner, former Marine Sean Mettler, on July 31, 2013. Mettler proudly stated, "I only book the best bands in town. We got voted three years in a row for best blues bar, and for the last four years, we placed fourth for best live music venue. There might be 100 motorcycles out front, but this is the safest place you can be."

Before becoming Smedley's, the location housed a series of different establishments. It was previously known as Kamm's Pub, Kamm's Picture This Bar and Grill, the Closing Room and Blue Lite Lounge; the latter featured topless dancers. In the 1960s, it operated as King's Lounge.

Crossing the street once more, we encounter West Park Station, a tavern whose evolution mirrors that of many establishments in the area. Opened in 2006, West Park Station has worn multiple hats, functioning as a sports bar, Irish pub and music venue and even experimenting with comedy acts. The building's history extends far beyond its current incarnation as a tavern. For nearly seven decades, from the late 1920s to 1990, this location was home to Riverside Hardware, a cornerstone of the neighborhood's commercial landscape. Walter Lucien, the store's proprietor, ran the business from its inception until his death in 1977, representing the kind of long-standing, locally owned enterprise that once defined many Cleveland neighborhoods.

Our final stop is the Public House, the cornerstone of this Irish bar community and the elder statesman among the cluster of taverns in the area. Established in the early 1980s, it predates many neighboring taverns. The Public House takes pride in maintaining its legacy as a welcoming neighborhood bar and restaurant. The history of this location brings us back to Joyce's Restaurant and Tavern, which operated for decades. Even earlier, this site housed the original Riverside Hardware before it relocated a few blocks down the street.

This pattern of repurposing buildings from practical, home-themed businesses to taverns continues with P.J. McIntyre's, near the corner of Lorain Avenue and Rocky River Drive. The bar opened in 2007 and was conceptualized with the neighborhood's character at the forefront, designed as an authentic Irish pub, from its ambiance to its draft selections and

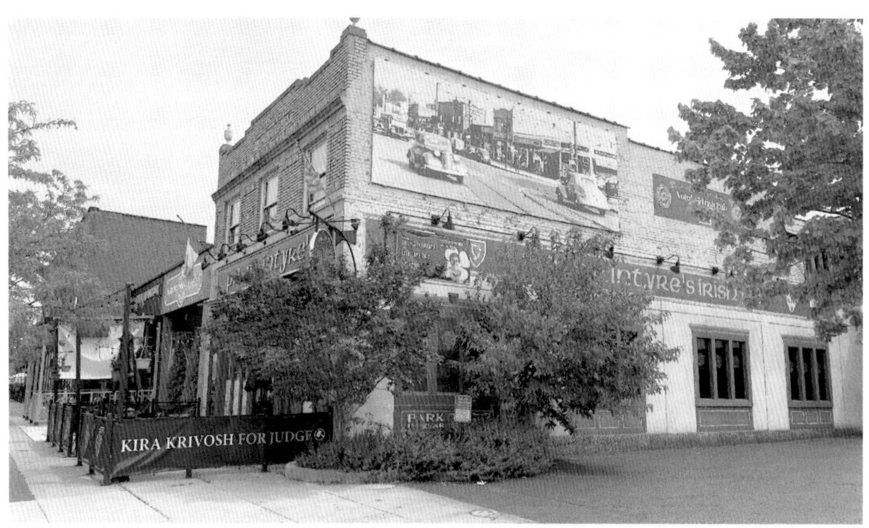

P.J. McIntyre's Irish Pub, center of Kamms Corner, August 2024. *Author's photo.*

traditional Irish fare. This attention to detail reflects the area's strong Irish American heritage and the owner's commitment to creating a genuine experience. Prior to becoming P.J. McIntyre's, this location housed the National Loan and Finance for many years, followed by the West End Appliance Store.

Interstates and Intersections: The Taverns of West Boulevard and Cudell

Our journey now takes us eastward along Lorain Avenue, into the heart of two distinctive neighborhoods: West Boulevard and Cudell. Nestled between I-90 and I-71, these communities offer a unique perspective on how Cleveland's tavern culture has adapted to urban changes and demographic shifts. The West Boulevard neighborhood is named after the north–south road that runs through its center. Once home to Hungarian, Czech and German immigrants, the area has, in recent decades, become a vibrant community with a growing Hispanic population, primarily from Puerto Rico, El Salvador and Mexico. The neighborhood is home to just under twenty thousand residents.

Adjacent to West Boulevard is Cudell, a neighborhood named after Frank E. Cudell, a German-born architect who developed the area in the early 1900s and designed several notable West Side churches, homes and businesses. Like its neighbor, Cudell has transitioned from a predominantly working-class, factory-oriented community into a diverse enclave. Much of the industry that once lined the railyards has disappeared, partly due to the construction of I-90 in the 1960s. The population has also declined, with fewer than ten thousand residents now nestled just north of the freeway.

We enter the West Boulevard neighborhood at the corner of Lorain and West 117th, once home to Tony's Diner, where Cleveland Mayor Dennis Kucinich held court during his brief tenure from 1977 to 1979. In the 1960s, this stretch of Lorain Avenue from West 117th to Clark Avenue was lined with twelve bars. The first bar we'll pass, located at 11619 Lorain, has gone through many names over the years, including the Norka Cafe in the 1950s, the Bow String Inn in the 1960s and Chevalier Lounge until the early 1970s; for the next decade, it was the Grapevine Lounge. In the mid-1980s, the building transitioned into a thrift shop and later became the Cleveland Mofongo Latin Grill. Continuing, we pass Mike & Addy's at West 110th and make a stop at Town Lounge Liquor at 10705 Lorain.

This location has a colorful history spanning nearly a century. The story begins in 1927 when it was raided by Prohibition agents, setting the stage for decades of intrigue and transformation. In the 1940s, it was Coffey's Lounge before evolving into the Town Lounge. The venue, which initially featuring weekend country music, adapted to changing tastes, adding polka and go-go girls to its entertainment lineup by the late 1960s.

The Town Lounge gained notoriety in January 1977 when it became the backdrop for an unusual incident. As reported in the *Plain Dealer* on January 17, police dramatically interrupted a wedding reception at the bar, arresting the bride, Eve Cipher—who also managed the establishment—and taking her to Central Police Station for questioning about a fatal shooting. Meanwhile, 125 guests remained at the venue, waiting hours for her release from jail.

The bar's history took another dark turn in the late 1970s, when Elmer Brittain, an associate of infamous Cleveland mobster Danny Greene, was found shot to death in an apartment above the bar. In 1983, the establishment reinvented itself with the grand opening of After Ours, which transformed into to Scaramouche Lounge in 1986 and operated under this name until it became Buggatti's Westown Café in the 1990s. In more recent years, the location has moved away from its bar roots, housing a Hot Spot fashion and tobacco store and finally becoming Better Uz fashions.

A few blocks down at 10510 Lorain Avenue stood the Hollywood Café. William and Helen Feyjes opened this working-class establishment in the late 1940s, nurturing it into a neighborhood fixture for over three decades. Their commitment to the community was evident in the café's longevity: it served as a gathering place for local residents until the building's demolition in 2017.

As we continue down Lorain Avenue, we encounter two bars that once faced each other, each with its own rich history. Ray's Café at 10416 Lorain was a popular spot during the 1960s and '70s. This building had previously housed Kilroy's Bar until the late 1940s. The building served as the home of the Cleveland Association of the Deaf from the early 1990s into the 2010's. Today, the building stands vacant, its deteriorating condition a stark reminder of the area's changing fortunes.

Directly across the street stood Norm's Tavern, owned and operated by Norman Skaroupka from 1947 until his untimely death in 1975 at the age of fifty-eight. For twenty-eight years, Norm was known for his generous sponsorship of bowling and softball teams, fostering a loyal crowd at his neighborhood bar. Following Norm's passing, the building briefly housed

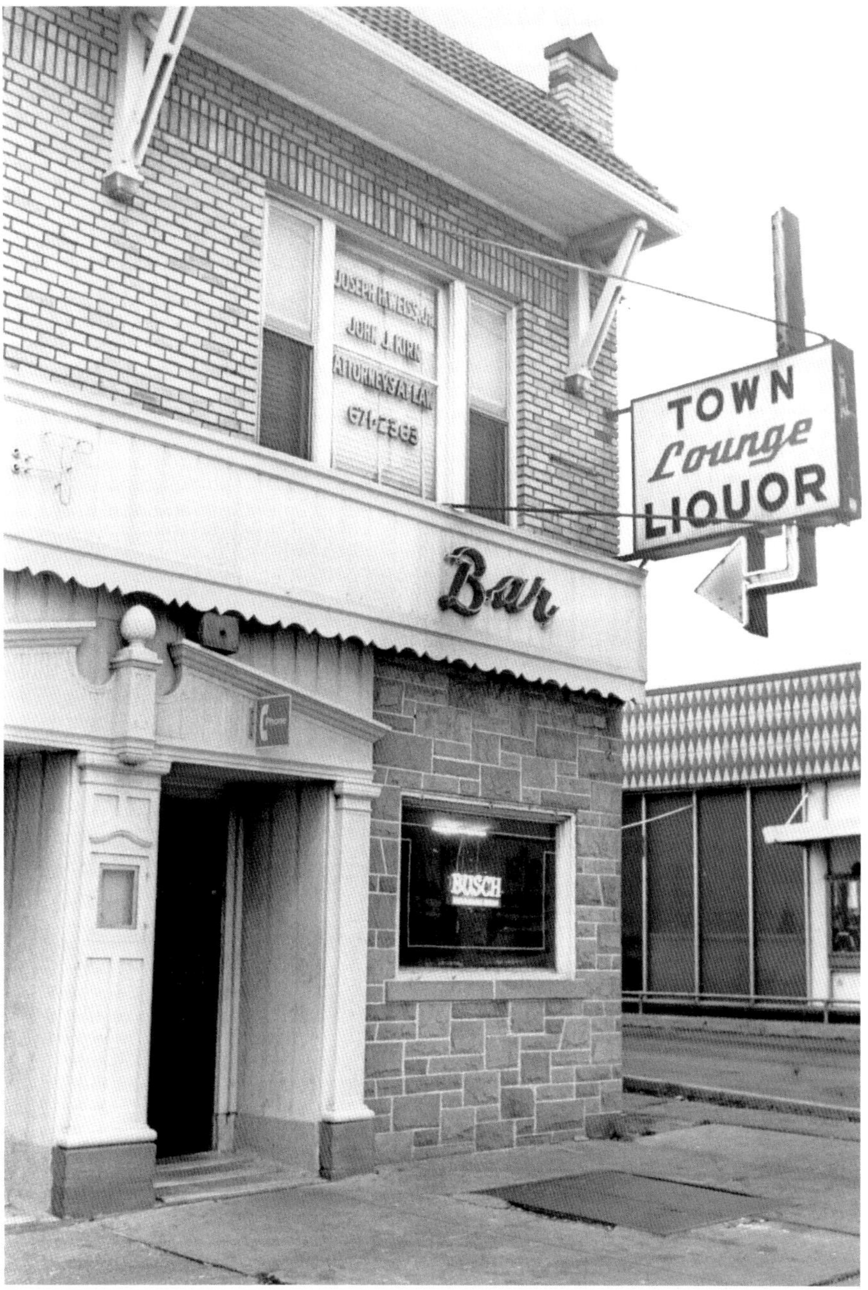

Town Lounge, 10705 Lorain, 1970s. *Cleveland Press Collection, Cleveland State University, Michael Schwartz Library Special Collection.*

the Moravian Restaurant before becoming the Deerhunter Bar in 1979. The bar's tenure was marked by tragedy. In July 1979, new owner William Howell fatally shot a customer who, after being refused service, lunged at him with a knife.

Subsequently, the establishment underwent several more transformations. It became O'Connell's Tavern in 1981, later evolved into McKenna's Pub and, most recently operated as Cheap Shotz. While the building still stands, it no longer functions as a tavern, marking the end of its long history as a drinking establishment.

Our final stop on Lorain Avenue brings us to Izzo's Café, a venerable neighborhood tavern that was a community fixture since 1936. Founded by Carmine Izzo, the establishment remained a constant presence in the community for over eight decades, with only three owners over that span. While the original sign may have been replaced, the Izzo name continued to grace the façade, symbolizing its legacy. However, in 2024, Izzo's closed its doors, marking the end of an era.

As we conclude our exploration of Lorain Avenue's tavern scene, we'll bypass several other notable establishments: Diana's Lounge, Marlo's Bar, Frank's Café and Mary's Café. We'll shift our focus to another long-standing neighborhood fixture, steering our journey toward Glunz Café on West 105th Street.

The Glunz Café was a neighborhood institution, serving as a cornerstone of the community for nearly half a century. When Fred and Irene Glunz opened this working-class tavern in 1953, the location had already been operating as a bar since the end of Prohibition. As reported by Michael O'Malley in the *Plain Dealer* on August 6, 1999, the establishment was known for its no-frills atmosphere: ordering anything as fancy as a sloe gin fizz was almost considered heresy. Fred, at seventy-six, and Irene, at seventy-five, were fixtures behind the bar, pouring Corby's whiskey for the "elbow crowd" and upholding traditions like closing on Sundays because "people should be home with their families."

The café cultivated a fiercely loyal clientele, including local softball players, who would often pack the bar after a game played by one of the teams sponsored by Glunz. By 1999, after nearly five decades of serving the community, Fred and Irene had decided it was time to sell the café. The announcement brought a mix of sadness and nostalgia from longtime regulars. As Fred poignantly remarked, "I don't want to die behind here," signaling the end of an era for the beloved establishment. After the Glunz family stepped away, the bar continued to serve as a neighborhood gathering

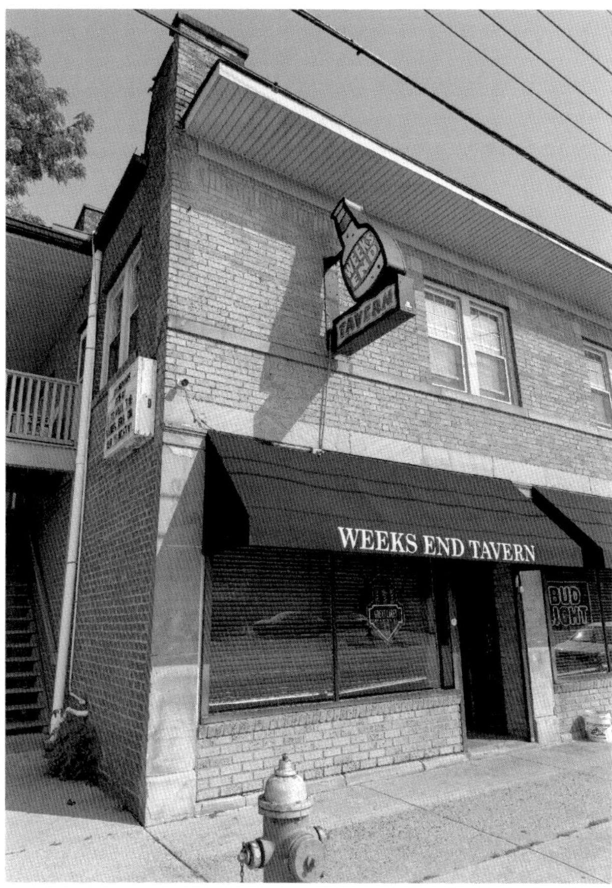

Left: Weeks End Tavern, previously Glunz Café for over fifty years. *Author's photo, September. 2024.*

Below: Judd's City Tavern, 10323 Madison, August 2024. *Author's photo.*

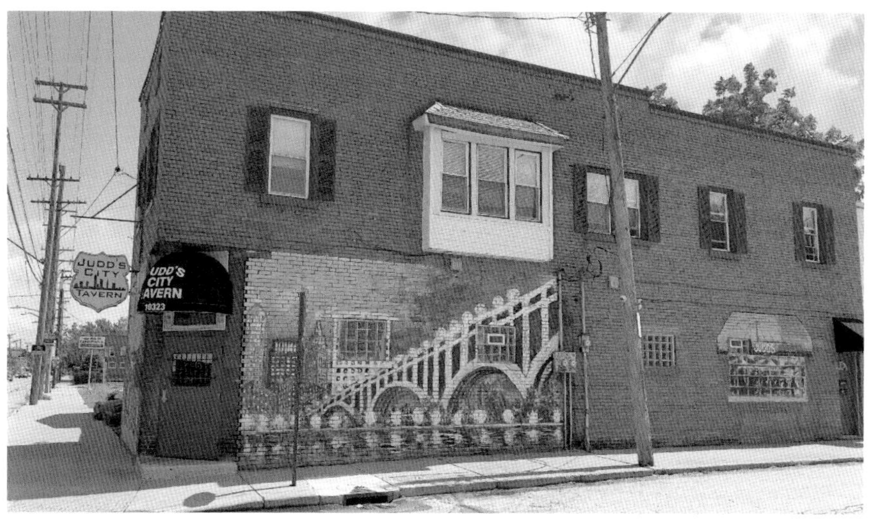

spot under new ownership as the Weeks End Tavern. Although this marked the end of the Glunz era, the transition ensured that the location remained a vital part of the community.

As we head north through the Cudell neighborhood, we stop on Madison Avenue, which had its share of taverns in the 1960s. There were four bars between West Ninety-Fifth and West 101st: Norm's Café (later known as Margie's, in the 1990s), McLaughlin Bar, Sam's Café and Rock's Café. A quick stop in the past reveals that several of these taverns had rough reputations. McLaughlin's was previously known as Murphy's Bar, and in 1957, a pool game dispute there tragically escalated into murder. The shooter was convicted and sentenced to life in prison. In 1996, the same bar, then operating as the Midnight Star, saw another fatal shooting. A security guard, angered by being forced to leave the bar for bringing in his own liquor, returned and shot CMHA Patrolman Derrik Lanier multiple times; he was convicted and received a thirty-three-year prison sentence. Just a block away, at Sam's Café, more trouble erupted in 1957. In a shocking incident, a woman fatally shot her estranged husband at Sam's Café after urging him to kiss their son one last time. She then turned the gun on herself, though she survived.

Let's leave Cudell on a brighter note with a visit to Judd's City Tavern, located at 10323 Madison Avenue. This corner spot has a long history, originally serving as a grocery and meat market dating to the early 1920s. Over the years, it was home to various taverns, including Triggers, Mariell's and the J&K Lounge. In 2018, it transformed into Judd's City Tavern, a bar with a nostalgic flair that takes patrons back to the taverns of yesteryear. Decorated with vintage Cleveland memorabilia, Judd's offers a glimpse into the city's bar history while providing friendly service and affordable drinks.

Although Judd's is a relative newcomer to Madison Avenue, its commitment to preserving the past gives it a timeless charm. Now that we've enjoyed a taste of history here, it's time to head over to the Detroit-Shoreway and Edgewater neighborhoods.

INDUSTRY AND RESILIENCE: THE EVOLUTION OF DETROIT-SHOREWAY AND EDGEWATER

The Detroit-Shoreway and Edgewater neighborhoods carry a rich history, shaped by industry, immigration and resilience. The northern edge of Detroit-Shoreway saw its first wave of development in the 1850s, driven by the construction of railroads that spurred the growth of local factories and manufacturing plants. By the 1860s, Detroit Avenue was flourishing, full of homes and businesses, laying the foundation for what is now known as Gordon Square. The area was a melting pot of immigrants from Ireland, Germany, Italy and Romania, who brought with them their traditions and established a vibrant community.

Just across Detroit Avenue, the Edgewater area emerged in the late nineteenth century as a haven for Cleveland's elite, known for its grand estates along the lakefront. As the twentieth century progressed, both neighborhoods underwent significant changes, including postwar economic shifts and the construction of major highways that reshaped the urban landscape. The effects of White flight and economic decline posed challenges, but the resilience of these communities prevailed.

In recent years, Detroit-Shoreway and Edgewater have experienced remarkable revitalization, fueled by community efforts to preserve historic architecture and encourage new development. Today, Detroit-Shoreway is home to a diverse population of approximately 17,000 residents, while about 5,850 call Edgewater home.

Leaving Cudell behind, we continue north on West 117th Street toward Detroit Avenue, a main thoroughfare long before the interstate system reshaped the city's landscape. Detroit Avenue stretches through the heart of three northwest Cleveland neighborhoods: Edgewater, Detroit-Shoreway and Ohio City. During the 1960s, this four-mile stretch was home to no fewer than twenty-six neighborhood bars. Let's select a few and explore their unique identities.

At 11619 Detroit Avenue stands a building with a history that stretches back to the early 1900s. Originally home to Lakewood Electric and Wilson's Drug Store, the structure housed various restaurants through the 1940s before becoming the Tudor Inn in the 1950s. In 1959, it took on a new identity as Brothers Lounge, which started as a neighborhood tavern and gradually evolved into the popular lounge and music venue it remains today. Brothers quickly gained a reputation as a premier spot for jazz and blues, attracting renowned musicians such as local legend Robert Lockwood Jr., B.B. King and Buddy Guy.

Brothers Lounge closed in the late 1990s. The building was sold at a sheriff's auction and given a second chance when new owners purchased it in 2004. After a complete renovation, Brothers Lounge reopened in 2008 and expanded to include the adjacent space. Today, it boasts three distinct sections: a pub, a wine bar and a music venue. Brothers continues to be a staple of the local music scene, offering live performances almost every night and showcasing top local talent.

Our next stop is Ninety-Three Hundred Café at 9208 Detroit Avenue. In 1971, the owner, Otto Kozak, was beaten and robbed of $2,500 he had on hand to cash customers' paychecks. In the 1980s, the establishment transformed into California Nites, a gay bar known for its lively atmosphere. However, tragedy struck in 1987 when a woman was fatally shot in the bar by her boyfriend's ex-girlfriend. By the 1990s, the bar had become Rockies, another gay bar, named after its owner, Rocky Archacki. Rockies featured a bar, patio, dance floor, pool table and game room, and it was very active in supporting the gay community through hosting themed events and fundraisers for LGBTQ+ causes, including the Northern Ohio Coalition's annual Easter Basket Auction.

After operating for nearly twelve years, Rockies closed its doors in 2006, and the bar reopened as Cocktails Cleveland. Sadly, Cocktails experienced its share of challenges, including violence, as reported in the *Plain Dealer* on September 13, 2013. Surveillance footage captured two separate hate crimes that month, in which groups of teenagers attacked both the bar and its patrons, including a physical assault on a twenty-eight-year-old man walking by. The incidents drew attention to ongoing issues of discrimination and violence against the LGBTQ+ community in the area.

Just down the street at 11217 Detroit there was another bar that catered to the gay community. It originally opened as the Tomahawk Café in 1934 and was owned by the Hoeller brothers for over thirty years. As the years passed, the bar evolved and became known as the Hawk, a well-known gay bar in the neighborhood. The *Plain Dealer* described the Hawk as a typical corner bar, reminiscent of *Cheers*. However, in this version, the theme song would end with: "Where everyone knows you're gay."

As we officially enter the Detroit-Shoreway neighborhood, we come upon the site of a very old-school bar at 7320 Detroit Avenue. The Cheerio Café opened shortly after Prohibition and quickly became a local favorite. However, its history was not without drama. In 1938, the café made headlines when a robber named Alvin Fletcher attempted to hold up the establishment. The proprietor, Edwin Arthur, defended the bar, fatally wounding Fletcher in a shootout. Unfortunately, Arthur was also seriously wounded by Fletcher's accomplice, though he survived. This violent episode was just one of several robberies the café endured during its first years of operation. The Cheerio Café continued to serve the community through the 1970s before eventually closing its doors. The building later became Banter Beer and Wine, which occupied the space from 2015 until it relocated farther down Detroit Avenue in 2019.

As we enter the heart of Gordon Square, particularly around West Sixty-Fifth Street, it's worth noting that by the late 1940s, this area had become one of the most tavern-congested neighborhoods in Cleveland. In February 1949, a *Plain Dealer* article highlighted the growing concerns of local residents and community leaders about the sheer number of bars and clubs saturating the area. At the time, the intersection of Detroit Avenue and West Fifty-Eighth Street alone boasted multiple taverns, and efforts to bring in more liquor establishments were met with strong resistance from neighborhood groups and churches. Despite the opposition, liquor permit applications continued to flow, reflecting the area's long-standing reputation as a hub for nightlife—a legacy that continues today.

The current site of Brewnuts, at 6501 Detroit Avenue, has seen many transformations over the years. In the 1940s, it was Lenihan's Grill, followed by the Avenue Bar and, later, the Detroiter Bar, in the 1960s. During its time as the Detroiter Bar, in January 1967, a violent incident occurred: four men were shot outside the bar after the bartender refused to serve five underage youths. A brawl broke out, and when the youths smashed the front door glass, loyal patrons followed them outside, where the argument escalated, leading to gunfire. Two of the men were seriously injured. By the 1970s, the establishment had become Rallis Lounge. It was a travel agency through the 1980s and 1990s before the popular Brewnuts finally settled in.

At 5801 Detroit Avenue, back in 1910, Patrick Gallagher made headlines for his unique approach to attracting customers. Gallagher offered free lunches at his tavern, charging one cent for ten tickets, which patrons could redeem for snacks. However, this promotion led to his arrest for violating Cleveland's new "no free lunch" law—a regulation designed to prevent saloon owners from enticing customers with food to encourage excessive beer consumption. Gallagher insisted he was within his rights, arguing that he should be allowed to give away lunches with beer if he wished. Gallagher's creative marketing exemplified the entrepreneurial spirit that has long characterized the area.

Fast-forward to 1949: the location at 5801 Detroit Avenue saw significant investment from John and Anna Socotch, who poured $120,000 into constructing a new building. Socotch aimed to transform the site into a modern venue but faced strong opposition from local community groups and clergy, who were concerned about the proliferation of taverns in the neighborhood. Despite Socotch's insistence that his investment was an

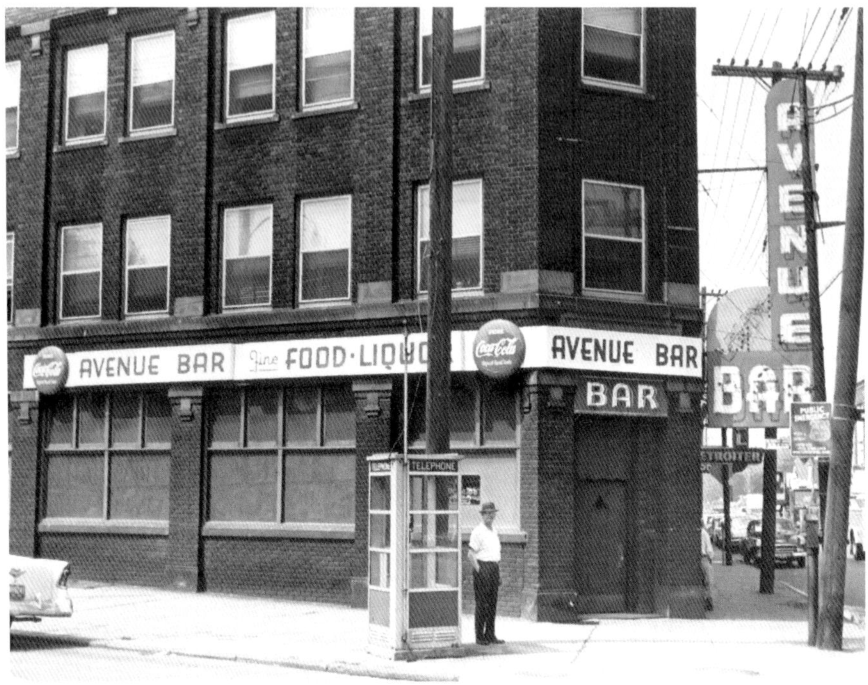

The Avenue Bar, 6501 Detroit, in the 1960s. *Cleveland Press Collection, Cleveland State University, Michael Schwartz Library Special Collection.*

improvement to the area, this dispute dragged on for over six years, leading to litigation that went all the way to the Ohio Supreme Court. Ultimately, Socotch never opened his tavern at the site. However, in 1960, William R. Krause acquired the building and secured the liquor license. Krause initially planned to open under the name Yankovic Bar—having purchased the license from the well-known polka band leader Frankie Yankovic—but intended to change the name later. This marked the beginning of a new chapter for the location, as Krause worked to establish the bar that Socotch never had the chance to open.

The bar eventually took the name Yankee Bar, and the Socotch family returned to operate the establishment. However, in 1966, John Socotch found himself in legal trouble again. This time, he was charged with violating a 1934 city ordinance that banned discrimination based on sex at public dances. The violation stemmed from a "Ladies' Night" promotion at the Yankee Bar, where women were admitted to a go-go dance for free while men were charged an entry fee. Socotch defended his actions, stating that he had waived the fee for women as a gesture of goodwill rather than a strategy to increase business. Despite his defense, Socotch was found guilty and fined fifty dollars plus court costs. His lawyer argued that the ordinance was unconstitutional and that Socotch could have avoided the charges by simply charging women a nominal fee.

The Yankee Bar offered nightly entertainment, including go-go dancers—and in 1972, the bar featured a particularly unique act. "Queenie," a 350-pound bouncer turned performer, captivated patrons with her snake-dancing routine. Draped in her size 54 dresses, Queenie danced with real live snakes, including a cobra named Satan and a garden snake named Gore. Her larger-than-life presence, combined with the exotic appeal of her act, kept customers coming back for more, adding a sideshow element to the bar's already lively atmosphere.

In 1981, the Yankee Bar went up for sale, and after a series of changes, it eventually became Happy Dog, which it remains today. Starting in 1998, the bar became a popular meeting spot for patrons gearing up for the North Coast Ghost Tour. In 2008, Happy Dog underwent a much-needed makeover when Sean Kilbane and his partners took over, transforming it into a vibrant music venue that continues to thrive. Today, Happy Dog is known for its eclectic live music performances and its famous gourmet hot

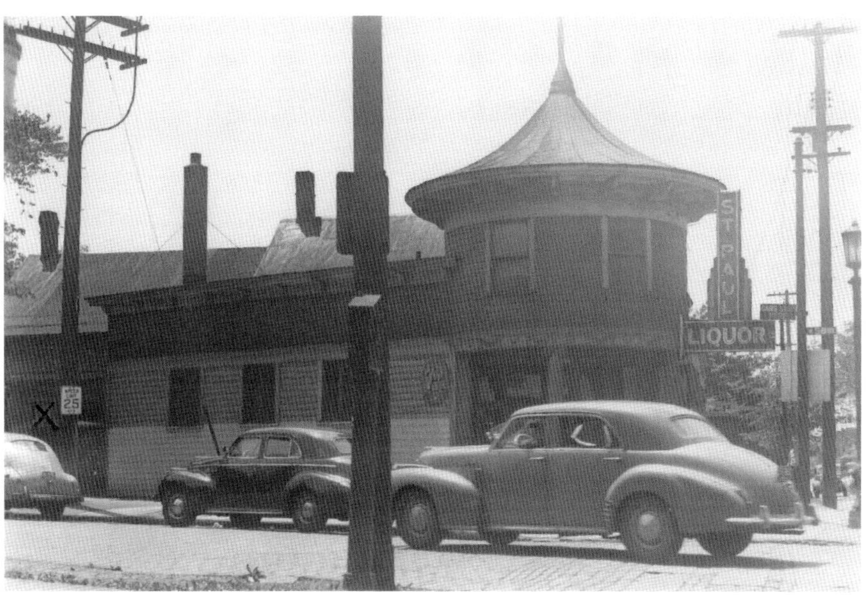

The St. Paul Tavern, 5801 Detroit Avenue, 1947—current location of the Happy Dog. *Cleveland Public Library/Photograph Collection.*

dogs, which come with unconventional toppings like Froot Loops. Whether you're there for the music or the quirky food, Happy Dog offers a unique and memorable experience.

Since we're already on West Fifty-Eighth, we'll head down the road to the Parkview Nite Club, which was also owned by John and Anna Socotch for decades, starting in the 1930s. The Socotch family remained connected to the bar; a family member tended bar there for decades. Nestled in the heart of the Detroit-Superior neighborhood, the building looks more like a nondescript brick structure than a dive bar. Although the area has seen signs of gentrification and is now surrounded by new apartments, the Parkview has retained the charm and grit that define both the neighborhood and Cleveland. Inside, you're reminded that this bar has been around forever by plush red booths lining one wall and low tables scattered throughout. The long, old wooden bar is surrounded by an eclectic array of wall art, from classic Cleveland sports memorabilia to framed tributes to the city's rich urban history.

The Parkview's blend of nostalgia and authenticity earned it a feature on *Diners, Drive-Ins and Dives*. As one 2016 review aptly described it, "It's a cool place for shady people." Whether you're drawn in by its storied past or the

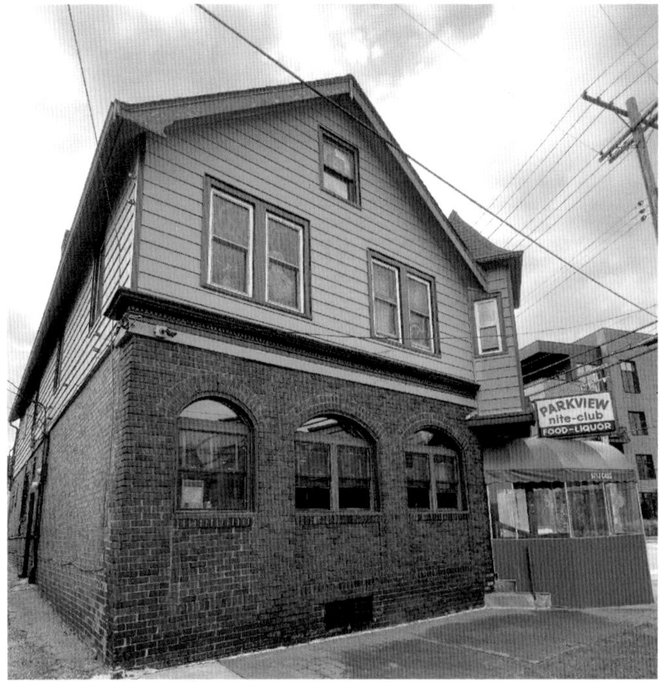

Parkview Nite Club 1261 West Fifty-Eighth, an iconic Detroit tavern for over ninety years. *Author's photo, August 2024.*

nightly specials, Parkview Nite Club remains a beloved fixture in Cleveland's bar scene.

Before we head back up to Detroit Avenue, we have a few more stops to make in the neighborhood. At 1306 West Sixty-Fifth Street, you'll find Stone Mad Pub, which opened in 2008. This location has a long history in the neighborhood, dating to 1912, when the building was originally constructed as a tavern and storehouse by the Leisy Brewing Company.

Leisy Brewing was Cleveland's largest brewery at the turn of the century, when it was common practice for breweries to own taverns to promote and sell their products directly to consumers. During Prohibition, the tavern operated as a speakeasy, which was known for its Romanian, Irish and Italian bootleggers. After Prohibition ended, the space transitioned into an Italian workers' social club, reflecting the strong ethnic identity of the neighborhood at the time.

In the 1960s, Italo DiRuggiero turned the establishment into the I&R Bar. Its name was short for Italian and Romanian Bar, highlighting the blend of cultures in the area. In May 1969, tragedy struck when DiRuggiero was gunned down while walking to his car after closing the bar for the night. He was shot by a gunman in a slow-moving car, a crime that rattled the community since there was no apparent motive.

By the 1980s, the bar had become the R&A Lounge, which continued to operate until the early 2000s. In 2004, Pete Leneghan and Eileen Sammon, who both grew up in Cleveland's Irish community, purchased the deteriorating tavern. Despite the building's poor condition, they were committed to preserving its history. After an extensive restoration and renovation, Stone Mad Pub opened in 2008, offering a fresh take on the neighborhood bar while respecting its roots.

Leneghan and Sammon, through the city's Storefront Restoration Program, restored the façade to its original 1912 appearance. They thoughtfully repurposed materials throughout the pub, using stones from an old city street for the patio and salvaging sandstone tables and seating. Light fixtures were sourced from a historic Tremont building, and the front room was designed as a traditional Irish pub with a black walnut bar. Today, Stone Mad remains a beloved neighborhood spot, offering a welcoming atmosphere that blends the rich history of the area with a modern twist on the classic pub experience.

Our last stop is at 5400 Herman Avenue, home to Tina's Nite Club. This small brick building may not look like much from the outside, but it has earned its reputation as one of Cleveland's best dive bars for cheap beer and karaoke. The unpretentious bar is often packed with regulars and visitors waiting to sing their favorite '80s songs. Now it's time to head east on Detroit Avenue and into Ohio City.

Tapping Into Ohio City: A Pub Crawler's Paradise

The Ohio City neighborhood, one of Cleveland's oldest, traces its roots to 1818, when it was founded as part of Brooklyn Township. Ohio City was initially an independent municipality, and its early years were defined by a fierce rivalry with its eastern neighbor, Cleveland, which even led to civil skirmishes during the 1830s. At that time, Ohio City had a population of two thousand. It was finally annexed to Cleveland in 1854 and was known as the Near West Side.

As the nineteenth century progressed, Ohio City's demographic landscape began to shift. The area, originally populated primarily by descendants of English and German immigrants, welcomed waves of eastern Europeans in the early twentieth century to work in the industrial flats. Today, Ohio City is home to a diverse population of nine thousand that continues to grow. At the heart of Ohio City is the iconic West Side Market, a century-old institution that draws Clevelanders from across the city and is a must-see stop for visitors. The neighborhood has become a mecca for craft beer enthusiasts, boasting the highest concentration of breweries in Cleveland. This brewing renaissance began in 1988 with the opening of Great Lakes Brewing Company, Ohio's first craft brewery, and has since expanded to include numerous breweries throughout the area.

As we head east on Detroit Avenue, we come to the Harp, a well-known Irish pub that has been an anchor of the neighborhood since 1999. The Harp sits perched above the West Shoreway, and its patio provides a panoramic view of Lake Erie, the Industrial Flats and downtown Cleveland. The Harp—built by Irish-born Cleveland contractor Michael O'Malley for his daughter, pub owner Karen O'Malley—is decorated with Celtic designs, including a mural of the O'Malley ancestral home, a stone fireplace for those snowy winter nights and stained glass that was salvaged from St. Joseph Church. The Harp continues to be a beloved spot in Cleveland and is considered one of the best places to enjoy a pint while taking in the stunning views of Lake Erie.

As we continue toward West Twenty-Fifth Street, we pass the former site of the Crow's Nest, located at 3801 Detroit Avenue. Before Prohibition,

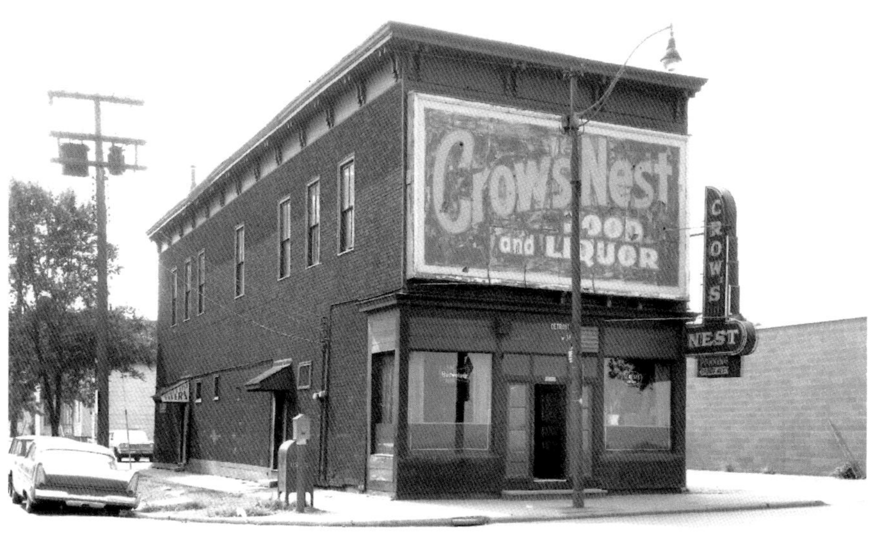

Crow's Nest, 3801 Detroit Avenue, 1950s. *Courtesy of the Old Brooklyn Historical Society, Frank Libal Collection.*

the building housed McIntyre's Tavern, which was forced to rebrand as McIntyre's Soft Drink Parlor during the dry years. However, this didn't stop the flow of illegal alcohol: police once confiscated $25,000 worth of liquor and wine from the owner's home. In 1929, the building was repurposed into a Studebaker and Nash car dealership; then Leo Crowe opened the Crow's Nest in 1935. The Crow's Nest became a beloved neighborhood fixture, operating for decades. Unfortunately, in 1986, the tavern suffered significant damage from a devastating arson fire.

At the corner of West Twenty-Sixth Street and Detroit Avenue, the old sign for Kiefer's Tavern still hangs on a century-old redbrick building in the now-revitalized Ohio City. Kiefer's, a German restaurant and tavern, operated from 1937 until 1991. Initially named Schwarzwald, the tavern was renamed Kiefer's during World War II due to anti-German sentiment.

Kiefer's quickly became a favorite, serving classic German dishes to nearly one thousand patrons a day at its peak. The tavern was known for its live music and vibrant social atmosphere, attracting politicians, businessmen and celebrities. In 1957, a ceiling collapse caused minor injuries and temporarily closed the establishment, but it rebounded when county treasurer Francis

Gaul purchased the iconic tavern. Kiefer's continued to thrive throughout the 1970s. However, despite efforts to modernize, the tavern couldn't withstand the economic challenges of the time, ultimately closing in 1991.

Just a few blocks away, near the corner of Detroit Avenue and West Twenty-Fifth Street, stood the now infamous Christy's Lounge. While the bar itself no longer exists, it played a notable role in Cleveland's underworld history. On March 29, 1975, notorious Cleveland racketeer Alex "Shondor" Birns was killed in a car bombing after leaving Christy's Lounge. Birns, mentioned earlier as part owner of taverns on Short Vincent, had been a fixture of Cleveland's criminal scene for decades. That evening, his life ended violently when a bomb exploded under the front seat of his Lincoln Continental. The massive explosion scattered parts of his vehicle across the street to St. Malachi's Church, marking the dramatic and bloody end of one of Cleveland's most infamous mobsters.

Like Kamm's Corner, there might be more bars on West Twenty-Fifth Street today than there were back in the 1960s and '70s. This stretch is now home to numerous brewpubs and bars, creating a vibrant nightlife scene. We've already passed Saucy Brew Works on Detroit and West Twenty-Ninth, and on West Twenty-Fifth alone, there's Bookhouse Brewing, Nano Brew, Market Garden Brewery and, of course, just around the corner, the granddaddy of them all: Great Lakes Brewing Company. But before we dive into the brewpub scene, let's make a stop at the Old Angle Tavern.

At first glance, the Old Angle Tavern might seem like a century-old Irish pub; however, the tavern's story is far more modern. The idea for the Old Angle, located at 1848 West Twenty-Fifth Street, was born in 2001 after a fire, along with changing shopping habits, forced the closure of a neighborhood hardware store. The vacant, burned-out Ohio City Hardware Building needed a new purpose to save it from demolition. The solution was to transform this 1906 space into a grand, old-school neighborhood Irish tavern that would help stabilize this prominent corner of the West Twenty-Fifth Street corridor, later known as the Market District.

Let's now stop at Bookhouse Brewing, located at 1526 West Twenty-Fifth Street. This building, dating to 1866, has a rich history that mirrors the evolution of the Ohio City neighborhood. Originally known as the Jacob Baehr Brewery, the establishment was founded by German immigrants Jacob and Magdalena Baehr. Tragically, Jacob passed away just seven years after opening the brewery, leaving Magdalena to raise their eight children while also managing the business. Magdalena carried on as "Cleveland's Widow Brewer" and successfully grew the brewery over the next twenty-

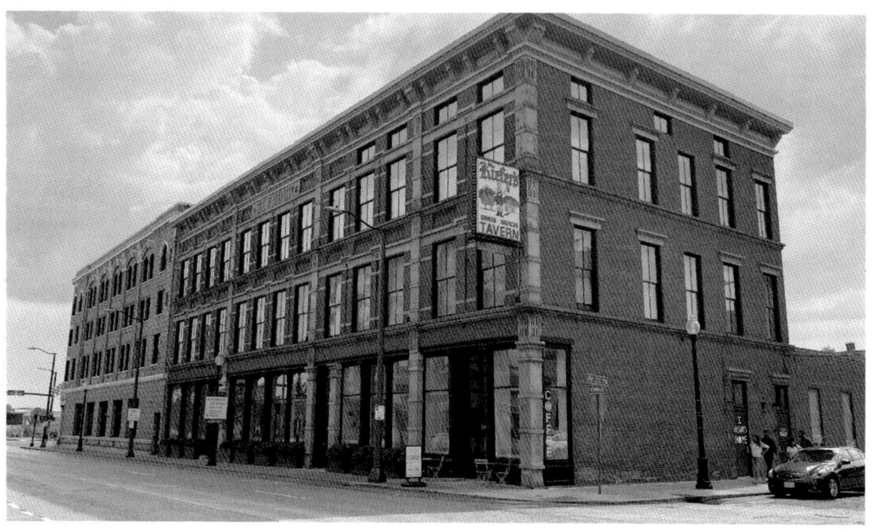

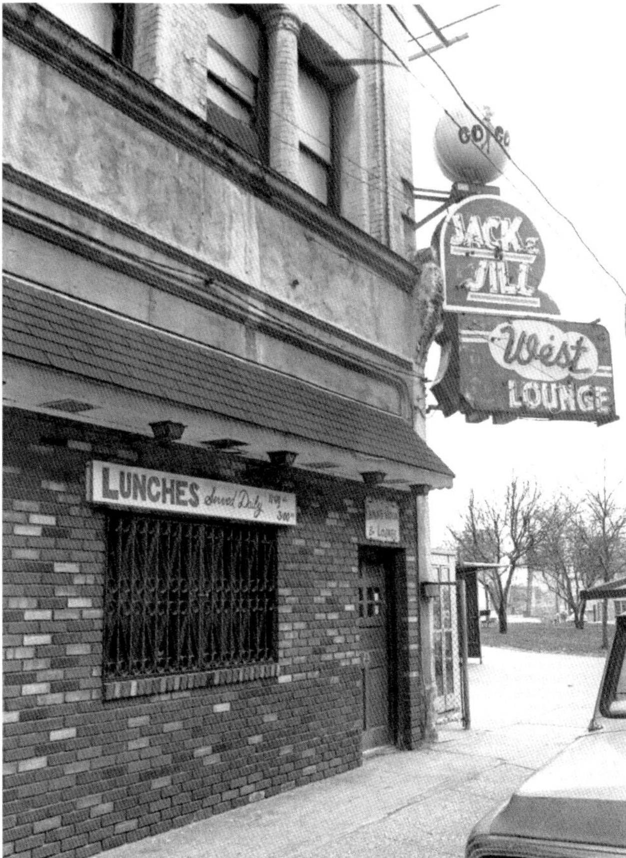

Above: Kiefer's Tavern on Detroit opened in 1937, and despite its closure in 1991, the sign remains today. *Author's photo.*

Left: Jack & Jill West Lounge, 2516 Detroit Avenue (its name later changed to Christy's Lounge). Shondor Birns visited Christy's prior to the bombing that killed him in the lounge's parking lot on March 29, 1975. *Cleveland State University, Michael Schwartz Library Special Collection.*

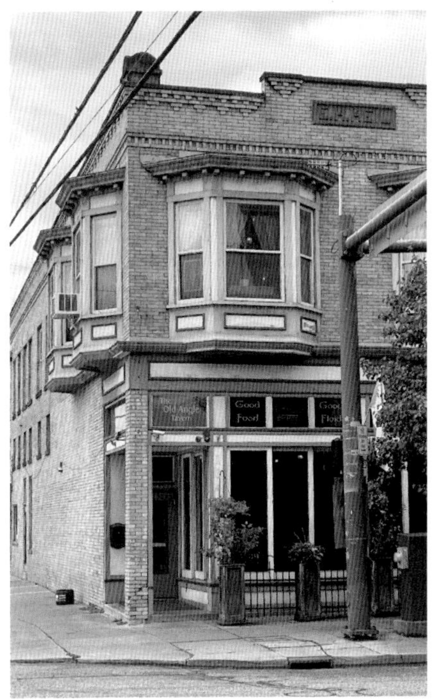

Above: Old Angle Tavern in the E.H. Heil Building, 1906. *Author's photo, August 2024.*

Opposite: Bookhouse Brewing at 1526 West Twenty-Fifth Street, September 2024. This building dates to 1866 and was the Jacob Baehr Brewery. *Author's photo.*

eight years. Her dedication paid off, and she became a well-respected figure in Cleveland's brewing scene before finally selling the business in 1901. One of her sons, Herman Baehr, even went on to become mayor of Cleveland.

After the Baehr family sold the brewery, the Cleveland & Sandusky Brewing Company operated at the site until 1907. In the decades that followed, the building housed a metalworks company and eventually fell into cycles of use and neglect, narrowly escaping demolition, much like the Old Angle. Finally, in 2014, renovation efforts began, and today, Bookhouse has brought the building back to its original purpose: brewing. The brewery has preserved many of the building's original architectural features, such as exposed brick, wallpaper and tin elements, paying homage to its storied past and continuing the Baehr family's legacy in the very place where it all began.

At 2516 Market Avenue, the building that now houses Great Lakes Brewing Company has a rich history dating to its early years as the Market Tavern. Over time, it became known as the Market Street Exchange, a significant fixture in the area near the West Side Market. In the 1970s, efforts to restore the historic structure were spearheaded by local investors James and Jane Bowers, who sought to revive the tavern's original charm. Despite challenges, they successfully restored the building, preserving its brick walls, heavy beams and historic bar. In 1988, brothers Pat and Dan Conway transformed the Market Street Exchange into what is now the iconic Great Lakes Brewing Company. As Cleveland's first modern brewpub, it marked the return of local brewing to the city after a long hiatus. The brewery followed the strict Bavarian Purity Law of 1516, which mandated the use of only barley, hops, water and yeast, ensuring the production of high-quality

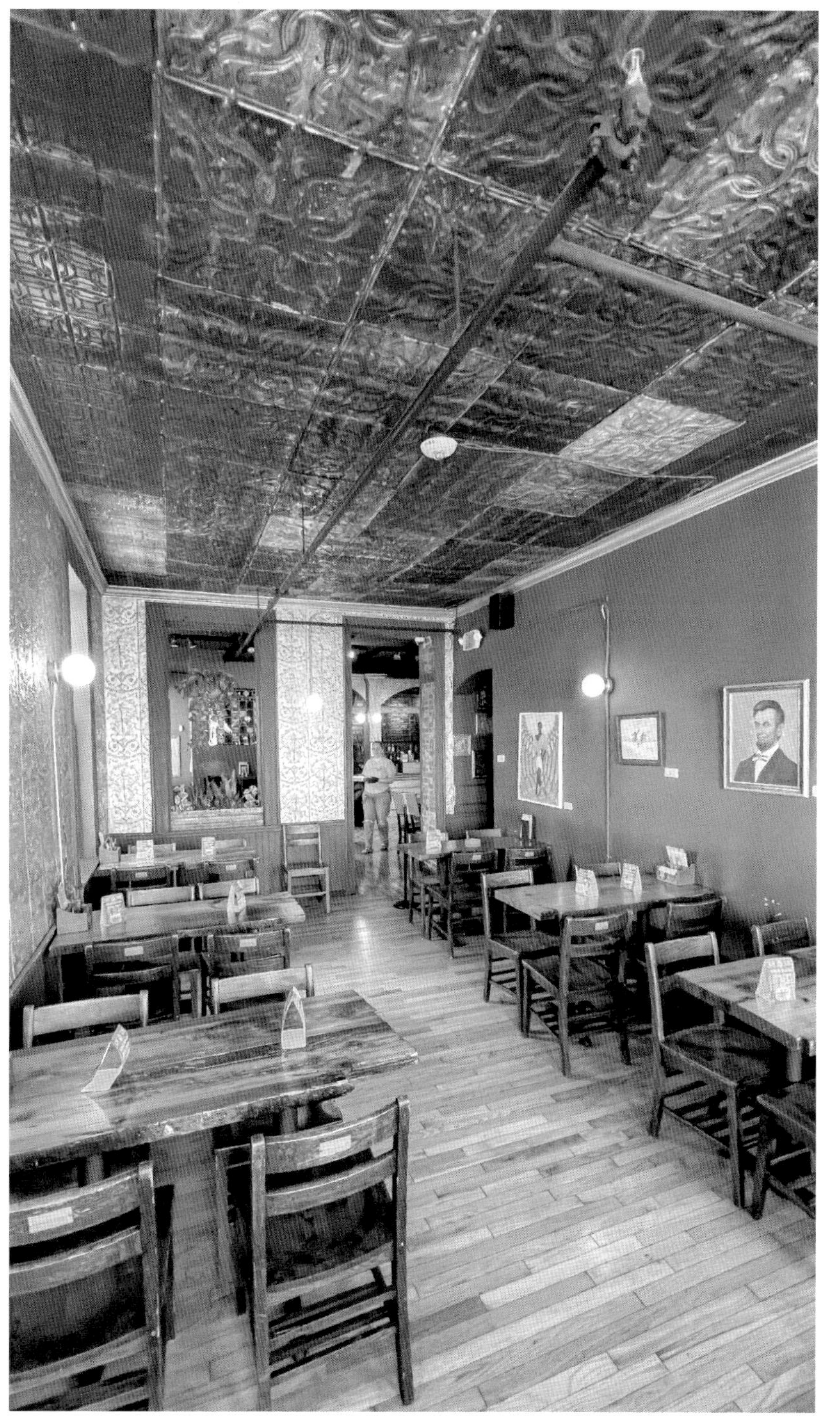

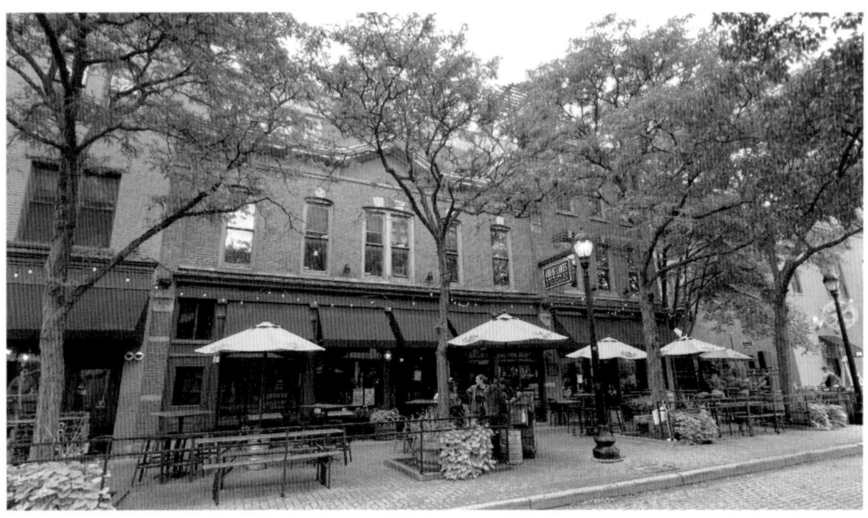

The Great Lakes Brewing Company in the historic Market Exchange Building started the craft beer resurgence in Cleveland. *Author's photo, August 2024.*

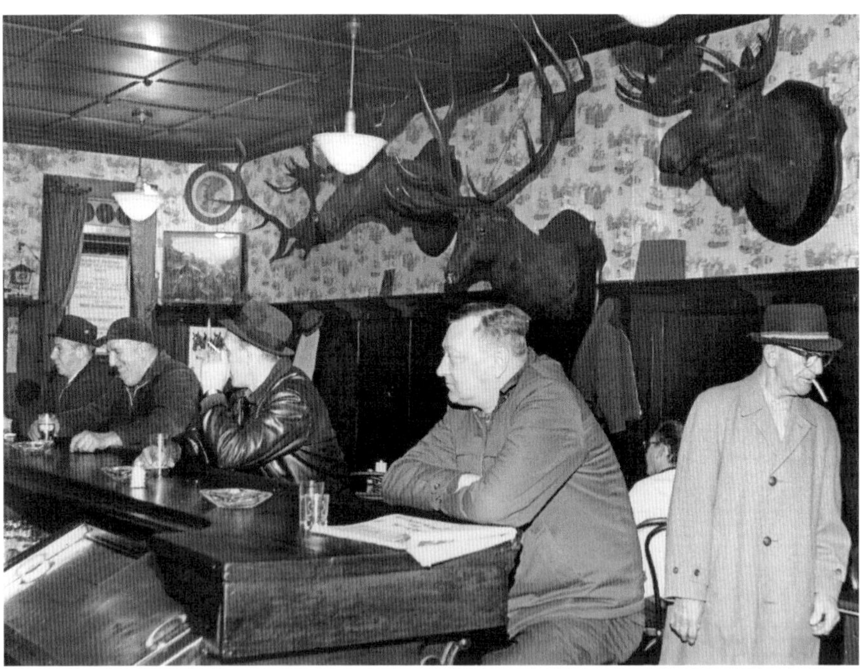

Patrons enjoying a drink at the Market Street Exchange in February 1968, home of today's Great Lakes Brewing Company. *Cleveland Press Collection, Cleveland State University, Michael Schwartz Library Special Collection.*

craft beer. The brewery and the beer—which is sold across the United States—have become a cornerstone of Ohio City's revitalization, growing and thriving as a beloved institution in Cleveland's craft beer scene.

Let's go around the corner and back in time to the late 1930s. At 3910 Lorain Avenue stood Jack & Eddy's Lounge, a popular spot known for its lively entertainment. In May 1939, due to popular demand, the lounge extended its run of the Beef Trust Girls, an exotic dance act featuring performers ranging from 250 to 400 pounds. The lounge proudly advertised the show, highlighting its 350-pound headliner as a unique attraction.

The lounge's story took a turn in 1941. Owners Jack Rogoff and Eddy Helstein were both called up to serve in the army, which led them to sell the establishment. Their departure marked the end of their six-year partnership, which had made Jack & Eddy's a well-known name among West Siders. The bar was sold, marking the end of an era for the lively and colorful Jack & Eddy's Lounge. Over the years, the building at 3910 Lorain Avenue transitioned through various identities, including stints as Gallucci's

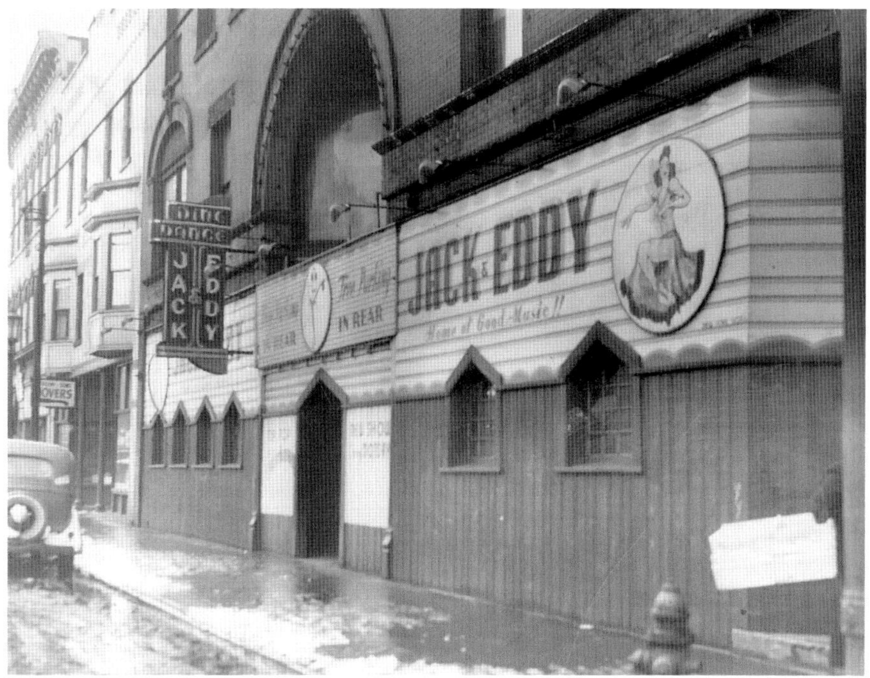

Jack & Eddy's, 3910 Lorain Avenue, 1939. *Cleveland Public Library/Photograph Collection.*

Motors and Pollster's Furniture. It housed a range of small businesses as the decades passed. This historic 1892 structure still stands, a silent witness to the neighborhood's evolving character.

Our final stop in Ohio City, located near the Tremont border, takes us to the historic Forest City Brewery at 2135 Columbus Road. This location is steeped in Cleveland's brewing heritage. The original Forest City Brewery operated from 1839 to 1880, and today's brewery and pub stand on the grounds of the Silberg Brothers Beer Garden, housed in a 1915 timber-frame warehouse.

In 2014, the new Forest City Brewery was established with the goal of re-creating the charm of a nineteenth-century brewery. The renovation incorporated reclaimed materials from the local area, including salvaged wood from nearby homes dating to the 1880s and bricks from the original Forest City Brewery. These materials were used to craft a brewpub complete with a beer hall and a restored beer garden to evoke the site's historical roots.

As we wrap up our journey through Ohio City, we head down to the West Bank of the Cuyahoga River, returning to the area where Cleveland's story first began.

Chapter 9

From First Pour to Last Call

A Final Toast to Cleveland

As we leave Ohio City and circle back to where it all began, we pass Carney's Top of the Flats, perched just above the West Bank of the Flats on Washington Avenue. Before becoming Carney's, the bar was known as Ginley's Top of the Hill, from the 1950s to the mid-1970s. The bar catered to a blue-collar crowd of dock- and ironworkers that offered inexpensive shots and beer.

In 1975, the bar made headlines for a dramatic robbery that could have come straight out of a movie script. Six armed robbers stormed the bar, forcing fourteen patrons into a small men's restroom. The nine men and five women were stacked on top of each other—some wedged into wastebaskets—as the robbers made off with $1,550 in cash and valuables. Remarkably, after the ordeal, the bartender, James Ginley, offered everyone free drinks while they waited for the police to arrive. Despite the chaos, the patrons joked about deserving a Guinness World Record for their bathroom pile-up.

The bar was also the site of a 1981 altercation that later surfaced during a federal drug trial. Testimony revealed that a fight had broken out at the bar between a member of the Hell's Angels and another patron, leading to allegations that the bar was a criminal hangout. These events only added to the bar's reputation as a rough-and-tumble place where hardworking locals could unwind and trouble sometimes followed. In one particularly heated altercation in 2001, an argument over a bar seat escalated into a shooting that left three men injured. Despite these incidents, Carney's has remained a neighborhood fixture, its regulars loyal to the bar and the neighborhood.

Farther down the hill at 1219 Main Avenue lies the Harbor Inn, often hailed as the king of Cleveland's dive bars. While it's widely claimed that it was established in 1895 and it's recognized as the oldest continuously operating bar in the city, the facts have been the subject of some dispute. Regardless of its exact founding date, the Harbor Inn undeniably exudes an old-school Cleveland vibe, housed in a sturdy brick building that has weathered the city's industrial past and social changes. The bar has a storied history intertwined with Cleveland's working-class roots. For many years, it was a go-to spot for third-shift factory workers, dockworkers and sailors, who would stop by for a drink after long hours on the job. As early as 1939, the *Plain Dealer* described the Harbor Inn as a place "where society rubs shoulders with ore boat sailors." Its legacy as a meeting point for locals and seafarers alike has helped cement its reputation as one of Cleveland's most authentic dive bars.

One of the Harbor Inn's defining features is its vast beer selection. During Cleveland's heyday as a bustling port, sailors from all over the world would bring beers from their home countries to the Harbor Inn. The bar began offering these imported beers for sale, gradually building an impressive collection of over 180 beers from places as far-flung as Japan, Germany and Mexico. Despite these worldwide offerings, in the 1970s, whiskey, Rolling Rock and Strohs were the most popular selections. Its diverse beer selection remains a hallmark of the Harbor Inn, though today, local craft beers and classic domestics are top sellers.

The Cleveland Dart League was founded at the Harbor Inn in 1972, adding another layer to the bar's rich cultural history. Regular patrons and dart enthusiasts gathered here, contributing to the Harbor Inn's reputation as a neighborhood hub. At closing time, owner Wally Pisorn would famously ring an antique ship's bell to signal the end of the night—a nod to the bar's nautical theme. Like any place that has been around for more than a century, the Harbor Inn is not without its legends. Stories of ghosts and local folklore add to the mystique of the bar, creating a unique atmosphere that is hard to find anywhere else. The bar's dimly lit interior, accented by Christmas lights and nautical-themed decor, creates an ambiance that is both nostalgic and gritty—offering a true dive bar experience.

The Harbor Inn, despite the changes around it through the Great Depression and multiple recessions, has remained a symbol of Cleveland's resilience. It continues to hold court over the West Bank, serving as a reminder of the city's industrial past and the enduring spirit of its working-class communities. Whether you're a local or just passing through, a visit

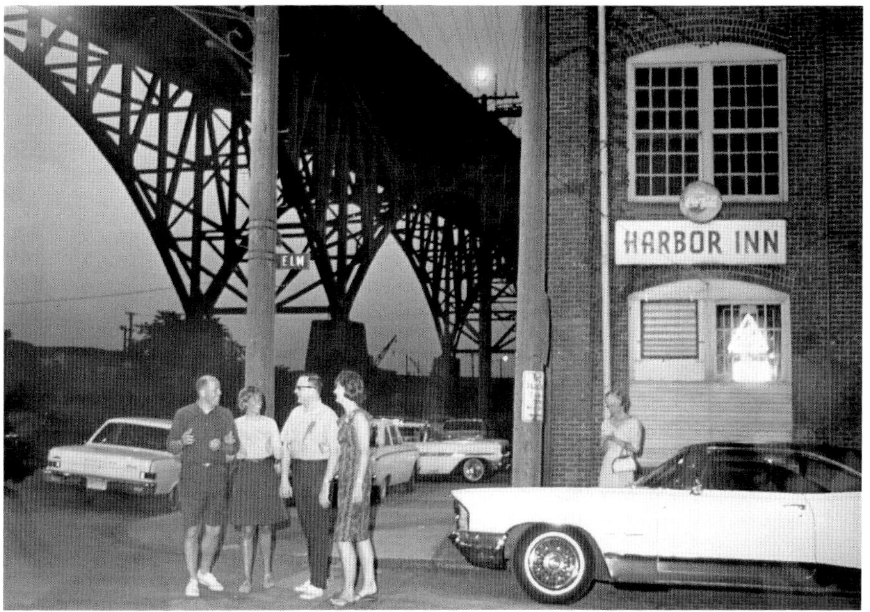

The Harbor Inn, June 21, 1965. *Cleveland Press Collection, Cleveland State University, Michael Schwartz Library Special Collection.*

to the Harbor Inn offers a chance to experience a piece of Cleveland's rich history.

As we continue along the West Bank of the Cuyahoga, we see Major Hoopple's, just a short distance away and nestled along a bend in the river. Since 1981, this beloved neighborhood bar has had stunning views of the city's skyline, the steel lift bridge and the winding Cuyahoga River. Interestingly, the owners originally had no idea that Major Hoople was a character in an old comic strip called *Our Boarding House.* On discovering this, they cleverly added an extra *p* to the name to avoid potential copyright issues. Despite facing its share of challenges—such as ongoing road construction, parking limitations and occasional bridge closures—Major Hoopple's has demonstrated remarkable resilience. For more than forty years, it has remained a steadfast part of Cleveland's ever-changing landscape in the Flats.

We now head back almost to where we started, near the site of Lorenzo Carter's Tavern, to the Flat Iron Café, located at the corner of Center Street and Merwin Avenue. This historic landmark has been a cornerstone of Cleveland's Flats district since it first opened its doors in 1910. The building, originally a blacksmith shop and four-story hotel, was reduced to two stories

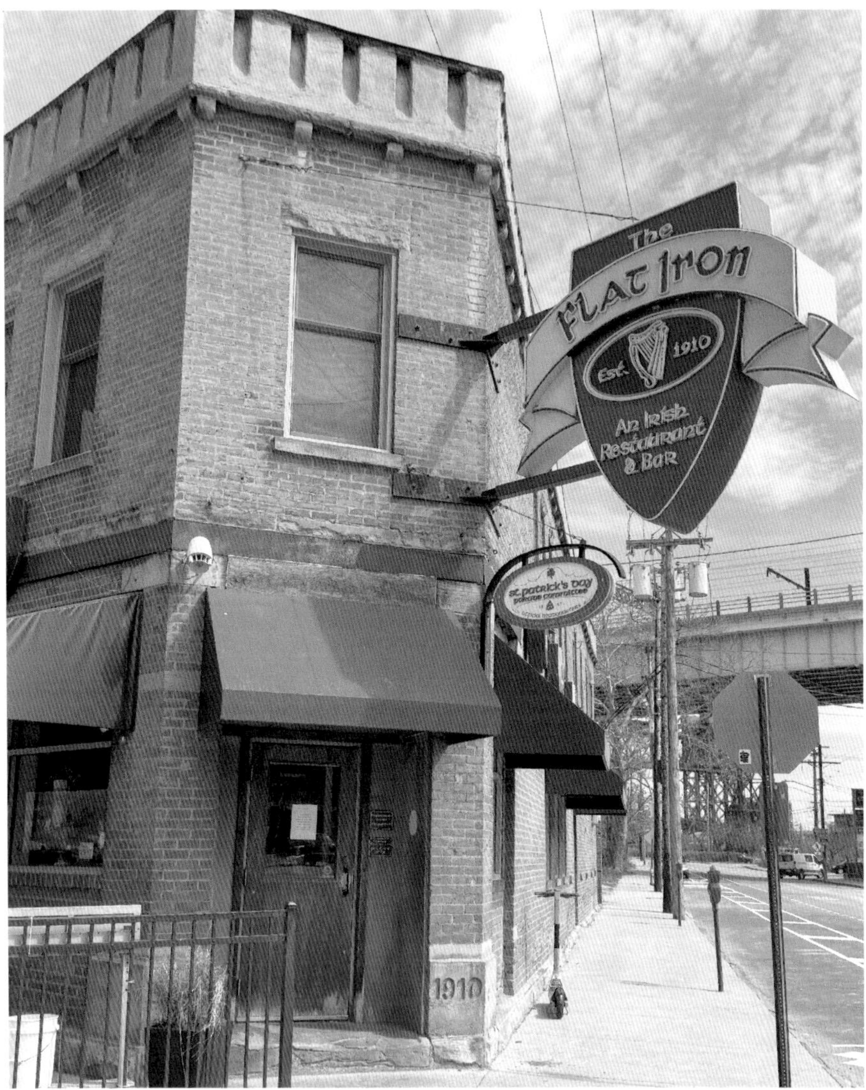

The Flat Iron Café, open since 1910. *Author's photo, April 2024.*

after a fire in the late 1800s that destroyed the upper floors. According to local legend, the blaze was started by a prostitute who fell asleep with a lit cigarette and tragically perished in the flames. Some claim that her spirit haunts the building to this day.

The Flat Iron Café initially catered to a working-class clientele, primarily Irish longshoremen, sailors and industrial workers who frequented the bar before and after their shifts. The café, known for its cafeteria-style dining, became a gathering place for a diverse array of customers over the years, from politicians to factory workers. Though the bar suffered another fire in 1980, it quickly reopened, and a more extensive renovation followed in 1988. The original bar was refinished, and the upstairs quarters were transformed into additional dining space. Today, the Flat Iron Café continues to serve its beloved traditional fare, including what is often hailed as the best perch dinner in Cleveland.

Full Circle on the Crooked River: Where Taps and Time Converge

As we conclude our journey through Cleveland's storied taverns, we must reflect on the waves of urbanization that have reshaped the city's social landscape. The East Bank of the Flats serves as a microcosm of this evolution, having undergone several phases of revitalization. What was once an industrial hub dotted with gritty blue-collar watering holes has transformed into a sleek, modern entertainment district. While we celebrate progress, we must also acknowledge the character and history lost along the way.

Before this transformation, Kindler's Saloon stood as the East Bank's oldest and most storied establishment. Founded in 1906, it served as a gathering place for generations of dockworkers, steelworkers and longshoremen. More than just a bar, it was a community cornerstone where workers shared meals and stories after grueling shifts. Kindler's embodied the spirit of the East Bank for nearly a century, holding on even as urban renewal projects began reshaping the Flats in the late 1990s. Yet, like many of Cleveland's original taverns, Kindler's eventually succumbed to the forces of change, disappearing in the wave of redevelopment.

The evolution of Cleveland's tavern scene mirrors the city's broader development. The first wave of urbanization brought iconic establishments like Fagan's, Pirate's Cove, Peabody's and D'Poos, which flourished in the 1980s. The second wave ushered in a new generation of bars catering to shifting demographics. Riverfront establishments like the Beach Club, Banana Joe's and the Odeon became fixtures of the city's nightlife, drawing younger crowds with live music and a more polished atmosphere. These newer bars thrived for a time, but with the exception of Shooters on the West Bank, most eventually faded away, leaving only memories of the Flats' heyday as an entertainment district.

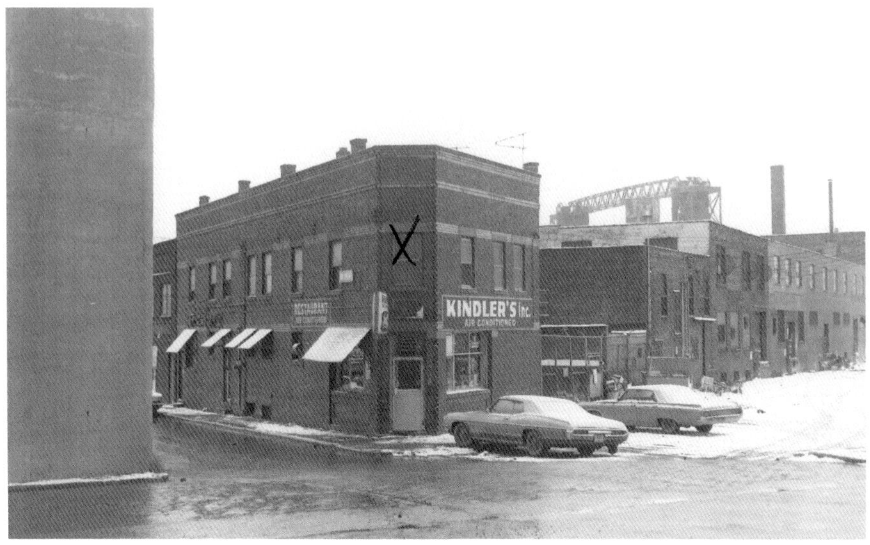

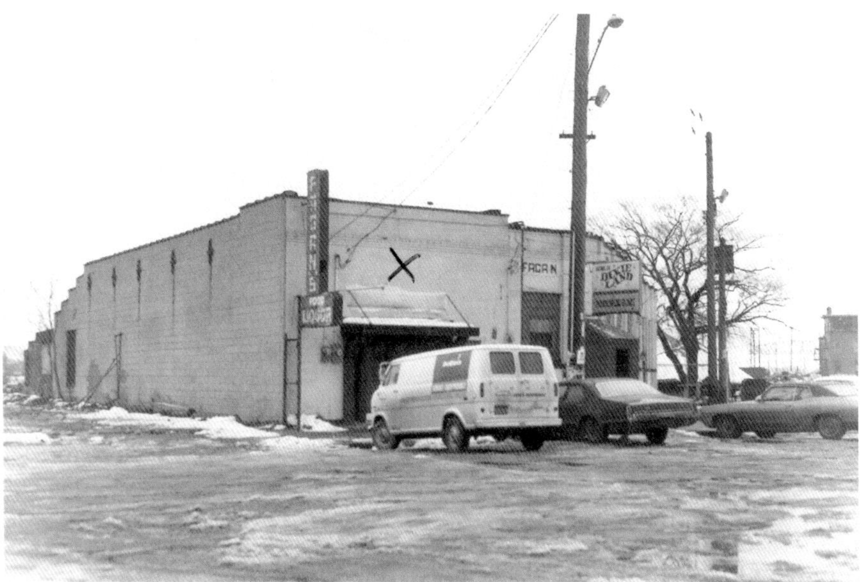

This page, top: Kindler's on the East Bank of the Flats in 1970. It survived almost one hundred years but not the revitalization of the Flats. *Cleveland Public Library/Photograph Collection.*

This page, bottom: Fagan's and the Flats in the early 1970s. *Cleveland Public Library/Photograph Collection.*

Opposite: Fagan's in 1980 during the East Bank's boom in popularity as a destination place. *Cleveland Public Library/Photograph Collection.*

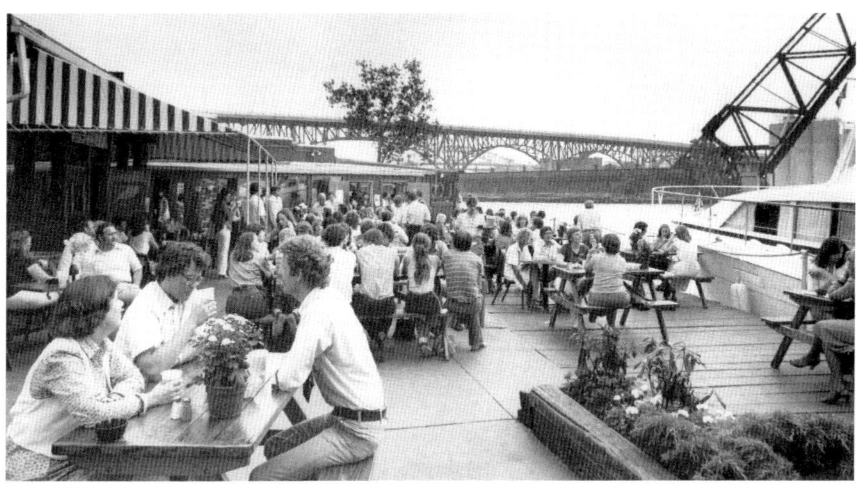

In recent years, corporate bars and chain restaurants have taken root, offering a more sanitized version of nightlife. However, something intangible has been lost in this process: an authenticity and connection to the city's roots. These modern establishments, with their polished façades and formulaic designs, cannot replicate the character that decades of history instilled in Cleveland's original taverns.

As we reach the end of our journey, we recognize Cleveland's evolution—both as a city and in its tavern culture. Establishments like the Flat Iron Café, Harbor Inn and Hotz Café represent more than just places to grab a drink. They are symbols of resilience, community and the working-class spirit that built this city. These taverns remind us that Cleveland's history is not just found in grand monuments or famous landmarks but also in these humble gathering places where people have long come together to share life's daily struggles and celebrations.

Through all these changes, some taverns have managed to hold onto their roots, serving as bridges between Cleveland's past and its future. These establishments, with their deep-rooted histories, remind us that true character isn't built overnight. They are Cleveland's living history, poured into a pint glass and served with a side of camaraderie—a testament to the enduring spirit of a city that continues to reinvent itself while honoring its rich heritage.

As we raise our glasses to Cleveland's past, present and future, let us toast in the languages of our immigrant forefathers who built this great city:

Cheers! *Na zdraví* (Czech)! *Prost* (German)! *Sláinte* (Irish)! *Salute* (Italian)! *Na zdrowie* (Polish)! Будьмо (*budmo*) (Ukrainian)! *Egészségére* (Hungarian)! *Živeli* (Serbian)! *Skål* (Scandinavian)!

Bibliography

Andrica, Theodore. "Friendship Glowed in Old German Cafés." 100 Years of Nationalities in Cleveland Series. *Cleveland Press*, November 13, 1950.

Basalla, Leslie, and Peter Chakerian. *Cleveland Beer: History & Revival in the Rust Belt.* The History Press, 2015.

Bonutti, Karl, and George Prpic. *Selected Ethnic Communities of Cleveland: A Socio-Economic Study.* Cleveland Urban Observatory, 1974.

Cleveland Memory Project. "Cleveland Breweries Remembered." Michael Schwartz Library, Cleveland State University. https://www.clevelandmemory.org/breweries.

Cleveland Urban League. *The Negro in Cleveland, 1950–1963: An Analysis of the Social and Economic Characteristics of the Negro Population.* Prepared by the Research Department. Roger Milton, Research Director, Ernest C. Cooper, Executive Director. Cleveland Urban League, 1964.

Coates, William R. *A History of the City of Cleveland: Its Settlement, Rise, and Progress, 1796–1896.* Imperial Press, 1897.

Dutka, Alan F. *Cleveland's Short Vincent: The Theatrical Grill and Its Notorious Neighbors.* The History Press, 2014.

Field, Edward. *The Colonial Tavern: A Glimpse of New England Town Life in the Seventeenth and Eighteenth Centuries.* Preston and Rounds, 1897.

Grabowski, John J. *Irish Americans and Their Communities of Cleveland.* Cleveland State University, 1978.

Hubbard, Harvey Rice. *Pioneers of the Western Reserve.* W.B. Clarke, 1883.

Lamoreaux, Naomi R., Margaret Levenstein and Kenneth L. Sokoloff. *Financing Invention During the Second Industrial Revolution: Cleveland, Ohio, 1870–1920.* National Bureau of Economic Research, 2004

Lathrop, Elise. *Early American Inns and Taverns.* Tudor Publishing, 1926.

Memorial Record of the County of Cuyahoga and City of Cleveland. Lewis Publishing, 1894.

Miller, Carol Poh, and Robert A. Wheeler. *Cleveland: A Concise History, 1796–1996.* 2nd ed. Indiana University Press, 1997.

Musson, Robert A., MD. *Brewing in Cleveland.* Arcadia Publishing, 2005.

The Negro Motorist Green Book. Victor H. Green, 1953.

Ohio Historical Records Survey Project. *Historic Sites of Cleveland: Hotels and Taverns.* Ohio Historical Records Survey, 1942.

Porrello, Rick. *The Rise and Fall of the Cleveland Mafia: Corn Sugar and Blood.* Next Hat Press, 1995.

Rose, William Ganson. *Cleveland: The Making of a City.* World Publishing, 1950.

Van Tassel, David D., and John J. Grabowski, eds. *The Encyclopedia of Cleveland History.* Indiana University Press, 1987.

Wallen, James H. *Cleveland's Golden Story: A Chronicle of Hearts That Hoped, Minds That Planned and Hands That Toiled, to Make a City "Great."* William Taylor Son, 1920.

About the Author

Tom Kaschalk was born and raised on Cleveland's Southeast Side, in the Union-Miles neighborhood and, later, in Slavic Village. After graduating from Cleveland State University with a degree in political science, he spent several years in local law enforcement before transitioning to a corporate career that took him across the country. Despite his travels, Tom's love for Cleveland always remained strong.

On returning to Cleveland, Tom rekindled his passion for the city's rich history. As the owner of My Cleveland History, he specializes in genealogy and helping others discover and connect with their Cleveland roots. Through his work as a volunteer researcher at the Cuyahoga County Archives, he has explored countless family histories and uncovered hidden stories that reveal the city's diverse past. Tom's dedication to Cleveland's history helps preserve the legacy of the city and ensures that future generations can connect with their heritage.